Ricky Ross formed Deacon Blue over 30 years ago, and 2022 saw the 35th anniversary of the release of their debut album, *Raintown*. A string of bestsellers followed it, leading to over 7 million álbum sales and hits including 'Real Gone Kid', 'Dignity' and 'I'll Never Fall In Love Again'.

Ricky also presents a number of radio shows, including BBC Radio Scotland's Americana music show *Another Country* (for which he has won two Sony awards and a CMA International Trophy in 2015) as well as *Sunday Morning With*, BBC Radio 2's *Ricky Ross' New Tradition*, and a podcast, *Ricky Ross Meets . . .*

Walking Back Home

RICKY ROSS

Deacon Blue & Me

HEADLINE

First published in 2022 by
HEADLINE PUBLISHING GROUP

First published in paperback in 2023 by
HEADLINE PUBLISHING GROUP

2

Cataloguing in Publication Data is available from the British Library.

ISBN 978 1 4722 8930 8

Designed and typeset by EM&EN
Printed and bound in Great Britain by Clays Ltd, Elcograf S.p.A.

MIX
Paper | Supporting
responsible forestry
FSC® C104740

HEADLINE PUBLISHING GROUP
An Hachette UK Company
Carmelite House
50 Victoria Embankment
London EC4Y 0DZ

www.headline.co.uk
www.hachette.co.uk

For everyone who has taken the time to listen.

CONTENTS

INTRODUCTION

In 1986, I started a full-time career in music that has lasted, so far, for thirty-six years. My earlier working life had been spent in youth work and teaching in my home city of Dundee and my new home in Glasgow. I spent these formative years learning how to write and play songs until it became imperative for me to make music for a living.

I've always written about people who've made an impact on my life. It often occurs to me that the song that changed everything for me, 'Dignity', came about because I was looking out the window of a flat I lived in at the time. In my early life, I failed at school by looking out the window too much, but in recent years I've realised how much of my future career was born from dreaming.

When my band Deacon Blue were working on their last album, *City of Love*, I found an interesting thread developing. Rather than simply trying to contain my thoughts within the traditional song structure, I stepped out of my usual habits and wrote a long spoken-word piece called 'On Love'. The song flits between stories of a school bully, my grandfather, and an early disappointment in love. It seemed to be the song that really connected with people when they listened to the record, and it sparked an interest in recalling stories from across my life that have stayed with me.

I started to write: about the years I spent putting the band together; about the first time we ever played in America; and about some of the musical characters I've met along the way. I gave some thought to growing up in suburban Dundee in a family with no record player and no sense that someone like me could, one day, make a record. I wanted to write more. One day in London, I took a small tour round the haunts of our early recording career in the West End, and I felt drawn to understand and explain why I had to leave the first band I'd joined on coming to Glasgow. Was it because one night in a Wishaw bar, I had experienced the Waterboys and knew there was still so much more to explore? Or was it simply that I was lucky enough to meet some amazing people at the perfect time for us all, and we went on to make the best music we could imagine?

That's one part of the story. However, I also want to talk about the smell of *Born to Run* when I first got it home, and the time I saw the Buzzcocks looking at a Cliff Richard album sleeve in a Dundee record shop window. I still want to tell the stories of my grandparents and parents, and the woman whose voice was so vulnerable when she got up to sing at our church – the church that formed the background to everything I knew in my younger life.

For all these years, I've told stories. These days, I sometimes tell them on the radio. I've met some amazing people, and their stories need to be told too. The first time Deacon Blue ever played Wembley Arena, I started to introduce a song, only to hear, 'Get on with it!' shouted from row Z. We proceeded with the song, but I often thought I'd quite like to finish that story.

Here it is.

Part One

I AM A CHILD

1

Whistlin' Past the Graveyard

Born Annie Ross Gray, she was known to the family as Nana and to her children as Mam. On any given Sunday in my late teens, once I had passed my driving test, I would pick up Nana, my grandmother, and bring her over to ours for lunch. There was a certain pleasure in visiting her house as a teenager. She didn't believe most of the things my folks adhered to, and my father, her son, found this friction a constant irritation. She smoked rather elegant cigarettes, bought pop records and spent far too much on fashion accessories, even in old age. In my time as a schoolboy, I'd often meet her, along with her stepsister Effie, in the town centre on my lunch break. Nana would be prowling the main shops on Reform Street, hoping to spend more money than was necessary on some item she really didn't need for her house or her wardrobe. I'd be consuming a Wallace's pie before returning to school to endure double chemistry.

Nana was everything my other grandparents weren't: cool, detached, superstitious and fashion-conscious. Her preferred band of cigarettes was De Maurier, which she enjoyed with a drink of something stronger than tea. Intriguingly, it was said she had once left her husband for an ill-fated liaison with a man in London before returning home with her romantic tail between her legs.

Her house was one of four in a short terrace on one of Dundee's steeper inclines. On the west side of the city, it was near enough Lochee, though she seldom shopped there, preferring the downtown charms of departments stores like Cairds, Draffens or Justice.

'They see her coming,' my mother would declare. They also witnessed her coming back, as she was wont to change her mind about a purchase by the time her key was in the door of her house.

A lot of this was to do with time. Her husband, my grandfather, who I barely knew, had died from a heart attack aged sixty-three. He'd been climbing that frozen hill back to their house after they'd been to the pictures one cold February night. My grandmother had thirty years of widowhood, and time presented itself as a vacuum that could never be filled. She must have had beliefs and a world view, but what they were, I don't recall. Any interests or passions she may have had seemed to demand very little by way of time or commitment. Instead, she would fill her days by livening up her house, acquiring wardrobe additions, which she'd then pass on to others, and spending time with her stepsisters.

It's easy to be slightly flippant about all of this now, but in retrospect I realise there was so much more she'd had to do in order to survive the hard life she'd been given. Like my other grandmother, Nana had been slowly sidelined by a new stepmother after the death of her own mother. Fearing what might become of them, she and her younger siblings had moved out of the family home and lived together in a small flat while Nana worked and provided for them. It was a common story in those days, and perhaps that's why, when the opportunity arose, she had no wish to return to a life of struggle.

Domestic chores she managed, but gardening, odd jobs and occasional shopping trips were arranged and carried out by my grandfather's younger brother, John, who was a willing assistant. John's beneficence was born of duty but carried out with grace and good humour. Perhaps the only socialist in the family, he'd estranged himself from my father and the family business. There was a rumour of 'creative accounting' in John's favour. This, it seemed, had kept family civilities to a minimum until a time well after my grandfather's passing, when John reappeared on the scene, to the great benefit of my grandmother.

Because she presented such a contrast to the fundamentalist side of the rest of the family, Nana was a source of constant intrigue to me and my sister. It was rare for her to babysit us, but when she did, she'd ask us to take away her ashtray after her cigarettes had been extinguished. This gave my sister the opportunity of inhaling the last dregs of the cigarette before running it under the kitchen tap in a suppressed explosion of coughing. She read Sunday papers (which were forbidden in our house), and we consumed them voraciously. She bought pop records and we would go round to her house and pile the forty-fives onto her small record player. I seem to remember her buying Petula Clark's *Downtown*, and my sister and I playing it endlessly.

Nana watched the kind of TV programmes we liked to see, and unlike our other grandparents, she didn't turn off the set when the sight of alcohol loomed or someone took the Lord's name in vain. She was also deeply superstitious. On Sundays, I'd take her home in the early evening, but always needed to make sure the route back didn't pass Balgay Cemetery. Her husband was interred there, but she never visited the grave to my knowledge. This superstition was understood to be a 'highland thing' – we were told she had grown up near Thurso in Caithness. It was with some surprise that, on looking into the family tree many years later, I discovered she'd not been brought up there at all. She was born in Queensferry, though her mother had come from Tongue.

Superstition was not encouraged in our Brethren household. Along with horoscopes and lotteries, it was understood to be diabolic in nature. The idea that anything happened by chance or that magic occurred outside the divine sphere of influence was frowned upon by those in our close church circle. We didn't even buy raffle tickets. Nana, on the other hand, embraced many superstitions, and was inclined to adopt more as time went on. Scarred by her own encounters with fundamentalism and my father's frequent proselytising, she took great satisfaction in holding views that were the polar opposites to our household's received wisdom. Spilled salt was thrown over shoulders, knives were never given as gifts, and any thoughts concerning death were never spoken aloud.

She seemed to me to have been happily married to a husband who was well thought of by everyone. I don't suppose it occurred to either of them that her widowed life would extend for such a long time. They were a well-to-do couple who enjoyed the good things in life. Cars, television and entertainment were within their hinterland, and although neither had had a formal education, theirs was an informed world. Bill, her husband, had been a man of invention and enterprise. He dreamed up and manufactured 'fancy goods', as they seemed to be called, which he'd sell from the family stationery business. He loved printing, produced candleholders and was good with his hands in a way his eldest son, my father, never was. My eldest cousin remembers their assured affluence, which, post-war in Dundee, was something to behold. 'I'm off to garage the Zephyr,' he'd say. 'Do you want to come with me?'

They were the only members of my family likely to go inside the picture house or cinema, and it was Nana who took me to one of the most joyous nights of my young life. My television heroes, Francie and Josie, played by Rikki Fulton and Jack Milroy, were to play one last tour and were booked to appear at the Queen's Theatre, just off the Nethergate behind the hotel of the same name that still stands there. Although it was the kind of thing that seldom happened, it seemed, at the time, to be the most natural occurrence that we should spend the night in a darkened palace of variety. It was a thrill.

She was given to disposing of memorabilia, but kept significant keepsakes. In the hall cloakroom hung my Uncle Tom's RAF officer's uniform and parts of Papa's First World War kit. (He'd been in the Highland Light Infantry, or some other unlikely regiment, rather than the local Black Watch because, according to my father, 'He didn't want to wear a kilt.' This family loathing of the national dress has extended down the generations. In my case, it's even extended to the national instrument.)

Other than that cloakroom, though, the house was a model of spartan minimalism. Paintings were hung, cushions were scattered and rugs fell loosely on parquet floors, but very little was allowed to linger. Instead, Nana would pass on furniture to my parents or her other children (my sister still has a very serviceable bedroom tallboy and dressing table). My mother would inherit rash purchases. 'It doesn't suit me, Catherine,' she would declare. 'I don't know why I bought it.' At this, my father would quietly harrumph and fold his paper, knowing that these retail errors would eventually appear in his own business expenditure. His own father, having died suddenly, left no will, but it was thought by the family that Nana should continue to benefit from the business. Roofing bills and general maintenance were taken care of, and although this was in the days before foreign travel was common, she managed to find creative ways to spend money. In retrospect, it was fairly minimal compared to the kind of debt a twenty-first-century person could accrue. There were no credit cards, and I suspect most of the spending was on an account at Jaeger or Thomas Justice, the Dundee bespoke furniture store.

At a fairly senior age, it was agreed by the family that Nana could no longer manage on her own, and she would stay in turn with each of her four children. Her three-month stay at our house was probably viewed by all parties as mutual torment. My parents were probably less than enthusiastic hosts, and for Nana, it was akin to Mary, Queen of Scots being quartered in the house of John Knox. She was hostage to all the evangelical indoctrination she'd spent the best part of her life avoiding, while those things she loved – shopping, smoking and seeing friends – were no longer possible. She had no independence, and I realised she was someone who had never expected nor wished to be old. None of us do, but some are better at ageing than others, and my Nana was ill-equipped for dotage.

Happily, it became clear she would be best placed with her youngest daughter, my Aunt Ev, down in the southwest of England. Selflessly, Ev devoted years to making her mother as at home there as she was ever likely to be. So, the final few years of Annie Gray's life were spent in the rural idyll of the Cotswolds, in a family home worthy of Mole and Ratty in *The Wind in the Willows*.

I visited once, when she was a good age but still alert enough to know what was what. My dearest cousin, Laura, was still at home and loudly searching for her shoes before departing on a night out.

'Where's my shoes?' she barked at anyone who caught her eye. 'Where's my bloody shoes?'

Aunt Ev sighed and quietly requested restraint with such language in front of her grandmother.

Nana piped up, 'Oh I don't mind if it's only that she's saying.'

When my father was less well himself, I took him to visit. He wasn't able to make the journey on his own, and I drove him from Dundee to the Cotswolds. We stopped for lunch on the way down at a motorway services, and he gave thanks for the food aloud above the Formica table. We were making the visit as Nana was going downhill fast and, as it turned out, it would be the last time we'd see her. She was frail and sleeping a lot. Although weary of life, she was probably still a little concerned about what the afterlife might involve. By this time, my parents seemed to have heard her say the right phrases for them to be satisfied that she was going to end up on the correct side of the pearly gates. This made my dad less anxious, and no doubt brought some relief to the rest of the family, who didn't want to witness some re-enactment of the *Brideshead Revisited* deathbed conversion scene.

Nana died soon after, and my father only survived her by a few years. The house she'd lived in had been denuded of its artefacts, and her clothing and possessions distributed among her children and grandchildren. Laura's older sister, Su, told me her own daughter, Kate, who died at a young age in 2021, still wore some of Nana's wardrobe; so stylish it never went out of fashion.

Annie Gray's funeral took place in the little parish church in Stow-on-the-Wold. In the great family tradition, I have probably only visited her grave once. She's buried beside her husband, high up in Balgay, overlooking Ninewells and beyond that the River Tay, in the cemetery she never liked to pass.

2

I Never Told My Parents I Went to the Regal

I must have been about ten. We'd decided to meet some girls. I didn't really know the logistics of meeting girls outside of the classroom or the Sunday school, but my pals hatched a plan to meet some girls on a Saturday afternoon. We were all to go to the pictures.

As innocent as this sounds, it's difficult to explain just how thorny a problem it was. Cinemas – like pubs, bingo halls, football grounds, social clubs, dance halls, sports clubs, Roman Catholic churches and even some Protestant churches – were pretty well out of bounds. Every other week, I'd hear the 'testimony' of a brother who had spent his youthful days in drinking, dancing and going to the pictures, only to have been 'saved' from all of that. Very often, the brother would paint such a graphic picture of what my father referred to as his 'unregenerate days', that one could feel a general out-breath of disappointment around the hall when the big conversion kicked in. My uncle (a missionary in Africa) once brought home from Zambia a man called Brian who'd been converted in the prison there. Brian spent a good forty minutes telling us of his nefarious deeds, before tacking on a swift 'and then I got converted' in the final few minutes. A few of the ladies were a little flushed at all that, but it was a wild night at the gospel meeting for us youngsters.

It would be many years before I'd ever venture into licensed premises, but the cinema was a temptation that beckoned you in. Driving through the Seagate on a Saturday to arrive at a Christian rally at the other Brethren Assembly my grandparents attended involved going past the old ABC, where we'd see crowds of young couples in a snaking line, queuing to get into the pictures. Above the line, the marquee would proclaim the title of the latest release. There would be a faint tut of disapproval from my parents as we passed 'the lost', all misspending their Saturday nights. We, on the other hand, were heading to a warm Gospel Hall, where tea would be served from steaming urns, accompanied by home baking, and Mr Cathcart would conduct some glorious singing. There was no competition.

The cinemas themselves were dying. This was the 1960s, and television was stealing their audience. My dad would pass the cinemas he'd frequented as a young man and tell me how they were now being turned into bingo halls. As if there hadn't been enough things we weren't allowed to attend, they were now inventing new ones.

Even if we didn't subscribe to going to the cinema, it was inevitable that it would inveigle its way into our hearts somehow or other. Film posters were everywhere, and they always seemed so exciting. As children, we were acutely aware of what we weren't seeing. I can still feel the pain of passing by the *Help!* poster from the cinema at the top of The Hilltown and echoing it inwardly as a personal cry I wanted to make to the Fab Four: 'Let me in, I want to see you.'

As reluctant as my parents were to break the *omertà* on their home patch, it eventually transpired that things were slightly different if we were in a different town in a different country.

It was a holiday in Southport. We were there as a family, with my grandparents along too. The weather was probably not all we'd have hoped for, and the longest cinema marquee was proclaiming one word: 'Supercalifragilisticexpialidocious.' It ran the length of a long pavement and even turned the corner into the next street. The summer of *Mary Poppins* was making it hard for my mother to resist my big sister's pleas to see the film.

It was decided that Mum would take us one quiet afternoon, while my father distracted my grandparents. We wouldn't speak of the visit to them, but we would go just this once, as a special treat. I can remember very little of the trip itself, except that general sense of awe common to any childhood cinema visits: amazement at the size of the images on the screen and, of course, the colour. We adored seeing the colours. All of life elsewhere was in black and white.

We loved going to the pictures, but we also loved our family. We were happy kids, surrounded by love, who accepted there were certain places we didn't go. Although I had loved *Mary Poppins* like life itself, the picture house remained a place of dark mystery. Towards the end of the sixties, we went to visit a young couple who were friends of my parents and had moved to the north of England. We broke the journey in Carlisle, and my parents tried to find a good place to have high tea. I remember them discovering that the best and most available option was to be found within the precincts of the local cinema. We sat eating fish and chips in an opulent art deco foyer, being reassured by our parents that, although we were using the facilities on offer, we were not on this occasion entering into the dark recess of the auditorium itself. I remember feeling comforted but also a little afraid.

The cinema was a strange and alien land, full of ideas and images that, as visiting preachers reminded us on a regular basis, would seek to bring us down into the paths of iniquity from which we'd been so relieved to be saved.

As the years went by, my parents' views on the cinema eased a little. There would be an occasional family visit to see a 'good' film. Before all that happened, however, I was secretly making my way to a Saturday matinee at the Regal to meet girls. In my mind, this was the most covert operation I'd ever carried out. Excuses were made, times were set, and a bus ride or long walk would have been taken to reach the Regal. Going to Dundee's most easterly picture house came with few frills. The local woman generously referred to as an 'usherette' was a beastly ogre who carried a torch like a baton and delighted in shining it on any miscreants and shouting 'Get your feet aff the seats!' at the most sensitive point in any drama.

I don't remember the movie I saw there that afternoon as we stumbled into the stalls. My only recollection is that it was again big and colourful, and everyone in it was suntanned. It may have involved Michael Caine, but I simply can't remember. I know I loved the adverts, though. Generically produced, they used exotic Mayfair locations for Chinese restaurants, then slammed on the local restaurant on Gray Street at the end. Believe me, the Chinese restaurant on Gray Street bore no relation to the one on the screen. We loved the actorly voice saying 'Brawttyferry' in plum received pronunciation though. We'd never heard anyone say Broughty like that before.

I could never tell anyone in the family about my visit to the pictures. It had been a normal Saturday afternoon as far as they knew. But I had been to the Regal – and now I knew there was another world out there I needed to find.

3

The Spanish Doll

He was an incomer who came to live quite near us in West Ferry. My dad liked him because he was a businessman and my dad had a built-in interest in retail.

We got to know him because he became the superintendent of the Sunday school. Being superintendent was a big deal in the Assembly. He'd made an impact on the children too. I remember him teaching us all 'How Great Thou Art', with the words printed out on a cardboard prompt that looked like a giant birthday card opened up. Behind the words were pictures of pastoral scenes, with the sun shining down upon gentle hills.

At the end of every session, the Sunday school would hold an annual picnic and also a prize-giving. The picnic, held on a Saturday, was one of the highlights of the year. Everyone came. My dad, along with many others who still worked on a Saturday morning, would join us. We loved going on the buses, with the streamers flowing out the windows and the Sunday school teachers in their grey sports flannels and newly whitened gym shoes. We loved the dads all behaving like children, ties off and shirt sleeves rolled up for the sports and a twenty-a-side game of football.

The prize-giving was on a Sunday. On top of the platform would sit piles of books, all organised in classes and graded as Perfect, First or Second. Prizes were given for attendance, and a perfect attendance prize was something special. The books were all Christian, and sometimes the older students would be given a leatherbound Bible as a reward for achieving the perfect grade.

A leatherbound Bible, sometimes zipped, was a coveted prize. Inside the book would be the certificate, stuck to the first blank page: 'Presented to [name], in recognition of [achievement]'. It was the job of the superintendent to introduce the prizes, and the job of the guest speaker's wife to present the prizes and receive the flowers at the end.

On one occasion the superintendent had invited one of his old chums to come and give the address. As most of the parents who came to the prize-giving were local folk with no attachment to our Assembly, they were often seen as a natural target group for conversion. On this particular Sunday, my own parents also invited our highly educated next-door neighbours, whose boys attended Sunday school with us. To the embarrassment of my folks, the visiting preacher proceeded to behave in a slightly eccentric manner, charging around the platform and taking on the role of the animals from his chosen Bible passage. As kids, we delighted in the whole episode. The point where the preacher knotted himself up to the railing at the side of the platform with his own tie to illustrate what happened to the donkey on Palm Sunday was a particular highlight. My parents squirmed audibly. The family next door never returned.

The superintendent was married to a slight, tall-looking younger woman who collected Spanish dancing dolls, that she displayed in their home on glass shelves. Her own look owed much to the appearance of the dolls: she had long, lustrous black hair and puckered lips, which only emphasised her fine features. The dolls wore elaborate chiffon skirts, and visiting their house to see his wife and the dolls was a joy for my older sister, Anne. The superintendent's house must only have been a five- to ten-minute walk down from ours. The young couple, though childless, kept a Shetland collie called Susie, who they allowed Anne and her friend to take on the lead to the local park.

As well as enjoying the new zeal he brought to our Sunday school, we also liked riding in the superintendent's car. He owned a large blue Vauxhall Cresta, which was the closest thing any British car came to looking American back in the sixties. It had sleek lines and rear fins, which at the right angle and in a fair wind gave it a passing resemblance to a Cadillac. My sister and I, the boys next door and an adult who often needed a lift would all get in the Cresta after Sunday school finished and share the ride back to West Ferry from Cotton Road, where the Gospel Hall was located. The car had long bench seats and there would be six or seven of us all squeezed in without any seat belts, as that was how we were all transported back then. On other days, Grandpa Harkness, who was still driving at the age of ninety, would drive us at the sort of hair-raising speeds that made us vow never to step into his car again. The superintendent's journey was statelier, with the big car rolling smoothly past the graveyard to drop off the first passenger. He and Mr Melvin would reflect on days gone by and Anne and I would be shocked by the superintendent's colloquialisms.

'We were never learned at the school, were we Tommy?' he'd joke with old Mr Melvin.

'Why doesn't the superintendent know how to speak properly?' we'd enquire of our parents.

One day, my sister brought home the news that the superintendent and his wife were to foster a boy with a view to adoption. In due time, the boy, who was about five, arrived and was brought with them to church and Sunday school. Dressed up in his Sunday suit, the new boy was welcomed and fussed over by Anne, who now not only wanted to visit their house to see the Spanish dolls and the dog, but also to find out more about the young orphan who was joining the family. She would return with stories of Gordon, marvelling at how many things he could do at such a young age. Such was the fuss over the boy,

I began to feel pangs of jealousy over this orphan who had so much attention thrust upon him.

It didn't last long. One day, Anne returned from the superintendent's house to tell us that Gordon no longer lived there; he had gone back to live at the orphanage. It just hadn't worked out after all. If we drove from our house along the Ferry Road into Dundee, we would pass the orphanage. It was an intimidating-looking building, standing alone on the south-facing part of the road, looking towards Fife. As interesting as Gordon had been, none of us ever wanted to darken the doors of the orphanage.

The superintendent's life had appeared perfect, but it became apparent that all wasn't as it seemed. One day, we were all driving down our road when Anne saw the superintendent's wife hurriedly walking alone. Surprisingly, Susie the collie wasn't on a lead, but was instead walking unattended a good few yards behind her mistress, who was unaware of anything other than her own state of distress. It was the crying that we heard first. As my mother reached out to her, the superintendent's car drove along the road in search of his missing wife. With the two cars parked at the side of the road, both vehicles became counselling rooms for the troubled couple, with the superintendent's wife pouring her heart out to my mother in our car and the superintendent, a slightly embarrassed figure behind the wheel of the Cresta as my father became his unlikely counsellor. The scales seemed to fall from my eyes and Anne's. No longer were we in awe of the superintendent, for now we knew that in that small bungalow, the Spanish dancers would shake on their shelves as he shamed and shouted his wife into tears; that she would beat her fists into the plasterboard while Susie slipped quietly behind the sofa. In my imagination I pictured the noise subsiding and the superintendent's wife quietly rearranging the dancers back on their shelves.

4

I Remember the Night My Grandfather Died

I remember the night my grandfather died. Even now, I don't remember the cause of his death; I simply recall him getting older and seeing less and less of him in the way only a twenty-year-old can. As I think on it now, I realise I let him slip away without ever really saying goodbye.

My grandpa, Joe Ford, had always been my confidante, my playmate and my great champion. He was the one that hoisted us up on his leg on the sofa and twirled us around like circus acrobats. He built the stilts we played upon during one Easter holiday, and he fixed our bicycles if they needed attention. In short, he did all the things my father never really wanted to bother with. The contrast between the men was marked. One was tall and effortlessly handsome, a First World War veteran who'd never really found his true vocation. The other, my father, his son-in-law, a bald, slightly overweight man with soft hands whose own father had passed on a family business and so set up his passage for life. And yet, unlikely as it seems, they were great friends. A bond of mutual respect kept them close and kept me in a state of contented bliss. There was joy and laughter and little worry when they were both together.

My earliest memory of Joe was his last place of work; appropriately, it was as a watchman in a monumental sculptor's yard, keeping watch over the gravestones. We'd walk up to see him from their flat in Hawkhill, my grandmother and me, and occasionally I'd get to stay over at weekends. It was these nights that were the best. I'd go to sleep in the spare room, which had a window over the door that allowed the light to shine in from the hall and let me hear their movements as they prepared for bed. The round alarm clock had a moving pattern that blinked in and out and gently hypnotised me to sleep, before waking early on a Sunday by the church bells at the top of Shepherd's Loan. Between their tenement and the church was a squat row of buildings topped with an array of chimneys and flues. In the distance was the river, and in the foreground the smell of porridge warming. Later, we'd walk to church together, my grandmother in her straw hat and him in his dark jacket and pinstriped trousers, Bible in hand.

Joe loved modern life. Where my father feared the invention of the pocket camera, the automatic car and the tape recorder, Joe rejoiced in every labour-saving device he could afford. A man of deep and considerable faith, he nevertheless bucked the trend of his Brethren roots to embrace television, FM radio and the electric shaver. In the mornings, as the radio played the Light Programme, he'd sit by the dresser and take out his electric razor, bringing me endless delight as he tickled my hands with its rotating blades. Later, I'd walk out with my grandmother, Kitty, along the Hawkhill until we reached Roseangle, where we'd sit for an age as I watched the trains shunting in and out of the marshalling yards below. It was really the combination of the two grandparents that made my time with them so perfect. He was the joker and fixer, she the storyteller, the worrier and – with her beautiful seamstress's hands – the dressmaker.

My mother's wedding dress and the accompanying brides-maids' outfits had all been hand-sewn by Kitty Ford. Before her marriage, she'd worked in one of Dundee's high-end couturiers, and often revisited the tales of late-night deadlines being met in hot, dark workshops with dramatic tension: 'Then the manager came in . . . and oh, he was raging . . .'

It was my grandmother too who was our favourite babysitter when we were young. The highlight of these nights was not any received presents or special favours, but in her acquiescing to retell oft-repeated stories of family trauma. There was a great shortlist to choose from: the one about the family picnic, where they left an unattended bonfire in Fife and could see the smoke rising across the river on their return (a classic); or the day her father's horse, pulling the family in the trap, heard the thunder over the Sidlaws before any of the passengers and bolted for home – 'His ears pricked up . . . and he was gone!'. But the tale we really wanted to hear was the grim recollection of the near-death experience of her only son (my Uncle Jimmy) during the war.

War stories were easily the best. You had to imagine a different world, one of telegrams, sandbags, secrecy and rations; all concepts alien to children of the early 1960s. Jimmy had been on a troop ship headed for the Front – no one knew where he was sailing from, or where he was going to. The telegram arrived to say he'd been lifted off suffering from meningitis and was in hospital in Greenock. So, the story went on, my grandmother and her prayers were all that stood between Jimmy and certain death. There was a strong sense each time the story was told that, on this occasion, he might not make it. It was my first living encounter with Coleridge's 'willing suspension of disbelief'. Bedtime would come just in time for Jimmy to be sitting up in bed and drinking tea.

On some mornings, the post would deliver an 'aerogram' from Zambia with a typed letter from Jimmy, who was out there with my aunt Dorothy. Jimmy had ended up in Kenya during the war and there had stumbled upon an open-air gospel preacher. Reflecting on his current life of drinking, dancing and motorbike rides, he had converted to the faith of his parents and dedicated his life to God. In particular, Jimmy had promised he would return to Africa and the mission field, and he had. Read out slowly and thoroughly by Joe as Kitty and I listened patiently, the letters were always signed off 'Jimothy', a compound of my uncle and aunt's names. Joe always liked that bit.

At some point, Kitty started to get mixed up. She'd forget a pot on the stove, or whether or not she'd already put salt in the potatoes. Joe began to compensate by taking over more of the household chores. Imperceptible as it was, my mother noted the changes and slowly the family started to anticipate Grandma's memory loss. Relief always came in her wonder at the mundane. She'd marvel at the cricket highlights on the TV news, imagining all the wickets were falling in real time. We'd all gather on a Friday for tea and watch *Crackerjack!* as a family. Wisely, Kitty never really saw the force in the many costume-changes, elaborate sets and custard-pie fights that epitomised the zenith of children's telly. As the credits rolled, she'd shake her head at the sheer amount of energy the cast and crew had expended on half an hour of light entertainment. Clearly, however, all had been in vain. She'd rise from her seat and move towards the stove, uttering the immortal words, 'What a work. What a work.'

As a teenager, I spent less time at theirs, although they'd sometimes be called upon to stay with us when our folks went on holiday without me or my sister. I remember one awful day when Kitty's forgetfulness had caused too much distress to Joe, and he confided in me about how hard it was all getting. I will never forget his tears and distress as he spoke. How little comfort I must have been. My old hero and my heroine were much diminished, and it was sore to watch.

By the time of his death in his mid-eighties, Joe and Kitty had been separated. Unable to cope, he had moved into a care home and she'd been hospitalised. So far advanced was her dementia that she knew very little of her husband's passing. My mother

helped her dress up formally for the day of the funeral, but there
was little point taking her to the crematorium.

We'd taken the long road along Riverside Drive from our
home in Broughty Ferry to the hospital on the other side of town
when the final call had come in that Joe's breathing was poorly
and we should be there soon. It was late at night in early winter.
I always remember not knowing what to do as we sat around the
bed of my deceased grandfather, lying at peace. My father stood
over his old friend and gently swept back Joe's silver strands,
which had fallen down uncharacteristically over his forehead.
I loved the ease my father had with the dead man. 'He's still
warm,' he told us, and somehow we all felt some small glow of
comfort.

5

Last Night I Dreamed of Henry Thomas

Lily love that's a
Beautiful name
Your precious gifts are not the same
Since they faded away
The song so distant
But it still rings true . . .

It's hard to work out exactly how pop music entered my world. I'm just so glad it did. My earliest memory is of a pal from along the road and myself standing with tennis racquets on the porch of our first house, pretending to be the Beatles and singing 'She Loves You'. I must have been five years old, and somehow, without a record player anywhere near us, the Beatles had come in to my life.

I grew up in a very strong community where the Gospel Hall was the centre of our lives. It wasn't as strict as some Brethren Assemblies, and nearly all my memories are happy ones, but a good proportion of modern life was feared or excluded. The list is quite long: cinemas, alcohol, places that sold alcohol, television shows that showed people drinking alcohol, swear words – especially ones with God's name involved – smoking, football matches, playing on Sundays . . . and don't even think about sex. Gay people didn't really exist, as far as we knew. The theatre was allowed, but no one thought to attend for fear that the people onstage might do any of the things mentioned on the list.

Music was slightly different, though. Music was everywhere in the church, and although my parents saw no real need for a record player (they owned no records) we did hear music on the TV and on dad's car radio.

My dad loved music. He hadn't been brought up in the strict faith, so he kept an open ear for a good tune. He loved certain songs on the radio, and when he was happy, excited or just doing the daft dad routine that all dads do, he'd start singing. 'Little Children' or 'Itsy Bitsy Teenie Weenie Yellow Polka Dot Bikini'. 'The Sun Ain't Gonna Shine Anymore' was a particular favourite one rain-soaked holiday in the faded seaside towns my father always favoured for our annual retreat. Pop music came in the back door: overheard on the radio, watching the TV and eventually on a little mono portable record player which came into our new house on a day as memorable as the one when our first refrigerator arrived.

The other music was all at church. Sunday morning worship involved unaccompanied singing. My mum often sang a descant, and although the service was improvised – there was no minister – different Brethren would announce a hymn to be sung and the precentor would lead the singing, occasionally having to clear his throat and bring it down a couple of steps for fear of the men not making the high notes.

The real singing happened at the children's services. My own dad led the most boisterous of these on a Friday night, at a thing called the Bible Band. There, he had a primitive PA system with a microphone and a little loud speaker so the local Hilltown kids could read out their memory texts and win some confectionery from the two large sweetie jars placed on the platform. My dad loved leading the communal singing on these nights. I found out later his main daydream at school had been to imagine the wall behind the teacher revolving to reveal a dance band and a conductor. I loved the sound of that dream, and often wondered whether his enthusiastic conducting of the singing was, in some small way, the closest he ever got to being Artie Shaw or Glenn Miller.

On Friday nights, we sang from memory, but in case there were any newcomers, two of the local urchins would hold up large cardboard chorus boards as lyric prompts. 'Wide, Wide as the Ocean, High as the Heaven Above'. We all loved that one. The actions were important too.

'For his word teaches me that his love reaches me . . .'

(Big pause.)

'EVERYWHERE!'

On that word, we'd all stretch out our arms as far as they could go, and the unfortunate child on the end of the pew would find themselves dumped on to the cold linoleum that ran down either side of the long wooden benches.

On special nights, a preacher would bring a soloist along to break up the monotony of the evening gospel service. This was the last formal meeting of the Lord's day (as it was often referred to) and the main thrust of the proceedings was to convert any Godless souls who happened to be in attendance that evening. Inevitably, there was a lot of attention on the young people who'd not declared themselves for Christ yet. Occasionally, this service would have an entertaining preacher, but for the most part we looked to any musical items to capture our attention. However, the real musical action happened away from Sundays, and took place on a Saturday night.

Rallies or big special meetings could mix it up a bit. For a start, there was always an interval after the first part of community singing, during which we'd have tea and home baking. Ladies in hats poured and served all manner of delicacies to the eager throng after they'd had a solid forty minutes or so of boisterous hymn-singing led by a gentleman in a natty sports jacket and cavalry twills. As it was Saturday, things were a little more informal.

I remember one particular night when a visiting choir came and nearly blew the roof off the hall with their singing. They'd come on a bus from somewhere in Lanarkshire (so many visitors seemed to appear from there) and they even had matching costumes, all provided by their wealthy patron, whose Jaguar car was the subject of close attention from the teenage boys in attendance.

However, it was the music in my house that made the strongest connection. My mother played the piano, and my sister and I took piano lessons. It was my sister who I remember being the more musical; she also played fiddle in the school orchestra, and one cold Easter holiday we went to visit her at a music camp near Aberfoyle, where they were billeted in what looked uncomfortably like a concentration camp.

Our piano at home was tuned as well as it could be by a small man with a very high voice who came out once a year. Unfortunately, he only ever managed to get it to a semi-tone below concert pitch, which made playing along with any records a little tricky. I formally gave up my music lessons around the time I was in my second year in high school. At that time, the piano teacher lived half a mile or so from Dundee United's ground at Tannadice, and the wait for my dad to pick me up and go to the football became my main focus. As always happened with me, throughout any learning experience, I spent a lot of time looking out the window.

Around the same time, however, it became possible to buy easy piano pop music books, and once more the Beatles came to the rescue. One Christmas, I received a book of Beatles piano music that was soon plundered song by song.

It's impossible to overemphasise the impact the Beatles had on my musical life. They were everywhere, of course. On the radio and TV, on my sister's wall, and eventually on a pile of forty-fives we inherited from a friend of my sister's, who'd moved on from the Fab Four and handed over all the early singles. We stacked them all up and played them in order, then we flipped the pile over and played them again. I loved the B-sides as much as the As – to this day, 'I'll Get You' is still one my favourites, even though it was only the other side of 'She Loves You'.

As time went on and the Beatles developed, I loved the idea of them writing their own songs and spending endless time in the studio. Years later, we would get to make our debut album at Air Studios, a facility set up by George Martin after he left his contract with EMI. The walls were adorned with black-and-white pictures of John, Paul, George and Ringo, looking over mixing boards and drinking tea from white cups and saucers as they listened to playbacks. I felt I was in the grand tradition started by the people who'd made me want to make records in the first place. They changed all of our lives. I once seriously went off a producer who I might have worked with because he dismissively said of a Beatles track, 'Before my time, mate.' Mate – they were before *their* time. That's the point.

One glorious year, my cousin Patsy, my Uncle Jimmy's daughter, came to stay for about six months. She'd grown up in Zambia and had eventually been sent to boarding school in England, and was now waiting to start her nursing training. It was 1969, and she arrived with *Abbey Road* and a couple of Jimi Hendrix albums. My life changed forever.

Abbey Road entered my consciousness in such a complete way. It was only years later I fully recognised the pain and deep love that infused these final songs of my favourite band. Perhaps too there was something about the piano being the instrument that opened so many of them.

With Jimi Hendrix, however, it was none of these things. It was simple, raw excitement.

Here was someone who seemed so otherly, and in his entire schtick represented everything my parents feared, and all the glorious, dark possibilities of rock and roll. It seemed miles away, physically and spiritually, from my life as a young boy in Dundee in 1968, but it also provided a deep longing to get there.

Reflecting now, I guess my parents were less able to control things coming into the house if they were supplied by the daughter of a beloved brother and missionary. The possibility of seeing any of these acts live was a bridge I'd need to cross at a later date. When I brought back the second LP I ever owned, The Rolling Stones' *Get Yer Ya-Yas Out!*, my father made disapproving remarks, but never went as far as removing the offending record from my small, but growing, pile of vinyl.

I was devastated when Patsy left, as her records went with her, and I never properly owned any of the albums until many years later. She left one with us: *The Rolf Harris Show*. It's still in amongst my vinyl, a curio of a different era when he was seen as an uncontroversial light entertainer.

One great year, a transistor radio (a Bush with an exclusive Radio Luxembourg button) arrived in the house. Taking it upstairs and tuning in to pop music after dark became my favourite escape. I loved being able to hear the radio before I went to school and after I went to bed. If Tony Blackburn loved something, he'd tell you to listen to the words, and on some days, he'd play it twice. I bought 'Ain't No Mountain High Enough' by Diana Ross on the strength of Tony's enthusiasm, something I was able to tell him many years later when we met at a Radio 2 event.

Radio One stopped at six pm, however. Radio 2 took over and often it would ease the gap by playing a country show or a folk programme in the early evening. It was probably here I grew to love the roots music I still cherish to this day. After dark, it was over to Radio Luxembourg's tiny playlist, which I listened to after lights went out on a mono ear plug. Kid Jensen was our go-to guy and artists like Hurricane Smith, Neil Young and the Faces were all part of the mix. During the day, Johnnie Walker became a lunchtime oasis of taste. I still remember the first time I heard Bob Marley and the Wailers' 'No Woman No Cry', Stevie Wonder's 'He's Misstra Know-it-all' and Steely Dan's 'Doctor Wu'. I went out and bought every album on the strength of one play.

Records were great, and we gathered as many as we could, but inevitably there were many we didn't have. My sister borrowed LPs from her friends and boyfriends. *Sgt. Pepper* came and went as often as the boyfriends changed. Sometimes we had Simon and Garfunkel, and other times we didn't.

The other music in our house was live. On Sunday nights, our home filled with young people from the church, who gathered round the piano and sang. Occasionally, someone would appear and really make the old piano come alive. I remember a visiting student who'd been invited over by my parents. He was Caribbean and would often arrive and just start playing. I'd no idea what he was doing at the time, but in retrospect it was my first encounter with real gospel music. The same raw material, now syncopated and voiced slightly differently, making all the hymns we thought we knew suddenly come alive in a completely different way.

We were also visited by a Northern Irishman who seemed the epitome of conservatism, but expressed a fondness for my big sister and took me in his car while he played Elvis's gospel album at full volume.

Often, people were coaxed into singing who weren't necessarily best qualified. Some singers were better than others, and some, though past their best, still had something that drew me in. There would be solos, duos, a trio or two, and even a quartet who did barbershop harmonies to selections from the *Golden Bells* hymnary. It kept things interesting. Occasionally, the younger generation would be let loose on a song they'd heard by the Sally Army beat combo The Joy Strings, and a guitar with a hand-woven strap would be faintly strummed. One day, a young fellow even accompanied himself on a Gibson SG electric, plugged into a real amplifier by a curly lead. He wasn't asked back.

The moments I enjoyed most were the occasional solos by Lily McArthur. Lily was a grandmother figure who'd been brought along by one of the stalwarts of the congregation. I enjoyed Lily, as I detected in her voice an otherness that suggested she'd performed solo but in slightly less refined company. There was a hint of showbiz vibrato pointing towards years spent singing more worldly songs, and perhaps cooing and sighing at crooners of a different tradition. Lily's was a starker performance, and there was an ever-creeping likelihood that the whole thing might just topple over at some point in the third verse. It gave her recital the element of danger, and I identified and loved the uncertainty in her voice. In a world where no question was without an answer, Lily's voice was a thing of wonder.

I never got involved in performing music at that age, except for one experience in my boyhood that has been seared into family memory. My teacher entered me into a piano festival in Arbroath. My mother had to take me on the train there, and it meant taking a day off school. I had prepared for the performance by learning the piece prescribed off by heart, but had been cautioned to look as if I was still reading it from the sheet music. Inevitably, halfway through the performance, I didn't know whether I was reading or remembering, and did neither. There was what seemed to my nervous mother an endless pause while I retraced my steps, before I picked up where I left off. None of this was overly traumatic for me, and the adjudicator offered me consolation for having managed to complete the performance. For my mother however, it was a nightmare from which she never fully recovered. No such festivals were entered again, much to my relief and Anne's, and for the rest of her life, my mum only ever came to see me play once. Although my own children find this fact a slight aberration, for my mother and me, it was a tacit agreement that was comfortable for both of us. I felt more relaxed knowing she was elsewhere, and she found plenty to occupy her without spending more time where she really didn't want to be. It served us both well for a good forty years until she died in 2020.

In her final days, all of this came together in a strange and beautiful way. Her hearing gone and only able to enjoy tiny pieces of food – mainly soup or ice-cream – we managed to comfort her by singing old hymns together. The ones we knew from the old days.

'Amazing Grace', 'Precious Memories', 'The Lord's My Shepherd', 'How Great Though Art', 'Softly and Tenderly'. Then a chorus we must have sung so many times on a Friday night at the Bible Band with my father conducting us. A hymn of hope for the unknown, the afterlife . . . the place where we trust all tears will be wiped away.

> Away far beyond Jordan
> we'll meet in that beautiful land . . .
> If you get there before I do,
> look out for me, for I'm coming too.

Finally, I realised, it was this music, always there at the beginning, that brought us together at the end.

6

Bob McKechnie

From memory he was taller than anyone else in the primary school and I have a recollection that he had a shock of blond hair but that may be because all alien species at that time seemed to have a shock of blond hair. He was the brother of a girl in my primary class called Gail McKechnie with whom I had almost no interaction in all the six years we spent together in a classroom. He, however, was a different proposition. As little as Gail affected our comings and goings, so in inverse proportion did the tall shadow of Bob McKechnie fall darkly on our young lives.

In our primary school, we were the last leavings of the baby boom. There were forty-five children in my own class. I had to remind my mother about this in her old age, as she had heroically taught one of the three streams of the 130 children in my year. In her class, as in mine, there were at least three sets of twins. Having my mother as a teacher at my own school was never an issue for me. Whether it was down to the serious lack of opposition or my real suspicion (that she was really good), my mother and I rolled along happily at Forthill Primary.

I knew this all too well when, one summer afternoon, on the upper deck of the bus home, two older girls surrounded me, seemingly aware of whose son I was. They moved into the adjacent seat and eyed me up accusingly as they declared me the son of the teacher they had been assigned for the following session. 'We are getting your mum,' they told me.

I was terrified about what they'd say next.

'We're dead glad,' they went on. 'She's the best teacher in the school.'

The ride home was a joy.

Bob McKechnie was in my mother's class, and he was putty in her hands. Too smart to cause any grief to the school's most popular teacher, his reign of terror and chaos, shock and awe was reserved only for the hours of leisure. The corridor, the playing field and most fearful of all, the boys' toilets, were all Bob-land. No one wanted to be found loitering in any of these theatres of Bob-war, and certainly never alone. Staying away from all of them led to a relatively peaceful life.

There is something, however, to my eternal shame, I have noticed about my own response to the external threat of the bully. Over a long life, I've been a little diffident, yet also a little enthralled by those whose superior social pull or physical might, coruscating wit or blunt cynicism all seem of a higher order than my own. I am, in short, too obsequious toward the bully. I noticed this first in my early days on Twitter, finding myself drawn not to the saints, but to the naughty boys who seemed to slap down easily any possible counterpoint with a verbal cuff or a metaphoric punch. I would look on in naked admiration – and, invariably, join in. This, it seemed, was the only way to be. Discovering, inevitably, that there were also saints on social media came as a late surprise and a period of repentance followed. It was always thus.

At school, I knew to be fearful of Bob, but so, too, was I drawn to his all-powerful presence. Bob, in my shallow ten-year-old opinion, was where I wanted to be at.

And so it was, on a rare, snowy afternoon somewhere around the back gate to our school, where I would often drift off with my best pal to play at his house before returning home, that I encountered Bob McKechnie in all his pomp. Snow, much like today, was the exception rather than the rule in Dundee in the late sixties. It was always a novelty, and it was always greeted with joy by all the children in my school. The possibilities were endless: slides (always banned within a day); snowmen (mildly tolerated); snowball fights (banned by lunchtime); and all sundry snow follies followed on from a heavy fall. We were all making our way through that back gate when (school rules no longer pertaining), Bob amassed himself the biggest snowball any of us had ever seen. It was more snowman than ball, and on that particular day the snow was in perfect condition for rolling, with an incremental volume quickly magnifying until it became more snow-giant that snow-sphere.

Bob was gleeful. Only Bob could carry the weight of such a snow behemoth, and proudly he raised it up above his broad frame as we all hurrahed aloud. There was a nervous laughter too from those who'd known Bob's past form, but by this time, my own excitement at being in the presence of the great one knew no obstacle. Bob was being Bob, and it was magnificent to behold. The snow giant was now testing the strength and deter-mination of the school bully himself. To any neutral observer, it was a simple calculation of gravitational force: there was only a matter of time before Bob and his ball would be separated. I was ecstatic. I looked up to see Bob's arms at full stretch, with the mound of snow atop his heroic hands.

'Bob,' I cried for all to hear. 'You're a genius.'

I'd heard the word recently and it seemed to sum up the situ-ation perfectly. I imagined too that the epithet would be taken on board by the triumphant Bob as the full endorsement of his bully status. He would recognise in my succinct encomium the bare facts of his higher order.

He looked around, vaguely puzzled. The words barely out of my mouth, his attention fell on me from his significantly esca-lated viewpoint. The crowd went quiet as his face darkened. In one swift motion, the giant snow mound came crashing down on my head. The waiting mass roared their approval as Bob's laugh echoed out across the school field. Off he went, as they slapped his back on their way to the dark lair of Bob-land.

The snow was gone by the next day, and I never shared the story with my mother. I did ask her about teaching Bob, however. What was he like in the classroom, I wondered. She looked mildly disinterested and paused to give me a brief summary of his academic progress, then looked away absently, saying something about him being simply 'a lovely lad . . .'

7

The Traveller

Middle-class fathers of my dad's generation were fairly similar. They tinkered in garages, cut grass on the weekend and played golf. Dads, in my little suburb, were often harassed figures who found leisure activity with their children a bit of a trial – unless, of course, the offspring played golf too. As much as I liked my dad and got on well with him, he was detached almost beyond belief. He spent his working life in the business that he'd inherited from his father and grandfather in turn. Keen to carry on the family tradition, he'd suggested I should be called William McLean, to make it the fourth generation of that name, but my grandfather, who I never knew, wisely put an end to the idea by declaring, 'What do you want to give the laddie that name for?'

Here's a list of things my dad didn't do: play football with me, engage with any of my toys, come to watch me play rugby, have any meaningful conversations about sex education (I have probably tried to emulate the last one, in all fairness). He also went away quite regularly, as he was a commercial traveller by occupation.

In the sixties, your father's job was something you often had to submit to others. On my return home from visiting a school friend's house for tea, my dad's only question, which was asked out of genuine interest, was always: 'What does his father do?' There would be days at school when we all had to say what our parents' occupation was . . . and in those days, it was often only dads who went out to work. However, beneath that dull 'commercial traveller' label lay a world that, in my friends' opinions, made my dad possibly the best dad on the block. He owned and ran a three-storey toy warehouse. A building so full of charm, intrigue and undiscovered mystery that even now, when I describe it to my own children, they gasp in wonder that such an Aladdin's cave was ever within my grasp.

The warehouse, as we always referred to it, was a wholesale business whose customers were small newsagents who sold stationery and toys. My father would visit the customers and offer personal delivery on goods they ordered, which, at a time when they could easily have found what they needed at their weekly cash-and-carry expedition, seemed to be the USP of the family business. In short, they trusted him, and he, along with my Aunt Margaret, who worked alongside him, gave them a personalised service that probably flattered their already inflated sense of self-importance. They were small shopkeepers of the kind that probably annoyed you when you were growing up. Suspicious of their customers and given to overcharging when a monopoly was in their favour, they would usually have the one shop on the scheme, the main street or the village. They were sub-postmasters or mistresses, small grocers, tobacconists, newsagents, confectioners and occasionally specialist card and stationery retailers. My father took responsibility for the toys and stationery, while Aunt Margaret, an elegant and tasteful woman, was in charge of the greetings cards. Valentine's day . . . they loved it, Mother's Day . . . they celebrated it. Births, marriages, deaths, anniversaries, retirements, christenings, good luck and congratulations all had their own drawers in my Aunt Margaret's small empire at the far end of the showroom. This was a small enclave: a hive of drawers, shelves and beautifully bespoke display cases into which only those who had gained Aunt Margaret's approval could be admitted or allowed to engage. In my father's prosaic estimation, Margaret's empire was more work than its income justified, but for Margaret and for those of us keen on her aesthetic, it was the crown jewel of the showroom, the Pitti Palace to which all other avenues and alley-ways inevitably led.

To confirm its special status, the back of the display cabinets acted as a flimsy barrier to the main showroom, a demarcation that here the pop-guns, skittles, rat-tat-a-tat bats, colouring books and plastic windmills ended and the real world, Marg's world, began. In truth, it was the women of the warehouse who were anointed to work in the greetings cards section, but there would be an odd day when Margaret would fix me with her win-ning smile and ask me to help out. I never refused.

The really exciting bit for me and for any visiting cousins or school pals was the careless magnanimity my dad adopted towards samples and stock. 'Do you collect Matchbox Cars?' he'd enquire of a chum as the delighted boy took home a brand-new toy truck or car in his pocket. There were shelves of buckets, spades, hula-hoops, small cycles, pogo sticks, jigsaws, dolls, toy rifles, and then, the best part, piled on the basement concrete floor: large brown paper sacks containing Frido footballs. 'Do you have a ball, son?' my dad would ask. No one ever did.

I loved my dad's generosity. He may not have been able to fix a fuse or change a spark plug, but he had kindness in him. It wasn't a lavish or ostentatious generosity, but rather the willing-ness to give a lift in the car, or pick up a bill, or – the quality in him that I loved most – to laugh and feign interest in the unfunny and the downright dull.

From secondary-school age, my sister and I would both spend at least a few weeks, working in the warehouse during summer holidays. On a Friday, Margaret would walk round the floors handing out the pay envelopes, and I'd love seeing her hand-writing on the wage slip enclosed. Margaret and her husband, Peter, added a certain glamour to the business that we all enjoyed. Peter smoked Benson & Hedges, and often let a long, king-sized train of ash dangle on the end of his cigarette as he arranged some of the newer lines in the showroom. Margaret smoked Silk Cut, and would send me out to replenish stock from our local tobacconist customer round the corner on the Arbroath Road. She wasn't a heavy smoker, but her office, where she typed the invoices and letters of complaint to suppliers, always had the slight whiff of the exotic brought on by lingering tobacco and eau de toilette. She'd often look up from her typewriter over her half-moon lenses and ask a question, having already made a decision on some matter of display around the place: 'What do you think, Richard?' And before I was able to fully form an opinion, she'd disarm me with: 'Oh, what do I know? Maybe it was better the way it was?'

Years later, I'd visit her in her house, which was kept like the pages from a Terence Conran catalogue. Peter had died, and she was going through his old war memorabilia, which included a fetching photograph of a young French woman who seemed to have been a little more than a passing acquaintance. She paused over the photograph just long enough to require a reaction from me. I was halfway through forming a suitably bland response when she turned the page and looked me in the eye knowingly. 'What if he did, Richard? What if he did?'

Outside Margaret's office, where invoices, accounts and sales were all gathered together, worried salesmen would hover, waiting for my dad's attention, with multiple samples ready to be leafed through testily by my frazzled father. In most of my experience my dad showed remarkable ability to suffer fools gladly, but not so when it came to visiting commercial travellers, whom he treated with impatience, bordering on outright hostility. It seemed to be an understood code of the profession to show a certain degree of mutual irritation, despite the fact each side understood the rules of engagement. For my part, I quite enjoyed the spectacle of my harassed father giving short shrift to these long-suffering traders, despite feeling a little sorry for them too. In the opposite position, Dad promised customers the earth, and often slightly exaggerated the scope and size of what was, after all, a small family business of no more than a dozen staff. 'Of course, Mrs Reilly, I'll have our dispatch department get on to that and your order will be with you tomorrow.' To be clear, the 'dispatch department' was two blokes called Bert and Jimmy on the ground floor armed only with some used cartons, a large ball of twine and a rusty pen knife. It was hardly Amazon HQ.

My sister and I were always put to work in and around the stockroom, trying to decipher the hieroglyphics of Bobby, the salesman, or even my own father, who refused to believe his handwriting was illegible. My sister loved the insight into the side of Dundee she had never known, growing up in the refinement of suburban West Ferry and getting her education at the exclusive High School. Showing surprise that the young man who worked beside her on the floor was once more going home to mince and potatoes for his dinner (lunch), he, equally surprised, pointed out that it was mince and tatties for dinner *every day*.

Margaret's younger son, our cousin, Brian would often be working in the summer holidays. It must have been 1970, and Bob Dylan's impending visit to the Isle of Wight had finally brought Bob to the attention of my father. Brian was studying geography at university and clearly this meant he knew what was what. 'Who is this Bob Dylan?' my father enquired of his nephew, as he passed through the gift stationery. I can't recall whether any explanation was ever offered, or whether my dad lingered long enough to hear it.

Other people's dads worked at DC Thompson, occasionally getting close to the wheels of power on the *Beano* or *Jackie*; many worked at Timex or NCR, while some were sailors on the high seas, who would come home bearing gifts every few months. They clearly had their uses. Others were professionals, like dentists or managers of some kind, whose work offered nothing back to their offspring or their pals. One girl, who sat beside me at school and once invited me for tea, had parents who were vaguely academic and took their children to see worthy science films at the museum on a Saturday morning. Over spaghetti, or something equally exotic that I'd never before encountered, while I stared in wonder at her parents' lava lamp, the girl in question explained concepts such as infinity, abstract art and her slightly haughty view of religion, which was nowhere near my own parents' beliefs.

People who had no faith were distrusted by my parents, although, in those days, almost everyone had a connection to a church of some kind. It's no exaggeration to describe our life as a binary choice of being saved or unsaved. To be unsure of either of these details was to position oneself in the second category. Rather like the old witch trials, the plight of those outside the fold was to be damned either way. Say you were a Christian, and our people would want evidence of conversion; declare you were not, and you would attract an onslaught of determined warnings of hellfire and certain damnation.

The official minister to our primary school was a gentle man called Mr McNab. I suspect my parents and others in and around our Assembly didn't fully accept that someone such as he would be on the roll when it was called up yonder, so vague was he on the crucial details of his conversion experience. The fact of his profession and his lifelong commitment to the Church would be interpreted as a mere smokescreen to his lack of true faith.

My dad loved this certainty. His had been an adult conversion, which had, in turn, been a form of rebellion against two parents who had fled as far from fundamental Christianity as they could go. My father had joined the RAF during the war and had a conversion experience, led to faith by a Scripture Reader in the bunkhouse on the RAF station where he was billeted at the time.

By the time I was a young child, my father had a key role in our church life, but preaching really wasn't one of the jobs undertaken regularly. All the men were asked to do it now and again, as there was no minister or pastor in Brethren Assemblies, but when called to preach, my father would usually opt to tell his own story. I loved it. I could almost recite it word for word even now. He'd tell us how he'd been sent to Sunday school with his cousin Dunc, and how they'd both tried to skip it as often as possible. How he'd heard the preachers calling him, but had gone his own way, smoking, drinking and dancing the night away. It all sounded so intriguing compared to the life he now led. Then one night, he had picked up the Bible of the guy in the next bed in the bunkhouse and started to ask him questions. I tell a good deal of this story in an early song I wrote that I have now recorded a couple of times, and I finally got round to a proper version on *Short Stories Vol. 1*.

> In an RAF bunkhouse I borrowed a Bible
> The fellow who owned it, he wanted it shared.

My dad, perhaps because of his own back story, was the one who gave us any chance of keeping up with the modern world.

My mum resolutely refused to learn or acknowledge the names of actors or TV stars who would certainly have been household names to other parents. I remember her physically recoiling when Mrs Prior, our cleaning lady, waxed lyrical about the dress Shirley Bassey had been wearing on the TV variety show the evening before. It was not a conversation my mum could engage in at all. Not only would she be determined to give the impression she had little idea of who Shirley Bassey was, she was dutifully oblivious to anything that wasn't on the BBC. My mother feared the modern world. The less she knew about it, the better. My father, on the other hand, knew his way round the outskirts of Hollywood and the obsessions of the tabloids. Like many people at that time, he subscribed to lots of newspapers. The local one, the *Courier and Advertiser* was delivered every morning, as was the *Evening Telegraph* later in the afternoon. At lunchtime, he'd pick up his daily national papers from the newsagent round the corner from the warehouse. His preferences were for the *Daily Express* and the *Daily Mail*. The *Express*, in those days, was a hugely popular newspaper with a readership of millions and star columnists like Jean Rook, as well as (my own joy) the Giles cartoons. Like the *Mail*, it was right of centre, and I grew up seeing the constant lampooning of the Labour governments of the late sixties and mid-seventies. Harold Wilson was ridiculed, but the real heat was always reserved for the man they insisted on calling Wedgwood Benn. Occasionally, my father would tire of one of these papers, and for a short period we'd get to see the *Daily Mirror* with its Andy Capp cartoons. He even briefly flirted with the *Telegraph*, but I suspect it was a bit too stuffy, and he went back to his favoured mid-market dailies.

It was from these daily rags that my father gleaned most of his knowledge of current affairs. He loved the bustle of politics. Though conservative, he was fascinated by the ebb and flow of

Westminster politics. In 1968, we went to London, and my Uncle Lawrie showed us round. One night, driving round pointing out the sights, he looked up to the light above St Stephen's Tower on the Palace of Westminster. 'It's on,' he declared. 'That means there's a debate and we can go in.'

Many years later, I chatted to my father about that night, and how dull the debate had been, but also how thrilling it was, nevertheless, to be inside this place we'd heard so much about, though never saw on television. I recalled how one of the Labour MPs had sat with his feet up on the dispatch box, half slumbering on the green benches.

'You remember who that was?' my father enquired.

I demurred.

'Sir Robert Maxwell.' He smiled wryly – we both knew the eventual outcome for that particular media mogul.

Looking back on that time, I loved my father's deep love of the mysteries of Whitehall and the nooks and crannies of government. In those days, you could walk freely down Downing Street and stand for a photograph outside Number 10. We all posed, with my mother as the photographer, while my dad instigated a conversation with a hapless constable on door duty outside the PM's residence. As we walked on, he pointed out a man walking briskly towards us. It was the foreign secretary, Michael Stewart, newly appointed that morning, unencumbered by a posse or a security detail, making his way towards his office in the spring sunshine of St James's Park.

It wasn't that my father necessarily liked any of these characters, but he was hugely interested in them. I preferred his interest to my mother's diffidence and outright fear. It always seemed to me my dad would have had some experience of something I was hoping to understand. I remember a deep disappointment on discovering he'd never been to America, when I'd assumed he'd been everywhere. In truth, he'd only been to India during the war, as well as a posting in Belgium but, in comparison to my mother, he was a globetrotter.

I'm also hugely grateful for this: my dad loved England. He loved their seaside holiday resorts with piers and putting greens. He adored their quaint, rural towns full of tea shops selling scones and homemade jam. He loved their regional accents, their northern grit, their southern charm, and, something I admire now more than anything, he loved their football and cricket teams. Almost all my life, I've gone with our own national pastime of hating the English national teams. Even now, I feel a sense of shame that I took the road more travelled when I could, and perhaps should, have stuck more solidly to my father's attitude of openness and tolerance. However, it's an easy bandwagon on which to ride. English teams are big and strong and pretty good, and Scotland . . . well, we're seriously never going to win anything given our size, so it's always going to be simpler to prick the pomposity of the next-door neighbours who have self-importance deep in their DNA.

My dad knew all of that, but still loved them. England winning the World Cup in 1966 was a cause for celebration, and we were gutted when they were beaten by Germany in Mexico in 1970. Still with him on the quest at that time, I was down for days. Inevitably, I spoiled it all and became like all the other kids, celebrating England's failure to qualify for the 1974 World Cup by cheering to the rafters. I guess my fifteen-year-old self saw it simply as icing on the cake of Scotland's own qualification.

In my later years, I've come to envy the magnanimity my old man showed to his neighbours. I'm pretty sure it came from their wartime experiences. They had all been together – Scots, Irish, Welsh and English, as well as all manner of Commonwealth servicemen fighting a common enemy. And even his wartime experiences didn't make him xenophobic to any significant extent, although it took him until his final decade to finally purchase a Japanese car.

It's only in hindsight that I realise how much theatricality I inherited from my father. He instinctively enjoyed putting on a show. I remember a friend of mine encountering him in my house late one evening, and half-jokingly asking where he'd got the drink from. My dad was a tee-totaller, and had been all my life, but would burst into song late in the evening and become palpably excitable in company. His enthusiasm was infectious. He'd want stories retold, even though we all knew the punchline, a trait I have inherited wholesale. He'd express a desire to start a song, but never complete it, and would embarrass his friends by loudly reprising it on their doorsteps late in the evening. He loved hearing the piano played, and if he knew how to turn on a record player, he would wallow in big band music. In the late sixties, we stayed with my bohemian aunt and uncle in the Cotswolds. My uncle loved jazz and was keen to play something my dad would enjoy. I'll always remember his request for something featuring the piano. I suspect he was looking for Oscar Peterson, whom he later loved, but knowing Laurie, he probably got Thelonious Monk.

My father and I grew closer as years passed. In reality, we seldom clashed over anything serious, as it was always my mother who drew the firmer moral lines over matters of faith. Although my father took no issue with her judgement on these things, there was always the hint, something my sister and I agreed upon, that dad was going to be a softer touch than mum.

We both seemed to spend hours sitting in the car, waiting for him. He'd go into work at the weekends, leaving us in the

Humber Sceptre parked outside the warehouse while he checked over the books. We'd try to switch on all the lights, the windscreen wipers and the radio, so that the car would come to life when he returned. He'd lock up the large double doors and push against them to check they were shut before half-crossing the road, then returning to check the doors again. Finally, he'd get in the driver's seat, switch on the ignition, and invariably fail to notice our delight as all the electrical contraptions in the car sprang to life.

The road was where he came alive. I don't remember him ever using a bus or a bicycle – it was thought he couldn't ride one. If the warehouse was my father's empire, his car was his castle. For most of our early life, he was the only driver in the family. Though he'd encouraged my mother to learn to drive, her success in the test brought a certain academic rigour to family outings that had been absent in the halcyon days before she'd had any working knowledge of traffic law. Now my dad could be chastised for breaking speed limits, overtaking carelessly or advancing into hatched yellow boxes before knowing how or when to exit. All these manoeuvres had been blithely undertaken with minimum fuss or damage in a selection of vehicles he'd owned since someone had given him a driving licence during the war. He'd never taken lessons, and had certainly never stooped to looking at or even opening the *Highway Code*. His only cardinal rule was to expect passing AA men on motorcycles to salute when they spotted his enamel Automobile Association badge glistening on the front grille of the car. The coming of seat belts in the mid-sixties was an additional hazard that brought untold misery on longer journeys, when my mother would insist they be buckled, only for my father to be unable to extricate himself from the apparatus at the next service station. Until they became mandatory – a dark day – my father avoided them whenever he could. It was ironic, therefore, that years later, in his last solo car ride, his life was temporarily prolonged by a seat belt, though an airbag was also involved.

His cars were all British. In the sixties, they were always Rootes Group cars: a Hillman Minx, a Singer Vogue, and then the beautiful metallic gold Humber Sceptre, which was perhaps my favourite. He moved to Fords after that, with a Corsair, then a run of Cortina GLXs, which were quite flashy with their alloys and vinyl roofs. All the cars had radios, and the radio was always on: Terry Wogan going to school, William Hardcastle and *World at One* at lunchtime. On the way home, it would be the full six o'clock news bulletin from Radio 4. We'd change the station to Radio One whenever we could, until the noise became too much, and he demanded it go back to something he could understand. On a Saturday, it would be the football reports and, if we weren't at a game ourselves, a match commentary, still one of the great joys of radio, in my opinion. He took the car everywhere, and it was always a special thrill on a family picnic or Sunday school outing when the car had to be driven over the grass; we'd squeal in delight at every bump and turn of the wheels on the unfamiliar surface. For a short while, it felt as if all the rules were being broken.

My dad enjoyed his own particular driving traits, which, when pointed out by a friend, did seem quaint. 'Are your dad's indicators not working then?' one of my neighbours asked as my father turned off the main road into our street. The driver's-side window was down, and his hand was out to signal a right turn. I hadn't noticed anything unusual. 'No,' I said. 'He just likes doing it that way.'

The car took him where he needed to go, but always with the possibility that a journey might coincide with a small diversion he could enjoy. Never one to be tied down too firmly, his position as boss of the family firm always allowed for a degree of laxity in his daily timetable. There were frequent visits to the accountant, customer calls to his best pal at one of the department stores, which would inevitably coincide with coffee in Grossi's on Victoria Road, a fine Italian café also know to the locals as Mike's. His bank was near enough Visocchi's Café in Broughty Ferry to allow him the occasional coffee there too.

For a few weeks of the year, he'd also return to his sales patch and take week-long journeys to visit his customers. His two main beats were the Moray Firth and the west coast, including some of his bigger accounts in Plockton and Skye. He loved driving the Highland roads, though never, to our knowledge, felt drawn to exit the car and walk some of the hills he must have passed at regular intervals. His route would take him up the A9 towards Inverness, then east through Buckie, Banff, Cullen and Peterhead, then back down the road from Aberdeen towards the Angus towns. His orders would be posted back to base.

Margaret was always there to run the shop while my dad travelled away, and she would point to some awful piece of tat my father had bought in bulk and shake her head in disbelief at his acute lack of taste. Margaret had style, but she also had to admire the fact that, despite the lack of merit in the line in question, the orders would still roll in for said 'tat': whatever my father had bought, he'd sell, and sell successfully. 'That's a winning line,' he'd proclaim, with a laugh in his voice.

By the time we went to secondary school, he would drop my sister and me outside the gates of Dundee High School just before the morning assembly bell at nine. Leaving the warmth of that car was a heartbreaking moment every day. How I envied his solo ride back up the road to his new warehouse in Kemback Street, listening to the wireless with what seemed like a day of freedom in front of him. We were imprisoned in unforgiving classrooms, surrounded by outsiders who didn't understand our insulated morning car ride, the voice of Terry Wogan, the simple stories of *Pause for Thought* and the lingering sadness that, as we closed the car doors, the radio show would carry on without us for all the hours we were trapped by the school day.

I only saw the last trails of exhaust fumes heading east past the museum as his rear lights faded into the morning mist of what passed for a rush hour in Dundee. I was the snared schoolboy, facing the vagaries of fragile friendships and overbearing teachers, with homework that hadn't been completed and lessons still unlearned. He was free from all of that. Behind the wheel of his car, he could go anywhere he liked, the radio playing all day if he so chose, the roads leading north, south across the river or west, to places free of timetables, rules, bells and uniforms. Little did I know that even then, under the hum of traffic noise and light music on the wireless, there was a worry in his world that would eventually overtake him.

8

There Was a Guy Two Streets Round From Us Who'd Been Stabbed in the Leg

There was a guy two streets round from us who'd been stabbed in the leg. In all the years we lived in our small housing estate (not scheme) I can't remember ever meeting him – or, for that matter, seeing him. It was, however, known to every one of us that this had happened and, far from feeling any sense of upset or grievance on behalf of the young man, there was instead a sense of respect, and a quiet but sincere awe that someone from an area as non-descript as ours had been part of such high drama.

Who had stabbed him in the leg was never ascertained. Why someone did the deed was also never speculated upon; and none of us ever thought to question why an assailant would aim quite so low. What were these unknown aggressors aiming *for*? Was the lad round the corner a giant whose Achilles heel was in fact his right thigh – I always imagined it to be that muscle – and did this wound render him incapable of jousting in future Broughty Ferry turf wars? I never knew, and I never sought to know.

His story was one of many things my friends and I never fully knew. Looking back, perhaps we enjoyed the dim light of the semi-known, the half-explained, the mysterious suburban mythology as compelling as Boo Radley's place. There were others: the man at the bottom of the hill who built his own kit car; Stewart Dunlop's dad, who always seemed slightly more jovial as the day progressed and never held down a steady job. And then there was Willie.

Willie, or Wullie, only really appeared in the summer. Even in the sixties and seventies, Willie was a character apart. Imagining him now would be impossible for a number of reasons. His job, even then, was fading out of practice and he may well have been the last of his kind. He was a leerie man. His job was to light up and maintain the last of the gas lamps in the city. There were still enough of these to give Willie a regular round, but even he knew that the lamps were a hissing metaphor for his own job, which was disappearing as rapidly as the old cobbles on the roads were being dug up and tarred over. You would see him down by the docks where the old lights still stood, marking the way to the shore as he pedalled along on his round. That was the other thing about Willie; he cycled everywhere.

Around the back of teatime in the summer months, when boys of all ages descended on the local park to play football, Willie would arrive on his bike, park it against one of the beech trees that doubled as bike racks and goal posts, and join in with any of the games that were going. Dusk would come, and Willie would be off on his rounds again.

To my surprise, a lad at my school who lived at the opposite end of town knew Willie from around his patch too. Wherever football games were played, it seemed Willie appeared and joined in, cycle clips still on. He was a good player, and the fact that he was thirty years or so older than the lads in the park only seemed to earn him respect. Arguments of hand-ball, foul play and general cheating were quickly sorted out.

He was also brilliant with bikes. When I wanted a racing bike, I managed to persuade my parents to buy a second-hand one from my sister's boyfriend, and Willie repainted it to make it look brand new. My sister and mother privately fretted about Willie and expressed doubts that the bike would ever return, until one great day, a few weeks after Christmas, Willie came strolling up our garden path with a proud hand on the saddle and handed over the spruced-up five-geared racer.

Willie's world, and indeed our world, was the park. On a Saturday, it was the epicentre for all the amateur football in the area, and the players tumbled out of a tiny pavilion smelling of liniment and boiling-hot tea to warm up in their faded strips. On a big day, a team might manage uniformity, but on any given Saturday, there would always be someone in the wrong shorts, older versions of the jersey or socks from teams and seasons past. We'd watch from the sidelines and occasionally get to pass a ball back that had been blootered out by a defending side, or more likely escaped the goalie's clutches and sped on past the netless posts.

Only on very special days would nets adorn the goalposts. Slowly and lovingly, after the touchlines had been marked out by sawdust, a groundsman would hook up a net for a special cup tie involving a visiting side from across the water or the outer glens of Angus. The nets would hang lamely down, as no one had considered stanchions or poles in those rudimentary times of amateur football. To us youngsters however, the nets brought joy unconfined. For the minutes between a net going up and the first whistle of the kick-off, we'd play shootie-in, trying to emulate our favourite moments of televised football. Our footballs, sometimes leather, but mainly plastic and misshapen, would be thudded into the goal again and again in those golden moments before the players arrived on the park and shooed us away. On one memorable day, the park keeper returned to his be-netted pitch to see us pounding the ball into the goal and was apoplectic with rage. 'Get awa' from that, ye dopey cunts,' was his succinct warning.

Only occasionally would a dark shadow cross over the green sward of football, cricket and hockey arenas. One morning during the summer holidays, an outsider had encroached. Parked on the small hillock that ran parallel to the main road, the wire mesh fencing had been breached and a broken Ford Consul slumped on the grass, body scratched, tyres burst and windscreen shattered.

'My dad raised the alarm,' Colin Glass informed us as we inspected the wrecked car.

None of us knew what had happened. It seemed the driver had left the passing A-road and crashed through the flimsy fencing surrounding our park. The blood on the bonnet and dashboard told us as much as we were expected to know. In those days, parents only shrugged at such incidents, if, as in this case, they didn't need to be involved.

In the same resigned fashion, we never knew the boy who'd been stabbed, where Willie lived or even if he had a house. We also never expected the goal nets to return, any more than we knew if Stewart's dad would ever work again. Curious but resigned to a state of blissful unknowing, we neither sought nor found out any more.

9

My Mother's Middle Names

My mother hated her middle names. She also resisted any abbreviation of her Christian name, Catherine. No Kate, Katy, Cathy, and certainly not Kathleen. That she shared a name with one of the most famous actors of our generation never occurred to her. Neither Catherine Ross was aware of the other.

She was born in April 1928, the last of four children to Joseph and Catherine Ford. My grandparents never used their own forenames in earshot of their own children or grandchildren. They were Joe and Kitty to their friends, but always Mum or Dad to each other, for as long as my mother or I knew them.

My grandfather had been charged with registering his youngest daughter's birth, and after discussing the merits of calling her after his sister, he took it upon himself to give her his sister's *full* married name. Catherine Jessie Bruce Ford she remained, until her surname was changed on her wedding day in 1953. It was only in her final years that she confided in me how much she'd hated the Bruce bit, and how annoyed her mother had been with my grandpa for adding it unnecessarily.

Jessie Bruce was a widowed aunt whose husband was never described in warm terms by my mother. They lived in Lochee, never having any children, and it seemed he had spent a good deal of time in bed with a long-term illness, which gave him the reputation within the Ford family as being something of a malingerer. After his death, Jessie moved into a small tenement flat on the third floor of the Lochee Road with her two unmarried sisters, and that flat, which they kept all the way through my mother's childhood and my own, became a place of real happiness for my mother and her sisters. Any stories of fun and laughter from her childhood always took place at the aunties', where the coal bunker at the bay window of the kitchen became the stage for children's plays and *Happy Families* or bagatelle were played each Friday night on their visits. The main charm for me was the tall, carved pump organ that dominated the front room and required the pedalling of bellows to make it play. We loved pulling the different stops that read 'diapason bass', 'dulciana' or 'flute', following in the tradition of the Ford children before us.

I took after my mum in many ways. It was to her I looked for advice on most things growing up. I knew her to be intelligent and educated, although she distanced herself from the modern world. Looking back, we've found the only way to describe her relationship with popular culture of all kinds as fearful. As I've said, she'd convince herself she knew none of the names of the entertainment stars who regularly appeared on television in front of her. Similarly, she took a distracted view of current affairs, leaving most of that to my father and his enthusiastic consumption of newspapers. Perhaps the real reason for her lack of interest in the wider world was that her life was so full with caring for her family and extending hospitality to the community of preachers who visited our Brethren Assembly at weekends.

She was also a brilliant mother whose time was always given over to her children. In the hours between school ending and bedtime, she was all ours. In the early days before the gas board came to install central heating, we'd both come back from the primary school, where she taught and I studied, on the number seven bus, getting off at the stop at the end of Fairfield Road. By the time we got home on winter afternoons, our hands and feet would be freezing, and she'd boil a kettle for us so we could gingerly insert our numb fingers and toes into the warm water and feel our blood circulating once again. Homework would be supervised as tea was prepared, and after or during, she'd encourage our reading, explain arithmetic and, in later years, take me through Latin and French verbs, shaking her head in disbelief that I didn't embrace foreign languages with the same enthusiasm she'd shown in her own school days.

She had been the only child in her family who had gone on to higher education, having attended the academy when the others had either not been allowed or not qualified. During the war years, she had learned German, singing songs in the language, and despite the blackouts, air raids and the fact that her brother and her father were sent away to assist in the conflict, she always separated her love of German culture from the country they were trying to defeat. When she was offered a place at St Andrews University, she had feared for her parents' ability to support her financially. The place she was offered had been deferred by a year to allow returning servicemen first choice after the war, and in light of this she opted instead to begin a course in primary school teaching, which she could start immediately while staying at home. Like many of her contemporaries, the cost of this would be augmented by part-time work, and any grant received was immediately handed over to become part of her family's household budget. As a young student, she had met and fallen for a young man who had visited her Brethren Assembly in Dundee. As they got to know each other, he asked her to marry him, and the engagement was announced on her twenty-first birthday.

It's sixty-four years later and we are driving through the north of England so she can join her friend on a short holiday in Lytham St Annes. I wanted to be reminded of the stories of her life I didn't know so well, and, to my surprise, she wanted to tell me one more story I *really* didn't know. She explained that her sister Margaret had reminded her about it at her ninetieth birthday celebration a couple of years before.

It was about the moment that her engagement in 1949 had been broken off. It turned out her fiancé had moved to London, and their long-distance correspondence didn't endear my mother to the idea of spending the rest of her life with him. He didn't take it well, but she knew it was the decision she had to make.

It was a moment of truth for us both, as we drove through the leafy roads approaching the coast that summer's day. She, explaining events from long before I was born, and me, hearing the forgiveness and love in her voice about my own failed first marriage. We'd both made mistakes. Critically, mine had brought about greater heartache and pain, but in her words that day I heard an understanding brought about by her reflection on her own circumstances some forty years earlier.

'It's a hard time being young,' she said. 'You know all about that yourself . . . It was bad enough being engaged, but it's worse when you go into a marriage and you have that problem, and you realise it's a mistake. But what do you do about it?'

We'd driven a long way that day. She'd been attending her sister Mary's birthday celebrations in Cardiff, and I'd volunteered to drive her up to Lytham afterwards. It seemed those miles on the motorway had allowed us both to talk honestly. We were both regretful, but both trying to make sense of our younger selves. It was a journey north that took us so much further than our planned destination. I drove the last miles to Glasgow alone, with a new understanding of the one person I had known all my life.

As a kid, you meet other kids' mums all the time, and you make comparisons with your own parents. A teenage girlfriend whose own bohemian mother wore maxi skirts and sported waist-length blonde locks once asked if my mum had brown curly hair and glasses. I couldn't believe how accurately she'd guessed, until she reminded me that ninety-five per cent of mums looked like that in 1972.

Despite – or perhaps because of – that conservatism, my mum was a life force for me. She was as surprised and confused as anyone when I became a musician and not a teacher, preacher or journalist, as we'd both talked of in my teenage years. She was an encourager who told me I was special when I needed to hear it and it was her kind of faith I inherited. It's kept me going in all weathers and in the final days and months of her life it gave us both the strength to face the future.

All of that was founded on those magical early years. It was my mum who taught me how to cycle, took the stabilisers off, took me into town to buy me a puncture-repair kit, then showed me how to change a tyre on the bike. It was she who sat down at the piano and kept me practising when I might have given up. One Easter holiday, she told me we were going to paint the kitchen together. She chose the paint, bought a roller and sewed the new curtains, and we all delighted in the fresh new feel of the bright back door on which I'd been let loose.

One bitter Christmas, I flatly refused to go to the Sunday school party. I had a dread of all parties, and I probably still have a slight nervousness of all occasions that require new clothes – to paraphrase E. M. Forster – but on this occasion, I wasn't for changing. My mum bribed me by taking me to David Low's Sports Shop in the Seagate to let me pick an item of my choosing. I picked a Dundee United tie. I still have it, hanging beside all the other useless ties, but, unlike all the others, I could never throw that one out. I still feel bitterly guilty about having had the upper hand, dragging her out of her way on a cold December Saturday and, worse still, extracting payment.

My mother had a way of covering any blushes in those awkward moments. If she dished out a treat to me when my sister wasn't there or a pal wasn't about, it was always accompanied by, 'Since you're not everybody.' Some of the best nights were those when she would read me stories from the children's Bible she used to read to her own classes at school. She knew them all off by heart, and I'd soak in the tales of walls tumbling down as Joshua circled the city of Jericho, or marvel at the faith of Naaman's servant girl, the jealousy of King Saul to David and the deep bond of trust between Ruth and Naomi. We'd laugh at the ridiculousness of the Sadducees, and I'd imagine Zacchaeus up his Sycamore tree. Most of all, I saw in her the humanity of a God who came as a man whose yoke was easy. My faith changed, ideas grew, and in my twenties, I felt I barely shared the same beliefs that she celebrated, but similarly to Mark Twain's wise axiom,* I was amazed at how much she'd picked up over the last couple of decades.

If there is one thing I tell my children about more than others, it is our Easter trips to Edinburgh. It would be my mother, my sister and me. We'd go from Dundee on the train, crossing both bridges, and spend a full day in the capital. In the morning, it would be the castle, then down the Royal Mile past St Giles to the Museum of Childhood. We'd enjoy a packed lunch of sandwiches and a flask of soup in Princes Street Gardens before we spent the afternoon at the zoo, the highlight of the day. I was always mesmerised by the flags hanging in the halls of the castle. Tattered, worn and bloodied-looking, they instilled awe in a young boy who dreamed of soldiers and fighting men.

---

* 'When I was a boy of 14, my father was so ignorant I could hardly stand to have the old man around. But when I got to be 21, I was astonished at how much he had learned in seven years.'

Something of their faded grandeur came through to me in a way that went beyond my understanding of the world up to that point. It would stay with me all through my life. Standing on the station at Haymarket, waiting for the train that would take us back home via Queensferry, Kirkcaldy and Cupar, clutching our Edinburgh-rock souvenirs and trying to delay opening them for fear we'd finish them too soon, in my head, the flags would still be gently waving.

The last months of my mum's life took place during the first phase of the 2020 Covid-19 pandemic. Should we have hugged, kissed, embraced or even just touched more? I really don't know. My sister, my wife and I simply tried to make her life as enjoyable as we could. For my part, I played endless games of *Scrabble*, and would sweep round tidying up while she figured out an epic triple-word score. She loved *Scrabble* and we played it until very near the end.

I live with one regret about which she and my family have been kind. On the first day we were allowed to leave our council area, I packed a picnic and took her out in the summer sunshine to Largs on the Ayrshire coast. She'd fallen asleep a couple of times on the way down, but we persevered, and, with her wheeled walker, we strolled along the promenade before taking a short rest. I've gone over this next scene a hundred times and still never fully understood how it occurred, while still blaming myself that it did. It was colder than I'd hoped, and we headed back to the car. I looked round towards the sea with my mother on my arm beside me and suddenly, to my horror, despite her leaning on her walker, she was falling over. As she tumbled on to the hard pavement, I could hear her cry of pain. We struggled to get her to a safe seat, but it became obvious some damage had been done. Miraculously, an off-duty auxiliary nurse, who knew mum and recognised me from my visits to her a few months earlier, was nearby, and he and his wife, also a nurse, helped me to look after her while we waited for the ambulance. I am still indebted to those two folks today.

As the ambulance pulled away and I thought through the awful certainty that she was about to be admitted to a hospital where we would not be allowed to visit her, I held my head in my hands and wept. I felt I had let her down when she needed me most. Those around me assured me that the wind had caught her and there was nothing I could have done. My sister and all the family too were full of consolation and understanding about what had happened, but I still go over that day in my head, again and again and again.

It's a while now since she died. The broken hip seemed to speed her decline. She died surrounded by her family. My sister was sitting beside her in her room, and my wife and I were driving up to the hospital. We were just minutes away, and were still able to hold her warm hand and kiss her face as we said goodbye. In the days and weeks after her death, I received cards from folks I knew and many I didn't, and I realised her life had touched so many people, who felt they knew her and that she was someone special to them. I felt a pride of ownership for the first time since that day, so long ago, when those two schoolgirls had declared their delight that my mother would be their teacher in the next term.

She drifted in and out of consciousness in those last few days. We sang all the hymns she knew, and each became more poignant than the next. She'd mouth the words with gusto, but there was no voice left to give out any volume. It's her singing I've always remembered. Upstairs in my childhood bedroom, I'd hear her singing sacred songs, the only songs she really knew, in the kitchen below.

We sang for ages, gathered around her. The Covid rule book

was abandoned or ignored by kind staff who had been down this road a few times. One day, she'd had enough. As she eloquently put it, 'I'm weary of the singing now.' It was an apt metaphor for understanding how to slip away from life when it seems you can no longer be part of it. We often thought she was going, but then she'd rally and the nurse closest to the family would express her disbelief that she'd pulled through once again. In almost the last thing we all heard her say, she spoke out the faith she'd always professed. It was both her mantra for living and her final words to us all. Faintly but firmly came the words: '*God is good.*'

Part Two

ONE THING LEADS TO ANOTHER

10

You Write One Song

By the time I graduated from college, I knew how to put a song together. Without a very clear career plan, I embarked on teacher training, which, halfway through, changed to a degree course, resulting in my qualification as an English teacher.

In my final two years at college, I spent as much time playing music in small piano-practice rooms and at home, as I did in any other part of my life. It was the need to see where the song might lead that nagged me into filling my life with music.

Knowing when a song is finished is always tricky. The most difficult audience for any song is one made up of your own musical partners. They are the fiercest judges and often the ones who can kill a song dead before it's ever really alive. Musicians will receive a new song in a very particular way. Unlike a typical audience, they will listen to see what they should be doing, and will often make no comment on the song at all. These days, I tend to demo things before I let others hear too much, but in the past I've always been a little guilty of showing too much too early. It's a natural thing to want to share a song, and I've learned (the hard way) that when music managers, A&R people or music publishers assure you they can listen to songs without any production, that is the polar opposite of the truth. Never, never let people hear a work tape, phone recording or something similar. (Unless, of course, you are letting someone hear it well after the final master has been successfully recorded, released and adored.) They just won't get it. Within minutes, you'll hear comments about needing harmonies, or strings, or brass; they'll say it's too slow or too fast, and you'll say, 'But it's a work tape – you said you wanted to hear it!'

But you really should have known better.

I still remember my first songs. There's one I wrote when I was about eighteen that I really like, and I can still play it and remember most of the words. It was written on my folks' old piano, which sat in the study (as we used to call it). They'd gone away somewhere overnight, and I'd been left to look after the dog. I made the most of this time to myself by making music at all hours of day and night. I'd just watched *Bus Stop*, a great Marilyn Monroe movie, and something about the western feel of the film (there's a cowboy who gets in a fight) must have rubbed off on me. A song called 'Don't Let Me Be the One' emerged. It contained no real reference to the film, but somehow both are locked together in my memory.

As well as trying to write songs, I was busy doing what all music fans do: constantly absorbing new music and checking out artists and bands playing live. Gigs were always fresh and exciting – even if they got slightly dangerous at various points. I remember being appalled at the antipathy and disdain shown by the crowd who'd come to see Alex Harvey support The Who at Celtic Park in 1976. The Sensational Alex Harvey Band fans around us were oblivious to Little Feat, who were the band I really, really wanted to see. They were drunk, loud and abusive, and we had to try and look over their heads to appreciate what was happening onstage while, all around us, fights broke out and general mayhem ensued.

If that was rough, then any given night at the Caird Hall in Dundee or the Apollo in Glasgow provided full-scale warfare between paying customers and fat, boozed-up bouncers who saw it as their duty to humiliate and intimidate the audience. It was a strange old routine that really exploded when punk rock came along, and mini riots in the mosh pit were par for the course. I remember Joe Strummer having to suggest to his fans that 'gobbing' was not really a great idea but, somehow, it had become standard practice in the years after 1977. Gigs were fuelled by testosterone and alcohol, and often the music had to be experienced while keeping a wary eye on what the people next to you were about to do. Bouncers took great joy in not just ejecting rowdy punters, but also giving them a good going over once outside any particular venue. My friend's brother was a plumber by day and a bouncer on the weekend. The main meeting point for the 'security team' was a pub round the corner from the Caird Hall, where the penguin-suited squad would assemble for a considerable number of drinks before commencing their night's work.

In my early days in Glasgow, Radio Clyde hosted an annual open-air show at Kelvingrove Bandstand, which attracted a crowd who saw lobbing bottles as a reasonable way to interact with the band onstage. I remember witnessing a Bluebells gig there one sunny Saturday. A fight broke out on the stage, and people were running round with blood gushing out of head wounds – but there was never any notion that the show might not go on!

I'd witnessed enough of this world as a paying customer to know which parts of the music business I wanted to sample and which parts I'd gladly skip. It's the reason why, in 1988, when Deacon Blue were invited to play at Reading Festival, I decided a quick exit was preferable to becoming the target for missiles. There was no great malice in the bottle-throwing – in fact, it was seen as a rite of passage that all the bands should endure – but I took the line that dodging festivals over dodging bottles would prove a better career move.

The only thing I have ever been fascinated by was the power of a song, and what a song could do to me when it really connected. I desperately wanted to do that to other people with songs that I'd created.

Songwriting is not a gift in the way certain motor or artistic skills are. It's something you learn about and keep learning over the course of your life. If you're lucky enough to have any success with it, the chances are you will have listened to good advice, and adapted and changed what you do. In 1980, the only discernible contribution I could make to any musical venture was some kind of instinct about what went into a song. I had written a fair few songs by this stage, but there were probably only two or three that I could confidently say were any good. Writing songs was the part I'd most enjoyed about playing with the only two bands I'd been in so far. That I never found any great satisfaction with these bands also explained my restlessness. I needed to find the right musical way forward for the thing I wanted to keep doing: writing new songs.

If you write a song, you need to hear it back. You can sing it to friends or at a gig – if you're lucky enough to get one – but ultimately, the way you hear it in your head is different to how it sounds in its raw, unvarnished state. The songwriter knows all manner of magic is yet to happen, and the only way that magic will be realised is if the song is recorded and properly produced. And that's why I needed to keep following the dream: so that I could hear the thing I heard in my head reproduced, in brilliant stereo, coming out of my own speakers. To do that, I needed more songs, better songs, and also some people to play them, someone to record them and someone to bring them out on a record.

None of these things seemed very likely to happen in 1980. Instead, I carried on writing and playing songs in my room. Some of these were merely passages, a means to get from one song to the next. Try, fail, proceed and fail again. I always felt the important thing to do was finish the song in question. So they're all still there somewhere, those songs that filled my room; roughly put down on cassettes, and scribbled in an old book of lyrics still lying in a cupboard in my studio. Some I could still sing from memory, knowing them better than songs that have gone on to become records. In the early days, it was important to sing a song enough times to be able to remember it the next time you came back to it. There are no lost gems, and this is not a case of false modesty. In the mid-eighties, I scurried around all these back pages to find things, anything that would take me to the next stage.

In the meantime, I remained in love with popular music. There's always so much to love.

11

Cockburn Street

In my final years of college and early days of work, I managed to play music with friends in Edinburgh. It was a loose arrangement that happened on and off for a couple of years. The upside, apart from the joy of making music together, was the ability to escape to the capital by walking to the bottom of the street where I lived in Dundee and getting on the first train to Waverley Station. From there, a short walk to my friend's flat in Tollcross. In retrospect, it was those walks to and from the station that left the biggest impression.

If you ever go to Edinburgh, you'll spend time in and around the Royal Mile, either dodging the tartan kitsch or fully embracing it on your way to or from the castle at the top of the hill. Halfway down, you might well pass John Knox's house, from where he made his way towards St Giles' Cathedral to lambast the French Queen Mary, urging her to repent of her Catholic ways and adopt the doctrines of Jean Calvin, so beloved of the old Scots preacher. Of course, she never did, and it is tempting to imagine what he would have made of his new neighbour, a storytelling and arts centre once run by the Church of Scotland.

The Netherbow, as it is still called, is a place I got to know quite well for a while in the late seventies and early eighties. One summer evening around that time, I heard the music of David Heavenor there for the first time. I'd known of David through a couple of friends, but had not yet listened to his songs. That night, I heard him play a short, fairly unrehearsed set supporting a band whose music I now can't remember. David, however, was something special, and I knew I wanted to hear more. It would be a year later before we hooked up properly and began an on/off band that we never fully formed, but never quite broke up either. We are still great friends and I still regard him as the best songwriter I know.

Quite how I ended up in a flat overlooking the Meadows that August night after the show, I don't know. It was late summer at festival time, and we were listening to music, with the sash windows pulled up to let in that yeasty, beery Edinburgh air. As ever with musical awakenings of youth, it felt as if anything and everything was possible.

Later, I tried to identify who I'd had this conversation with, and my friends felt they knew the person. All I could remember was I'd been talking to a guy who was Canadian, and I'd asked him which Canadian musician he loved most. Slowly, he said, 'Bruce Cockburn.'

'I have never heard of him,' I said. 'What does he do?'

The Canadian paused, then looked me straight in the eye and, as if disclosing the whereabouts of the Holy Grail, he slowly intoned: 'Rain rings trash can bells, and what do you know, my alley becomes a cathedral.'

To understand owning and playing records in the seventies, you have to understand the economics of the time. To have a large record collection, you either needed to have lots of money or share a house with enough fellow music fans to allow you to double or quadruple your own collection. Friends from big families were usually those with the best music collections, and each new album collected was accounted for, catalogued and cherished. Other than that, the only other way to collect music was to borrow and tape your pal's albums, or to record things off the radio.

That didn't work with Bruce Cockburn, however. His albums weren't in the shops, and he certainly wasn't played on the radio. The Canadian had, unintentionally, sent me on a quest.

With the opening of Groucho's, a great second-hand record shop on Perth Road in Dundee's West End, new possibilities of owning more records – pre-owned, cheap records – came about. I walked into Groucho's one day to find an album called *Sunwheel Dance* by Bruce Cockburn and nearly collapsed with excitement. My best pal Doug knew a guy who had a good record collection, and this guy owned albums by Bruce Cockburn (and Nick Drake – despite the ubiquity of Nick Drake's music now, back in 1978, his was a name on very few lips). Piecing it all together, Doug now thinks that copy of *Sunwheel Dance* must have been his friend's, which had been traded in. In all Christendom, I was the only person I knew who owned a Bruce Cockburn album. I took it to heart and passed it round lovingly to my friends.

Within a couple of years (I'm not entirely sure of the timing) a wonderful thing happened. I was now making music with David Heavenor. It so happened that the reason I'd seen him that night at the Netherbow was because he worked there; it was a magical place that attracted artists, musicians and poets of all kinds. David befriended many of them. I remember encountering the beat poet Alan Jackson in David's flat one day, and all of my middle-class sensibilities being shaken. The poet was standing among the debris of his week-long residency, and the place looked how I imagined a hotel room might be left behind on a Steppenwolf tour. The unmade bed was crisscrossed with pieces of clothing, empty bottles and overspilling ashtrays. I must have asked him about himself, as I can only recall him telling me: 'I'm a poet. I'm a good poet.'

That stayed with me. It felt anti-Scottish and quite the reverse of anything anyone was meant to say, and I liked it. If you were going to try to do anything in the arts world, surely you had to know whether you had the basic requirements. I took it on as a mantra. I wanted to be – and I guess I still want to be – a songwriter. A good songwriter.

It may have been that day or another, but one afternoon after hanging in Edinburgh with David and assorted others, I was making my way down towards Waverley Station through the old town. Halfway down the hill, on Cockburn Street, was a great record shop, which, for reasons still unclear now, was displaying a Bruce Cockburn album in the window. I went inside and discovered they had taken stock of five of his albums. I took out my chequebook and bought all of them, including doubles for my pal Doug, who was, by this time, a massive fan.

In fact, a little while before, Doug had decided to write to Bruce via his record label in Toronto. In a moment that filled us all with joy, a postcard came back from Bruce himself, saying how pleased he'd been to get the mail. Doug had asked if he might be interested in playing this small music festival we were organising in Dundee. We had no idea how to book any bands, but we were looking for artists who might understand that tricky dynamic of music and faith, and Bruce matched our profile. He declined, of course . . . but hey, it was a classy reply, and frankly he had no idea how little money we had, even if he'd fancied it.

By the time these records arrived, we'd become slightly obsessed, and the albums only served to confirm our deep love. The haul that day was made up of *High Winds, White Sky*; *Salt, Sun and Time*; *Joy Will Find a Way*; *In the Falling Dark* and *Night Vision*. For us, they filled in the missing years between the only album we'd managed to find before now, and the current one, which was actually starting to get him some radio play. It was called *Dancing in the Dragon's Jaws*, and featured an airwave-friendly reggae song, 'Wondering Where the Lions Are', which could be heard on Radio 1 on a good day.

The discovery of those early Bruce albums was a moment for me that might be hard to understand now, in this age of immediate streaming and downloads. The idea that we can now access all these recordings with such ease still fills me with a slight sliver of excitement akin to finding buried treasure in the garden.

In time, we got to see Bruce Cockburn. Although it would be many years before he came to Scotland, he played in England at Greenbelt Festival in 1984, and we all went to see him. Five years later, I even managed to meet up with him when he dropped in for the soundcheck at our one and only show in Toronto.

Years later, I hosted a show on BBC Radio Scotland, and persuaded my producers that an hour's conversation with Bruce would make great radio. By this time, Bruce was living in San Francisco, and we talked over the phone. It was such a pleasure, even though I'd departed a little from my ardent fandom of the early years and hadn't quite kept up the same enthusiasm with the numerous releases of his later career. It's difficult to do that with any artist, and I totally understand people who enjoy our early work and have no real interest in the later stuff.

Bruce's music has continued to move and challenge, and despite having some favourite early albums, I always listen to what comes next.

As for the beat poet, Alan Jackson? I never saw or heard of him again. I liked the 'good poet' thing, though and found it handy to explain myself. I clung on to it for dear life whenever I was in an artistic trough of one kind or another, using it as a self-help mantra.

When I checked through my vinyl albums recently, I was pleased to find that some of those early Bruce Cockburn albums had survived. I also found one that I'd bought as another second-hand discovery. For the life of me, I can't remember where I got it, but the price is still on it: £1.75 for a beautiful gatefold 1970 copy of his debut album, simply called *Bruce Cockburn*. Track two is called 'Thoughts on a Rainy Afternoon', and it was a particular joy to find the lyric that started off the whole quest:

> *Rain rings trash can bells,*
> *And what do you know*
> *My alley becomes a cathedral.*

12

Back Here in *Beano* Land

*I studied for my teaching degree at Dundee College of Education.
It took until my final years for me to enjoy my time there. It was
then I realised I should have made more of an effort to leave home
after school . . . I suspect my parents were of a similar opinion.*

I had no real idea of what I wanted to do with my life, and part
of me feared teaching. As it happened, I was quite good at it,
although I was better with the kids than the subject.

By this stage, making music had begun to dominate a good
deal of my spare time. My two teenage friends, Mhairi and Rod
Gordon, had invited me to join a band with them. They'd heard
me play the piano round about the church and, thanks to them,
and their parents' generosity (they moved the family piano into
the garage so we could rehearse there), I was in my first band.
Their cousin, Dave Walker, was the drummer for a short time,
while Rod played guitar and Mhairi sang. We have remained
lifelong friends. Without their encouragement and kindness, I
wouldn't have had the courage to let anyone else hear my songs.

Perhaps because I was starting to play music and ask questions, much of what I had known and assumed began to change,
and the parameters of my youth and childhood were shifting
fundamentally. Having grown up within a conservative evangelical theology, I'd always accepted many of the precepts of that
style of faith. Now, I began to ask whether it was able to answer
the questions I seemed to be facing.

I'd finally left the Brethren church in which I grew up. Looking back now, I realise there was a multitude of reasons for this. Essentially, I stopped fitting in, but most of this could have been solved by leaving home and finding my feet in another town. However, I still lived at home, and needed, in some way, to make sense of everything without wanting to alienate my parents . . . even though that did, inevitably, happen.

My move away from the Brethren brought me to a Church of Scotland church in the centre of the city, where the minister seemed to understand some of what I was going through. He'd offered to host The Other Door outreach café we'd started, and which had caused a little consternation within the Assembly due to the music and the clientele who came and sometimes performed.

With the new location came more questions than answers and on Saturday nights in the heart of Dundee a few of us tried to bring a little piece of church into the city centre. Did we all have the same vision? Possibly not. For me, what had started out as a straightforward evangelistic outreach project became slightly blurred.

For a start, we booked bands to play in the café. At first, these were acts with some kind of Christian ethos, but this changed over time to include anyone who felt they were happy to be part of the set-up. For young punks and electronic acts from the city, it became a place where they could perform, though the risks of a fight breaking out or an act being shouted down were worryingly high. In addition, many of those coming into the café were clearly young people who had few places to go and were frequently being dragged into the criminal justice system. Kids who were there one week were absent the next, and that absence was often explained by a short time in custody of some kind. All this was new to me. I'd dealt with secondary school adolescents who needed to be excluded from the classroom, but I'd never given much thought to what happened beyond that.

The majority of the young folk attending the café came from an area close to where our Brethren hall was situated in Dundee's Hilltown. In the sixties, this area had been cleared of the tenements that surrounded the Gospel Hall of my childhood, and they'd been replaced by four high tower blocks and an assortment of low maisonettes that ran between Cotton Road and The Hilltown itself. In fact, it's a tiny area of land, which then housed thousands of families without any real thought of where they would spend any recreation time. The old housing had closes, back greens, common streets and pavements where folk could mingle. It may not have been salubrious, but nevertheless, it was socially cohesive accommodation. The new scheme had nothing.

It was from these newish flats (now ten or twelve years old) that the young people who came to the café escaped on a Saturday night. The possibility of cheap food, warmth and a place to hang must have seemed an attractive prospect.

It was their presence and what we were failing to do in the café to engage further that worried me most. My strongest priority was to find a way in which we could make a positive impact in the lives of that group of young people. I was also a restless figure who had all kinds of schemes in my head, and the minister, Jock Stein (not that one) took me under his wing. Jock became a father figure to me: a mentor and an enabler as well as a counsellor. At some point, I must have told him about my concerns for the young people coming to the café and my uncertainty about my own future. In the winter of 1979–80, he made me an offer to come and work with him in the church. His way of putting it was to invite me to come and be a volunteer (with a small salary) and to work wherever I felt the need was greatest. I could concentrate on the young people who came to our café, but he also needed someone to do something with the young people who were officially on the church roll. As the church concerned was actually a union of three city-centre congregations, he wanted us to find a common purpose for the offspring of all three. Should I take up the post, I could do some of this and some of the outreach café work, depending on what seemed to be most needed.

As I was still heavily involved in writing songs and being part of a band with David Heavenor and other friends in Edinburgh, the new job seemed to offer the possibility of carrying on with all of that at the same time. The gigs we played at that time were an odd assortment of worthy causes and the odd student union. I was the keyboard player and sometime singer and, if memory serves me correctly, we didn't last much longer than a year or so, although the friendships with the others remained.

I liked the sound of the job, as it allowed me to put off any real career plan for the time being, while still giving me space to explore music. There was, however, one caveat I insisted upon. If I was to carry out youth work around the church, I needed to live near it, and I was currently living out in a little village with my parents on the outskirts of Dundee. I would need a flat, near the centre, to use as a base for whatever work we were to do.

Jock saw no problem with this and immediately got the church to buy a derelict attic apartment on Union Street, which ran down towards the station in the centre of town. The flat was in a great location but needed to be completely refurbished. To pay for it, Jock used some money from the church coffers, but assured his board that I would find a couple of lodgers whose rent would offset the costs. To this end, I approached a young post-graduate student from Malawi who came to the church and was currently living in halls of residence, and another friend who was also a student in halls at the time. Zedi Nyirenda and

Andy Thornton became my two flatmates. For the three of us –
and also for the church, who were breaking new ground – it was
a fairly big adventure.

I now knew where I would be working, and where I'd be
living after graduation. The deal was free accommodation and
phone rental for the flat, along with a volunteer salary of £75
per month. I have no idea why I thought this was good at the
time, other than the fact I had no real material ambitions. In that
phase of my life, I was content to have a role and a plan for just
a few months at a time, and had no real need of any additional
resources. I was probably aware too that my parents' relative
affluence might get me through the odd tight financial scrape.

In the final months of my degree, however, I was shown
another opportunity that pulled on my heart strings. I'd become
very involved in drama at college and loved working on and
acting in productions. Alongside this, my degree was in teaching English and Drama, and my final teaching practice was at a
wonderful school that had a dedicated drama department and
full-time teacher. His name was Larry Young, and I was completely happy being his student assistant for the weeks I spent at
the school. So much so that, at the end of my placement, he told
me he'd been offered a new post and suggested I should apply
for his job, as he'd recommend me. I was tempted, but in my
heart I'd already decided my next step was to be involved in the
church project, so I declined.

Starting in early August, there began a two-and-a-half-year
period during which I learned almost everything worthwhile I
have ever known. Before this time, I knew almost nothing of how
people really lived, or what I was supposed to think or believe.
All the simplistic ideals and explanations that had seen me
through my teenage and early adult life were inadequate when
working with people whose lives were, at best, precarious, and

often so impoverished that I could barely understand how I had coexisted in the same city streets as them for all these years and not been aware of how they lived.

This was the summer of 1980. Hard drugs had not yet entered the everyday lives of young people in the city in the way they would later that decade. After I'd left, friends and colleagues told me that so many of the kids with whom we'd been associated later went on to die of drug-related causes. At this time, however, there were no hard drugs on the scene, and the only real outward sign of substance abuse was the growing popularity of glue-sniffing, which was a frequent recreational pastime for the clientele of the Saturday 'Other Door' Café.

The flat, whose refurbishment was still a work in progress, very quickly became the centre for the youth work I was tasked with carrying out. The young people knew where I could be found, and within a few months, the flat was the go-to location for group meetings and drop-in conversations, and occasionally an extended crash pad for those whose fortunes had taken a downward turn. Andy, who was still in his final year of a biology degree, had befriended and aided a number of homeless people, and now felt able not only to help, but also to provide them with accommodation when it was needed.

I was new to all of this. Despite my own outpourings on socialism and general Fabian leanings, I was and remain a middle-class boy from Broughty Ferry with very little experience of hard times. My first year in the Steeple Flat (as it came to be known) was a baptism of fire. Alcoholics, con-artists, destitute teenagers and the mentally and socially marginalised and excluded formed a large proportion of our visitors' book, which was also supplemented by charismatic theologians, clerics, social activists, writers and musicians.

On one memorable occasion, some pals from Glasgow who'd been playing a gig at one of the colleges were crashing with us, and were only able to get access to the flat by stepping over a sleeping, drunken homeless guy called George, who we'd had to refuse accommodation to until he dried out. George's protest at this involved camping out on the landing outside the front door until his 'appeal' could be heard again. At one point, he was given a 'hearing' at the front door, going round each of us to make his case. We had to keep straight faces as he came to Zedi (whose name George had always found a bit tricky to pronounce, invariably plumping for 'Desi'). As he was now courting favours, he looked pleadingly around the hall until his eyes fell on Zedi. Wishing to formalise things, George perhaps decided his case would be more successful if he gave Zedi his full Sunday name. He got as far as: 'I'm asking you . . . Desmond.'

At this time, I was really helped out by someone who became a lifelong friend. Lance Stone was an assistant minister at a city-centre church in Aberdeen, and was running a similar café and outreach project there. We all got together for a weekend to share our experiences, and he told me about a book I needed to read. *Geoff*, by Ron Ferguson, was the story of a Gorbals minister called Geoff Shaw who had gone in at the deep end of inner-city living in the fifties and sixties, and whose experiences had ultimately led him into politics. Tragically, he died of a heart condition as quite a young man, but before then he had become the leader of the largest local authority in Scotland, Strathclyde Regional Council. In 1979, as Scotland debated whether it wanted a devolved government, it was Geoff who was tipped to become the first-ever First Minister. Of course, neither the parliament nor Geoff's leadership were to happen, but the interesting thing in the book was the work he did with his other Gorbals Group partners in the early days. Years later, I got to know some of the other surviving members of that group, and I remain very close to them.

With my grandfather, Joe Ford.   With my parents, Catherine and Bill.

On our way to Church with my cousin David Tossell and my sister Anne.

My mother, sister, Aunt Mary – Mum's sister – and young cousin David Tossell.

Church picnic in Monifieth.

Alongside Anne, my sister, in our garden in West Ferry.

The Annual Easter trip to Edinburgh.

Long trousers, our Spaniel, Penny and a dress my sister can still remember.

With my dad on holiday in Bournemouth.

Aunt Margaret in her empire of cards.

Early Radio Love. In my friend Douglas Kerr's house where we made tapes on Radio Rose. Rose Street, Arbroath.

© Douglas Kerr

Me, at seventeen.

My first band, which started as Under The Sun, then became Disaster Movies. With Mhairi and Rod Gordon.

First recording session at David Heavenor's parents' house, Crieff.

The first Deacon Blue show, with Jim and Dougie Midas, 1986.

Early Deacon Blue gig, at Queen Margaret Students' Union, Glasgow University 1986. Graeme was now with us.

The early days, with 'The Captain', David Pringle – Deacon Blue FOH Mixing, 1987. He started with us in 1986, and continues to be the band's trusted sound engineer. On the far right, Gill Maxwell, our tour manager – a vital part of our success.

With Dougie V, arriving in Los Angeles for our first time in California, 1988.

Shooting the 'Fergus' video.

Playing in my home town, Dundee, with Deacon Blue, 1989.

For me, the book opened up the possibilities within other traditions of faith, and Lance himself became someone with whom I could meet up and receive wisdom and encouragement. Years later, he'd move to a church in Hackney, and I would stay with him and, his wife Sally on my guerrilla missions to London while prising my way into the music business.

At the same time as we were establishing a full time youth project, music was still eating away at my soul. The songs, even the ones that found no audience, kept coming. I was, informally, playing music with some friends based in Edinburgh. I'd become good friends with David Heavenor from the Netherbow, and we'd hooked up over the last few years to become a loose band, along with Sam Wilson on bass and Simon Jaquet on drums. We only played occasionally, but it was enough for me to realise some of the songs I was writing in my spare moments. There weren't many of these spare moments, as much of my time was taken up with the youth work, but I had the keys to the church halls, and in there were pianos. I'd go in when no one was around and write and play throughout all the time I was working on the outreach project.

The band with David, Simon and Sam fizzled out after the girl I was seeing, who'd briefly sung with us, decided she no longer wanted to go out with me (a very understandable decision, in truth). For reasons now lost to me, that put an end to what we were doing as a band, though we all remained friends.

What stayed me from that time was a conversation David and I had late one night outside the Netherbow. We were all a bit frustrated at the lack of focus within our music, and I remember asking him what it was he'd really like to do.

'I would love to make an album,' he told me.

That moment is now burnished in memory for me. I can feel the cold of the wind off the Forth. I can sense the night air, and vividly picture the expression on his face as he let me into his dream. What struck me was how perfect an answer it was. It was a dream I hadn't allowed myself to enjoy, as I'd never seen how that could ever happen. But from that night on, I too only ever wanted to make an album. It would be six more years before that would happen for me, and around another ten before David and Simon would produce one together – made, ironically enough, by my friend and old flatmate Andy, in his studio in Glasgow.

While I was working at the youth project and the church, I also met my first wife, Zara. We were married at the tail end of 1981, and were together for the next six years.

The youth project was still the biggest part of my life. Along with the staff who became part of it, we went on to have some great times with young people who needed support and encouragement. My dream had always been to find a place we could go on holidays with the kids, who often had never been on one before. We did take them to Frontier Camps in Arran, which became a regular summer activity, and Jock had a family cottage in Boat of Garten in Speyside that he generously allowed us to use, but I was determined to organise something more ambitious for the youngest group.

Andy had taken over running the Slessor Centre, which had now replaced one of the big churches in the city centre. He had also found additional funding for a minibus which became a vital part of our work, as it allowed us to pick up the kids from home and make sure they were returned safely after each activity. It also allowed us to dream about taking them all to a youth activity centre in two old fishing cottages on Camas Bay on Mull. We started fundraising in earnest, which involved me directly appealing to local businesses associated with the church, and what with one thing and another, the trip of a lifetime was on.

The adventure involved taking the children out of school for a week and essentially camping in the cottages, which had no electricity or mainline gas supply. What they lacked in basic amenities was compensated for by adventure and joy. It was a complete release for the kids concerned, and I still remember the beautiful evening sessions upstairs in the attic, as they sang songs in the chapel of the nets (a small improvised oratory). I have often said it was one of the happiest weeks of my life, and it seemed to me then to reflect everything we'd been hoping to do: giving young people alternative experiences to balance out some of the negative influences in their lives up to that point. Reflecting on it now, however, I realise how much deeper many of their adverse childhood experiences were, and how much more work was needed earlier on to give the children the possibility of a fair start in life. I also recognise how cavalier all of us were with other people's children. Risks around travel, outdoor activities and basic child protection were all largely ignored, as there were no regulations in place. I'm pleased to say that no harm ever befell any of the young people involved in the project but really, all of us should have been instructed to safeguard the children more thoroughly.

One story from that time still resonates. In the summer of 1982, Zara and I took a summer holiday to Ireland. Before we left, one of our regular volunteers was a young man who had clearly gone through a few addiction issues, resulting in separation from his family and a period of homelessness. Now in the process of getting his life back together, he presented as a bright guy who had everything in front of him, and he was making big strides towards reconnecting with his wife and two young children. Needless to say, he received great encouragement from the staff around the centre and many of the church volunteers. Not long before our holiday, we heard the terrible news that his son had been killed crossing a road. As the news filtered through, people rallied round and various offers of financial help and support were made to the young man. These he received, but he made clear that he and his estranged wife wished for the funeral to be private. As so many characters like him had past lives and connections that remained a mystery to us, it was accepted that this private grief should be respected, even though one or two of us wondered why he wasn't asking Jock to assist with the funeral in some way.

When Zara and I returned from holiday, at least part of the mystery was resolved. One of the other volunteers, himself a recovering alcoholic who volunteered at a children's club for associated families, had seen the little boy we were all grieving running around quite healthily. It was clear there had been no accident, no death and no funeral. The man in question admitted the truth, life moved on, and the only explanation found was that his need for attention and sympathy outweighed his knowledge that the truth would emerge. For me, it became another illustration of how fragile so many of the people's lives were. It affirmed too, that by opening the doors and looking out, rather than simply inviting people in, the church would reach and help far more people who really needed it.

During the summer of 1982, the chairman, Jim Howden, and I, with help from Jock, tried to put the youth project on a more secure footing. With a lot of advice from friends, including my dear pal Simon Jaquet, who worked at a programme called the Canongate Youth Project, supported by the Old St Paul's Episcopal Church, we journeyed to Edinburgh to talk to the Scottish Office about funding what was now called the Slessor Youth Project, or the SYP. It was an exciting time as we tried to see our dream become reality. With proper funding in place, we would be able to employ staff on longer contracts and offer greater support to the families and individuals with whom we worked. I have no memory of the meeting other than the outcome, which was a detailed assessment and report on our work by the commissioners of the Social Work Services Group, who came to Dundee and inspected everything we did, as well as holding extensive conversations with other agencies who worked alongside us.

By the end of the summer, Jim called me to tell me the big news that our application had been successful, and that I could now head up a fully funded youth programme – for which, as team leader, I would finally receive proper remuneration. It was an amazing moment, but one that had been rather clouded out by other events in my life.

Over the same summer, we had organised the Street Level Festival, which brought together a wide group of people involved in the arts and took place around the city churches where we were based. It had a mixture of music, poetry seminars and miscellaneous cultural events, all broadly from a Christian tradition. In time, I had plans for it to move towards becoming a community festival that was less for visitors and more for Dundee people.

After the festival, Brian McGlynn, a friend from Glasgow, came to stay with us and, over the course of one long night, we sat up and talked about his plans for the future. Brian was a singer-songwriter, and was putting together a new band in Glasgow. For reasons that are still unclear, I found myself getting caught up in the story. I admired Brian's music a lot, and he was aware of some of what I'd done with my friends from Edinburgh, as well as my various other occasional outings along the periphery of the Christian music scene. So, between us, we conceived the idea of being in a band together.

It was a hare-brained plan that really had no deep logic to it. I probably wasn't the guy Brian needed, nor was he the best reason for me to make a move to Glasgow – but the timing was everything. My wife was coming to the end of her studies and would soon be looking for a job. I had established the SYP on to a secure footing, but still wasn't sure my own future lay in youth work. I was a good enabler, but I'm not really certain I was a great day-to-day foot soldier. I think part of me had lost the drive needed to be so closely involved every day, and, as time went on, music kept nagging at me.

At the time, we lived just off the Perth Road in Dundee, and I'd become aware of Michael Marra's solo work. I knew Michael from his old band Skeets Boliver, but I was aware he'd gone to London and done that great thing my friend David had planted in my head: he'd made an album. *The Midas Touch* wasn't the album Michael really wanted to make, and it sounded, even then, slightly dated. But he was a huge character on my horizon, and the fact he'd succeeded in his own adventure was an inspiration to me. I also loved his solo shows, where he was doing something I'd been trying to do myself for a while: sharing songs about the things around him. In Michael's case, this became more pronounced on the songs he wrote after *The Midas Touch*, and although they probably ended his mainstream record career, they set him off on a different trajectory, which brought him love and support from people who accepted his work for its humour, human warmth and deep honesty.

One night, I bumped into him in the Hawkhill when he was smoking a pipe, sheltering from the rain in the doorway of a local pub. He'd had a few drinks, but we struck up a conversation that began a correspondence that continued into a friendship over many years. Michael was always in my mind when I'd decided I wanted to make music, but I was determined not to become that well-loved local musician whose songs were appreciated but never really known beyond a small group of people. The thrill for me was in the possibility of a wider audience. I wanted to do something on a much bigger scale.

During the Street Level Festival the previous summer, Tom Morton, latterly of BBC Radio Scotland, but at that time a full-time singer-songwriter, had played at one of the events. To my surprise and delight, he had played a song I'd written a couple of years earlier called 'Surprised By Joy', which he'd go on to cut on a record.

This summer, in August 1982, he had asked me to support him on a run of solo shows at the Edinburgh Fringe. Although this should have been simple enough on my own, I overcomplicated it by asking a new resident of the Steeple Flat, Jean Marc, if he'd like to accompany me. He played a variety of instruments, including saxophone and keyboards, and we performed a fairly downbeat batch of songs that my sister, very fairly, told me gave her one of the most depressing nights of her life. I have an eternal respect and gratitude for that honest feedback, as since then I have always known if she genuinely likes something I do.

However, one person who came to see the show enjoyed it. His name was Charlie Irvine. I didn't really know him well at that point, but a year or so later, he'd be able to tell me how much he'd admired those songs, and would enable me to make my first-ever solo tape album, which was eventually to become the thing that would bring me my first taste of success in the music business. As unlikely as all this seems, that miserable run of three nights in a basement in Edinburgh, boring an audience to tears and propelling me to forget any solo career in favour of joining Brian's band, was the key event leading to any future success.

On that long night when Brian and I had sat up and talked and imagined a band together, I had also begun to hatch a plan to end my work in Dundee. I had a good teaching qualification, which meant I could apply for a proper teaching job and use that work to keep a roof over our heads while we worked out how to become successful with music.

And so that September, I had to break the news to Jim that I wouldn't be the person to take the SYP forward, despite our newly secured funding. I explained to him that my future lay elsewhere and that I might be leaving as early as Christmas.

I began to apply for teaching jobs in Glasgow, and one post came up that seemed to have my name on it. It was for a teacher at a truancy project, and my experience in youth work was clearly attractive to the employers. I very nearly got the job, but it went elsewhere at the last minute. I'm grateful now that I didn't, as I would have been thrown once more into something that required more energy than I wanted to give to anything outside music at that point. Eventually, after the most bizarre interview, which I had to complete despite being up all the previous night with food poisoning (I must have appeared to the interview panel to be close to death), I was offered a teaching post at St Mungo's Academy, a secondary school in the East End of Glasgow, starting in December.

I left Dundee having written a couple of songs that would eventually surface on my solo tape album, and later on a solo album proper. Before I went, I read about Gary Clark, a guy who was making waves in the local music scene. I realised later I'd seen him at a gig, where he and lots of other great Dundee musicians played in a big band celebrating the official release of Michael Marra's *Midas Touch* album. At the time, Gary's band was called Clark's Commandos, and I think I'd read about them in the local paper. Years later, we'd become great friends, as his new band, Danny Wilson, and ours both brought out our first albums within a couple of weeks of each other. Around 1987, when Danny Wilson first appeared in the music press, I loved hearing the story of how they'd busked in and around Dundee, but been moved along by the authorities because they were making too much of a disturbance. According to the article, the local paper had carried letters of support from elderly ladies for the up-and-coming young buskers.

I put all of this and many more memories into a song I wrote around that time. It eventually became a B-side, but I still perform it regularly, as it tells a lot of my own story of growing up and eventually needing to leave my home city of Dundee.

Back Here in *Beano* Land

Every day they write the headlines
Talking diamonds talking steel
Don't talk things that folk don't know about
Talk about money and stuff that's real

Back here in *Beano* land the bubble is bursting
All things get busted, some things get builded
Old ladies write letters old men dream memories
Back here in *Beano* land all things are real

Every day my neighbour drives
For the company from the south
Tells us stories of how things are there
Talks about their life, talks about ours

Back here in *Beano* land the bubble is bursting
All things get busted, some things get builded
Old ladies write letters old men dream memories
Back here in *Beano* land all things are real

I've been trying to find a reason
Like I've been trying to leave this house
Every day they cross that great bridge
I watch those trains pull in and out
Those trains, those trains, those trains
Yeah, those trains

Back here in *Beano* land the bubble is bursting
All things get busted, some things get builded
Old ladies write letters old men dream memories
Back here in *Beano* land all things are real

13

How Do You Spell Protestants?

St Mungo's Academy was an all-boys Christian Brothers school on the Gallowgate. The building was relatively new, and as I sat in the headteacher's office on my first day, I tried to sound positive about the surroundings. He agreed, then let his head fall dramatically on the desk.

'Oh, Mr Ross, it's a beautiful building,' he said. He lifted his head, then let it fall once more. 'If only it weren't for the boys.'

I was to replace a man called Frank, who, for unexplained reasons, had been moved to the other Christian Brothers school in the city. That school was led by the familial brother of the desk-butting headteacher Brother and, according to the staff, their rivalry on all things scholarly was intense.

In those days, academic school league tables were not part of the learning outcomes for the staff, but had they been in place it's hard not to imagine you'd have had to look a good distance down the stats to find St Mungo's results. The school, it seemed to me, was in an educational, moral and social slough, and it would take more than an enthusiastic, useful idiot from Dundee to reverse the trend.

Looking out the window at the surrounding expanse of brownfield wasteland, the principal English teacher waved a resigned hand and told me, 'This is one of the worst areas of multiple deprivation in Europe.'

I hadn't been expecting the Eton Wall game but the stark reality of the scale of poverty in the East End of Glasgow was still overwhelming, notwithstanding my experiences of the children and families I'd encountered at the SYP in Dundee. It wasn't an auspicious start, but I was ready to roll up my sleeves and get on with it.

The good news was I'd been offered my own classroom and, given some thought and imagination, I felt I could make it look like a place some of the boys might want to be. Frank, however, had clearly left in a hurry. Every drawer and every cupboard was stuffed and scattered with used stationery. Past papers, pupils' work sheets, crisp packets and the detritus of years of boys' excess baggage filled every available space. I looked out the window. Within a few hundred yards stood Celtic Park, a place mythologised in Scottish football. I'd only been once in the 1970s, when Dalglish, McNeil and Macari all played in front of 70,000 fans in a midweek European Cup quarter final. Now it was where the local football team played, and I stood transfixed. Soon after, a couple of lads knocked on my door to ask if anyone wanted a Christmas raffle ticket to win a ball signed by the team.

However, it turned out I wouldn't even be in the school long enough to hear the raffle drawn. It seemed that, completely unexpectedly, Frank was to return to his original post, and my only priority now was to fix a meeting with the man in the education office who had appointed me in the first place.

Glasgow in 1982 was still a lot like the Glasgow I'd passed through as a kid. The buildings were dark and formidable, and the heavy winter weather – essentially a cold blanket of grey cloud and rain – didn't make it any less imposing. And yet, there was something essential and vital about the city. The long, wide boulevards reaching out for miles from the centre suggested a grandeur and self-conceit that augured well. This, it seemed to me, was a city that liked itself. It didn't need to be explained or apologised for; rather, it knew itself to be the second city of this old kingdom, and no one was about to usurp it.

That was borne out in the people too. They knew they were right at the centre of things. I remembered being affectionately patronised by Rangers supporters in the old days at Dundee United's home ground, Tannadice, when there had been no segregation and we'd all stood together. My favourite player was a midfielder called Jimmy Henry, who had a mod cut and generally looked cool as he stroked the ball around the centre of the park.

'Aye, yer gallus son, but it's getting you nae place.' Spoken by a middle-aged Rangers fan behind me, this one apt but derisory comment summed up Jimmy's career. It was too accurate for comfort, and I had a horrid realisation my team weren't going to win that day either. I must have said something. He looked at me kindly and said, 'That's OK, pal. Quite right. You support your local team. Here.' He offered me a half-opened packet of Polo mints. 'Do you want one of these?'

After learning of Frank's unexpected return to St Mungo's, I walked up the long, gentle slope of Bath Street to the education department office. I knew I wanted to stay in the city where strangers engaged with you, even when you were happy in your own company, and where the old, wise supporters of the big teams offered you their Polo mints. When I'd first stayed with my sister in Hyndland years before, I'd gone for a bus on Great Western Road and, for no reason at all, an old lady had just started a conversation with me. This rarely happened to me in Dundee, and I knew there was something magical about Glasgow. It's a feeling that's stayed with me for nearly forty years, ever since I first arrived; every time I think about leaving or express irritation at the mess the city can be, Glasgow will suck me back in. Someone will make me laugh or cry, or do something that will make me succumb once again to its grand old Victorian charm. Cities have come and gone throughout my life; I've thought of a move to London, spent significant time working in LA, New York and Nashville, and visited many others, but somehow, despite having the freedom to choose somewhere else, I feel the same way about Glasgow as my friend Ruth Wishart described the late Donald Dewar feeling when he came towards Harthill on his way home from Edinburgh on any given evening. My heart lifts when I see the lights of the city.

On that dark, rain-soaked December day, with the old orange buses spraying the pavements as they ground up the hill through the puddles, and the Christmas lights bouncing around in the cold wind around George Square, I realised I had been lured in and I wasn't going back.

In the office on Bath Street, the man from the education department was in a bit of a fix. He'd warmed to me and my situation. It was unprecedented for a teacher to have been transferred, then immediately transferred back to his original school, as Frank had. Reading between the lines, it seemed he'd had a number of personal issues (which didn't surprise me, given the state of his classroom) about which his new employer knew nothing – until they became clear upon Frank's arrival. The new school had promptly set him packing, in the grand old caring tradition of Christian faith and the Marist Brotherhood. I, it seemed, was an innocent from the east who'd been caught up in the machinations of a sacred teaching order's politics.

'Mr Ross.' The man from the education department looked at me with the eye of someone who was about to offer a solution to an intractable problem. 'There is a post for you at St Columba of Iona Secondary School in Maryhill. If you were happy to go there, we could offer you a permanent contract.'

The words 'permanent contract' were rare at this time. New teachers weren't offered them, and many teachers were unable to negotiate such terms. Essentially, it meant being paid for holidays and knowing your job was secure.

'Can I see the school and come back to you?' I was pushing my luck. No one got offered this kind of post, but I felt they owed me, and for this short window of opportunity, I could push a little harder.

The man agreed to me seeing the school and meeting the staff, so I immediately caught the underground up to St George's Cross and walked through the wasteland of demolished housing and factories surrounding the school building and playground. I met the man who would become my immediate boss and good friend for the time I was there, John Lawson, and a recently arrived headteacher who was a brave servant trying to turn round a failing school. There was no blaming the pupils, and certainly no praise for the building (it was fit for demolition), but this was a man who wanted to make the lives of his students fairer and better. I knew it was the right place for me. I would start on the first day back after my (paid) Christmas holiday.

During my last days at St Mungo's, I was walking up to the staff room one morning when I heard a beautiful noise coming from the sixth-year common room. It was so loud I followed the music filling the corridors of the sterile building. It was 'Someone Somewhere (In Summertime)' by Simple Minds, and the song echoed along the walls and spilled through the doors on that dark December day. It changed everything. I was so happy for a minute or so that I just stood there, drinking it all in. It was a beautiful noise that landed just when I was on the cusp of trying to do two things at once. I needed a teaching job to earn a living, but every other part of me longed to be making music. Hearing that song, at that volume, on that bleak December morning thrilled my heart and quite possibly gave me the courage to carry on dreaming. The song and that moment on a cold Glasgow morning would stay with me, and many years later, I'd be able to tell Jim Kerr just how it made me feel.

Although I began working at St Columba of Iona in January, I didn't receive my own timetable or my very own classes until the following August. I loved the idea of getting a first-year class of my own who I could work with in the way in which I felt comfortable. For once, I wouldn't be inheriting a class from another teacher or sitting at the back wishing I could do the thing myself. Now, I would be the person answerable to the students.

There were two great positives to teaching in a Roman Catholic school that I came to admire. First, there was always a strong sense of community and shared purpose. Although our school population had little excess income, there was still a real sense of social concern and generosity of spirit for anyone in need. Secondly, a school gathered around a common faith had an openness to mystery, which, in my experience, expanded rather than diminished imagination. Our youngest pupils loved the books of C.S. Lewis. My pal Craig, who helped me enormously with resources, as he had years of experience teaching at a non-denominational school in the East End, would balk in amazement when I told him how much my first-year pupils loved *The Lion, the Witch and the Wardrobe*. How, he'd query, could kids from Maryhill buy into all of that posh Oxbridge mythology? In fact, they didn't much bother about the culture or setting of the story, but simply loved the magic and the myth. They'd been steeped in it and, whatever their own current views on faith were, their years of Catholic education had allowed their spiritual imaginations to take flight. For children steeped in the mysteries of the Mass and the spirituality of Catholicism's saints and martyrs, there is very little disconnect between miracles and magic.

For this, I was hugely grateful. I would read the book aloud to my class, using different voices as they gathered round in rapt silence and delight. I taped a version of it too so that any kids who'd been absent could quietly catch up. Having your own first-year class who accept and trust your ethos and methodology is a great gift. I was grateful for the thirty-odd eleven- and twelve-year-olds I first taught in 1983, and I still remember many of the faces from that time.

This all came as an unexpected bonus. I had taken a teaching job to try and make myself more available for making music, but again, despite myself, I'd fallen for the age-old axiom of getting more back from it than I was giving. Being with kids, seeing them come alive as they hear stories and explore new ideas is an experience like no other, and spending forty minutes reading a book or a play together, and seeing and hearing them getting caught up in the story, is as good a slice of life as you'd ever wish to have.

The catchment area for the school was drawn from some of the poorer areas on the west side of the M8 as it bisected the city. The children came from Anderston, Maryhill, Ruchill, Possilpark and Somerston, and the city had already built a glistening new Catholic secondary school just up the road. It was sometimes mooted that the only pupils coming to ours were those whose parents hadn't managed to enrol their offspring at the new academy. There was also an imbalance of male and female students. An all-girls Catholic school was situated not far from us, and many parents (wisely) opted to send their children there. All of my teaching experience was in the days before I had a family of my own, and most of my opinions on what priorities and outcomes I would emphasise have changed radically. I now realise it's more important than ever to make schools places of safety, happiness and confidence. Children need to be encouraged to aim higher and wider than the goals they might otherwise have been happy to settle for. I'm not sure that was the educational experience most of the students got at St Columba's at the time, and I often reflect that I would have been the first to remove my own children from there should they have had to endure some of what went on in the playground or classroom, or on the way to and from school.

I believed then, as I still believe now, that fair access to education is wholly desirable, if very difficult to pull off. St Columba of Iona had been earmarked for closure, and there was a feeling abroad that the new headteacher, Jim Doherty, had been put in place to either facilitate its demise or bring it, Lazarus-like, back from the grave.

I met Jim on my first visit to the school. I was still getting used to the priorities of Catholic schools and the place RE had in the curriculum, as well as all the inevitable pictures of the Pope and the saying of grace before meals. Jim was an English teacher who had worked with a man many consider to be one of the biggest influences in modern Scottish education, Brian Boyd. Both Doherty and Boyd believed in mixed-ability education. It was a core issue for my new boss, and he was right in the middle of enforcing the ethos in the current timetable. Charismatic, ambitious and funny, he immediately broke the ice in our first meeting by cracking the old W. C. Fields joke about drinking water ('I never touch it, fish fuck in it') within minutes of my arrival. He told me about his vision for the school and what he wanted to create there. As I was coming from a background of youth and social work, I was a willing and natural ally. His vision was music to my ears, but as I came into the staff room on my first day, I realised he was fighting a rear-guard action to bring the staff along with him. That sense of tension ran alongside our work for the entire time I taught there.

Despite this tension, though, I have nothing but happy memories of the time I spent at St Columba. I had great friends on the staff and still keep up with some of the pupils, who will stop and chat if they meet me on the street. The senior staff have almost all passed, and sadly, Jim Doherty himself died a couple of years back. We exchanged Christmas cards for thirty years after I left teaching. He was someone who cared about young people and bringing out the best in them, and was truly an inspiring character to be around.

For me, everything was new. Glasgow, the weather, teaching, teachers and pupils all had to be understood. The staff were easy. I was one of a few younger teachers who'd started at around the same time, and we all went to the pub on a Friday – and often on other days too. The Friday get-togethers were christened by my pal, Jean, a much-loved PE teacher, as 'The Friday Nights of St Columba's'. Jean, like me, was a Protestant, though more nominal. The kids loved her, and she was great fun to be around. The film *E.T.* hadn't long been out, and her favourite gag to the pupils was, 'How do you know E.T. is a Catholic? He looks like one.'

'Aw, Miss!' they would cry.

On my first day with my first-ever first-year class, in August 1983, I handed out a worksheet that asked them to tell me about themselves in the form of a questionnaire. As they set about filling in the details, a hand went up from a young boy called Eddie. His face and name have never left me. A cherubic smile and earnest desire to engage are what I remember, even though, as he informed me later, his primary school teacher had told him he was 'a bit of a character'.

Eddie had reached the question: 'Tell me some things you hate.'

'Sir.' (It was always sir.) 'How do you spell "Protestants"?'

Eddie liked to tell me tales of what life was like around where he lived. 'You should have seen my bit last night, sir. Big fight. Guys with guns and everything.'

He wasn't exaggerating. The neighbourhood immediately west and north of the school was a tough part of town.

Eddie's own school career was beginning to unravel. His primary school teacher's assessment of him as a 'character' had been a clear example of understatement. Soon, Eddie was getting into trouble and found himself suspended from classes. Jim Doherty rejoiced in telling the staff how he'd tried to explain the situations to Eddie's mother after she'd been called up for a meeting about the boy. Storming straight out, she'd swept loudly through the main door, shouting back to the headteacher that he may have been in charge of education, but he was, nevertheless, 'a speccy bastard'. It was to Jim's credit that he was also slim, which probably saved him from an additional epithet. Years later, at a mini reunion with some of my old teaching pals, I learned that Eddie hadn't left the school for very long before he was found dead after suffering a heroin overdose.

The only class I was prohibited from teaching at St Columba was RE. On my arrival, the chaplain to the school had been a little put out that Religious Education classes had all been timetabled at the same time, first thing in the morning, as part of a new pastoral care programme Jim was trying to roll out. All the students from across the six years of the school were put into pastoral care classes, which also acted as a basic registration period. As far as I was aware, there was very little actual pastoral care happening, but because the headteacher wanted to create the ethos of a Christian school, he had organised the timetable in this way. It meant that, as a non- Roman Catholic, I and other similarly religiously handicapped staff were never needed first thing in the morning. It was fifteen minutes of grace I grew to appreciate.

There was, however, a shortage of music staff in the school. The one music teacher, who had a kind way of encouraging those who were interested in studying individual instruments, was not available to play piano on one particular day. At least, that's how I remember finding myself being drafted in for a particularly large Mass one morning on the feast of Corpus Christi. Always a tricky piece of theology to explain to the laity, Jim Doherty opted for, 'Today we are bringing Jesus (in the form of the host) down from the oratory into the school hall.'

I checked in later with the school chaplain on his comfort levels with that explanation, and his knitted brow told its own story. The headteacher, however, was not a man to let theological details get in the way of some homespun Catholic apologetics. There may have been a visiting bishop and a couple of extra priests on duty, but there was no doubt who was leading this from the front. I could feel all my reformed muscles slightly tensing as the Mass gathered pace. Well beyond my comfort zone, I was there to play the piano, and with the headteacher leading the singing, we were getting some gospel going. Incense, harmony and religious fervour were all mingling and rising in the room. Jim wanted the kids to raise the roof, and he reminded them that they'd all sung the next one with full voice when the Pope had come to Glasgow's Bellahouston Park a couple of summers before. He said he wanted to hear it as loud as he'd heard it that day. It was as good as lighting the touch paper for children or adults of that generation. Pope John Paul's visit to Glasgow was up there in the consciousness of the locals with Celtic beating Leeds United at Hampden in 1970 or Billy Connolly appearing on *Parkinson*.

'Our God Reigns' was the hymn in question. We all set off, with the chorus lifting higher and higher, the volume shooting through the decibel meter thanks to Jim's mention of the Holy Father and the (by now) holy park. The headteacher himself seemed to get carried away by the spirit in the room.

'Our God reigns,' we all sang.

'Whose God?' Jim shouted back.

'Our God,' came the response.

God, it seemed, had been claimed, and on that merry morning, was owned by the staff and pupils and in particular, the headteacher, of St Columba of Iona Secondary.

Jim Doherty knew that to get the staff onside, he needed to build a bond with the ones who were willing to take a chance on change. His great mantra (which was a good line of attack) was: 'Experienced teachers should take the most difficult classes.' This was to guard against older, lazy heads of department timetabling themselves with classes of more academic pupils while avoiding those troublesome fifteen-year-olds who were not going to take any qualifications in the given subject, but were simply killing time until they turned sixteen and could leave. For Jim, organising the school into mixed-ability groups was a way of addressing this, as well as making pastoral care a bigger priority. To this end, he arranged a weekend away at a teachers' residential centre near Pitlochry. It worked well to bond those who felt closer to the ideals Jim was trying to encourage. Most staff, however, simply wanted to find out why they couldn't get a promotion, and many suspected they were working in an educational backwater. Jim's plan was that on the Sunday morning, after Mass had been said, the head of the education department for Glasgow would come and take questions from staff about 'career development'.

The man from the education department outlined why he thought the school was taking the correct steps towards renewal, and added his own take on the ethos behind a successful educational institution. By sheer chance – and for the first and only time in my life – I'd found myself sitting beside Jimmy, one of the heads of department, who, apart from being on the more sceptical side of the staffroom, was also still quite drunk from the night before. At each proposal by the education department boss, Jimmy would turn to me and comment in too loud a voice. I tried to look as if I wasn't his pal, but being squashed in beside him made this rather awkward.

Undeterred, the director continued. 'All I'm looking for,' he explained, in a plum RP voice, 'is a little humanity.'

'Humanity?' Jimmy blurted out, as the entire staff looked over, 'Humanity?' His voice grew slurred. 'How can you have *humanity* . . . in a Catholic school?'

I saw his career-development prospects leaving the room, followed, in quick succession, by my own.

Whether the reimagining of the school and its ethos ever really changed anything is a moot point, which can probably only be answered by those who were at the receiving end of what was on offer at the time. Over the years, I've met a few ex-pupils who have shared their stories with me, and it's been heartening to hear from those who remember at least some of what we tried to do in a positive light. I was visiting an electrical appliance showroom a couple of years ago and got into a general chat with one of the staff who, I assumed, knew who I was via my music. It was only as I was leaving that he came back and said: 'There's one more thing I need to thank you for.'

There was a pause, and he could tell I was curious to hear the answer.

'You took us to the theatre. I'd never been before, and I really loved it.'

I couldn't have had a better testimonial from an ex-pupil. It isn't always as straightforward. At the height of the band's success I was in a supermarket I'd never been to before, which wasn't far from the school's old catchment area. Walking towards me was one of the biggest troublemakers I could remember from my time teaching. He'd been scary as a pupil, but now he was my biggest fan whose only desire was to get my autograph.

'Thing is,' he said, laughing. 'I huvnae got a pen or a pencil.'

I felt it incumbent to point out how little had changed since we'd both been in a classroom together.

14

When Will You Make My Telephone Ring?

In early spring 1985, I arrived at Victoria Bus Station in London, having tried and failed to sleep on the overnight bus from Glasgow to London. I was armed with a Walkman and a few cassette tapes, and was on my way to talk to a music publishing company who were interested in offering me a contract for my songs. I'd had to take the overnight bus because I could only skip one day of my work after phoning in sick.

The deal, when it eventually came, was, in the words of my new music lawyer, 'Not very good . . . but Ricky, it's short.' By the time I got to having any success, he informed me, I'd be out of the deal and able to negotiate a new one.

Very few promises made to me in the music business have proven to be as accurate as this one was.

A year or so before, I'd left Woza, the band I'd come to Glasgow to form with Brian McGlynn. Although I had learned a lot about putting music together – and a whole lot about how the music business worked – I had realised I wasn't the keyboard player the band needed, and, realistically, that I didn't care enough about what we were doing to invest all the time it was taking. I left because, somewhat naively, I thought I knew what I wanted to do with my own songs and how to sing them.

At around that time in Glasgow, there was a new scene emerging, and it felt as if songs with stories and a structure that seemed rooted in the music I knew – country/R&B, rock 'n' roll/

folk – were coming to the forefront again. Was it possible, I began to wonder, that I could simply follow my heart, go where the songs wanted to go, rather than chasing what was popular or fashionable? Could it be that simply doing what I wanted to do might be the way ahead?

Woza had played every gig in town. We'd done the student unions up and down the country, the only clubs that put bands on, and we'd traipsed north, east and west in search of some recognition. Along the way, we'd met a manager who seemed to have connections, but also got so drunk on each live outing that after the amps had been loaded, he too had to be carried out and deposited in the back seat. At the same time as he looked after us, he put on a regular night at the Heathery Bar in Wishaw. He offered us the support slot for the Waterboys, who he'd managed to book. I'm not sure how often they'd played at this point, but it seemed to be an early gig, and they only managed to get their gear on to the tiny the stage once a number of beer crates and other accessories had been assembled to form an apron in order to accommodate them. Turning up early, we watched as the soundcheck ran its course. I was stopped in my tracks. Here was a band that didn't try to sound or look like anyone else. They were just doing what they wanted to do, and it sounded amazing.

'You must love Bob Dylan too,' I said to Mike Scott.

He looked a little sheepish, as if someone had told him his slip was showing, and shrugged it off with a casual, 'I used to.'

Gigs in Scotland were often pitched battles as much as they were celebrations. In a corner of the room, a local guy heckled Mike every time he found room to be heard. 'Mick Jagger lookalike,' he bellowed from the bar.

Wishaw, beer crates, morons . . . it was rock 'n' roll, and I wanted it. I looked around at the band I was in, and I didn't feel the heat or noise of any A&R people from London flying up to see us. For me, it was a moment akin to when Toad's caravan is forced off the road in *The Wind in the Willows* and he blinks in startled delight at the motor car that caused him to crash. He loses interest in the caravan immediately. That night, realising I was in the wrong band at the wrong time, and seeing a better, more exciting model, I too wanted to unhook myself from the caravan.

I never properly met Mike again. In truth, I lost interest when his music went a bit folky – probably around the same time as a lot of people took up interest – but our paths did cross once more in the early nineties when I was with Deacon Blue and we both passed through Heathrow airport. He couldn't have been more distant or strange. I didn't read too much into it, as there wasn't much to say. But recently, I came across an article in *Hot Press* where he spoke in glowing terms about a Burns song we'd performed a while back, and though I never really rated that version myself, it was kind of him, and kindness is underrated.

Wishaw would figure in my life once again many years later, but that night – and the next day, and the next day after that – I realised the only way to make music was to make the music you had in you. It seems obvious in the cool light of hindsight, but it's impossible to be good at something you don't believe in. I realised that meant following my own dreams, writing and singing my own songs, even though I had no idea where to begin.

In the autumn of 1983, before my road-to-Damascus experience in Wishaw, one of the adventures I'd had with Woza was a trip to London, where Brian and I went round different record companies and publishers playing our three-song demo. Realistically, I don't think we convinced any of the A&R types to come and see us, but it was a wonderful week. I think I loved it even more because it was such a colourful contrast to the black-and-white world of my Glasgow life at the time. In the depths of the miners' strike, the mass unemployment of the eighties and the deep pessimism that surrounded our life in Scotland, stepping out in London was like landing on a different planet. Where so much of grey Glasgow seemed to be about decay leading to a sense of despair, London, certainly at first glance, seemed full of light and colour. Everything was brighter, bigger and bolder. It was impossible not to be caught up in the widescreen spectacle of it all. It was on this trip that I first met music publishers, as well as the usual music business types. Where the record people were occupied with chasing every single new twist and trend, the music publishers still seemed to be locked into the idea of songs and songwriters . . . heck, in some offices they still had pianos!

In October 1984, a year on from that London adventure, I retraced the steps on my own, this time with my own tapes in my bag. I'd made a cassette album called *So Long Ago*, which had been under discussion with our friends Dot Reid and Charlie Irvine (who had attended my support show for Tom Morton at the Edinburgh Fringe in 1982). They had a small label called Sticky Music, and I'd recorded the cassette album for them in a mixture of studios. The band tracks are pretty much unlistenable now. In truth, I didn't have a clue about what to do in a studio, or how to make the musicians do what I heard in my head, so the result was unfocused and often fairly anodyne. I'm also not sure I could really sing back then . . . my voice didn't really know what it was doing most of the time. Apart from that, though, the cassette is a heartbreaking work of staggering genius!

There were a couple of songs on it that I thought I could use to show music publishers what I might be able to do on my own. The album contained 'Surprised By Joy' which Tom Morton had gone on to record, and another song that I'd written when I was only twenty, 'Checkout Girls', which had featured on a record by (now Episcopal priest) Steve Butler.

I went to see ATV Music, which back then was still a small office in Brook Street, just off Park Lane. I met a couple of people who seemed to take an interest in what I was doing, and I left them with the cassette. To my surprise, when I phoned them up a couple of months later, they told me they'd been trying to contact me as they were interested in talking to me about a publishing deal. I couldn't quite believe it.

In the meantime, I'd put a small live band together for my tentative solo career, and we'd cut a new demo. Dot, Charlie and Steve from Sticky Music had had a conversation with the mastering people at Linn records, then a jazz label and home to the newly minted debut album of Glasgow's The Blue Nile. The people at Linn had taken an interest in my music, and had given me money to make some demos, which I cut at Palladium near Edinburgh in a day with some friends as the band in late 1984.

It turned out that Linn preferred me solo, with piano only – something I didn't want to pursue at the time – so they passed on the relationship. However, ATV in London liked the sound I'd created at Palladium, and by the summer of 1985 I had that 'not very good' publishing deal signed and some money in a bank account to get my solo career started. The next thing they told me was, 'Get a proper band.'

The hunt was on to find some committed musicians.

My personal life at the time was an extended car crash of gloom, restlessness and unfulfilled desire. I was in an unhappy marriage, which I wasn't really dealing with at all well. My life was filled with work, which was mainly enjoyable but time-consuming, with music fitting into what little time was left over. Most people I knew in teaching were desperate to leave it behind. Colleagues who had come in at the same time as me made it clear they had no long-term plans in the profession. Although I enjoyed the time I spent teaching, I always felt that I was eventually going to leave and follow the music. Any despondency I felt was not down to the day-to-day grind, but simply a sense of frustration at not being able to make music all day and every day.

And now all that was about to change.

Andy Brodie was one of the few musicians I knew in and around Glasgow. If I was going to get a good keyboard player, I needed to start with someone who was better than me. Andy was all of that and more. He'd played saxophone in a brass section for a few gigs where I'd chopped and changed the line-up, but he was – and still is – also a brilliant pianist. I felt that the only way forward was to build a band who were as strongly committed to the plan as I was. That plan was to be successful, but I still had no sound and no real identity other than a few disparate songs, which hinted at a few possibilities.

In reality too I wasn't writing about anything other than what I thought people wanted to hear. To that end, I was avoiding the subject matter that was right in front of me. I needed to write from the heart, and I needed this band to say something. In the early days, the songs I wrote had a life-or-death certainty, based more around the evangelicalism of my upbringing than anything else, but now that 'certainty' had gone. I needed to express something about the world I knew, about the disappointment in love I'd experienced, and about the sense of escape I wanted to dream about. That trip to London, the promise of something other than the life I was living, was nagging at me. I knew there had to be something in the songs that conveyed who I was. If I was going to be any good as a songwriter, I needed to find a way to tell my story.

In the early summer of 1985 I asked Andy if he wanted to help me put a band together. Malcolm Lindsay, who is now a producer and film composer, had been playing guitar for the pick-up band I'd had at this time, and I asked him if he would join the mission too. Andy knew a young drummer who was then studying alongside him in the music department at the RSAMDA (Royal Scottiish Academy of Music and Dramatic Art, now the Royal Scottish Conservatoire) who was, in Andy's words, desperate to start a band. Dougie Vipond, the drummer in question, came over to my flat in Pollokshields one evening for a chat, and memorably came bursting in telling me he'd nearly been run over by Billy Connolly on the way over. Dougie and I hadn't played together before, but I knew from Andy he was a great musician, and I could tell he had the energy and commitment I needed to feel from anyone who was going to be part of the plan.

I'd given the project a name by now. I'd been walking down Tottenham Court Road on one of my recent trips to London, imagining different names on fly posters. I loved the idea behind the lyrics to Steely Dan's 'Deacon Blues' and, for whatever reason, the idea of using that for the band name stuck. No one really liked it when they first heard it, but as there was no one else properly in the band when I picked the name, it came as a fait accompli, and therefore no extended discussion or hat ballot needed to take place.

We still didn't have a bass player, so Andy brought in a guy with whom he played club gigs, Stuart McEwan, who has since sadly died. Stuart played with us as we started rehearsing in the basement of a printshop just below Buchanan Street. At that time, there were few places in Glasgow to rehearse, so I was grateful to a benevolent friend of a friend who lent us the space for a peppercorn rent. It meant we could all get to rehearsals in the middle of the city easily. We spent that summer preparing to put on a gig at one of the few places that promoted bands in Glasgow at the time. Most of the gigs available were either nightclubs or student-union support slots, but the Fixx, a pub on the street parallel to our rehearsal space had agreed to put us on. Ironically enough, it was at this same venue, with an augmented line-up, where the band would finally convince an A&R man to sign us around nine months later.

We were a little nervous about doing a show for the first time without trying out our set somewhere else first. Stuart had a deep knowledge of the west of Scotland's cover-band scene, and found us a pub in Yoker (between Glasgow and Clydebank) that agreed to let us play two nights to their regulars on a Monday and Tuesday when there wasn't much else going on. My suspicions then and now are that there is seldom very much going on in Yoker. It was a deep learning experience summed up by requests for 'The Sash'. To reach the toilet, the punters had to walk through the front line of the band and past the drum kit.

Despite these inauspicious beginnings, by the end of September 1985, we'd played a show at the Fixx and cut our first demo at Park Lane Studios, which contained one song that would eventually surface on the project that still seemed a million miles away, our first album.

In the meantime, the 'bad publishing deal', which was helping to fund whatever the band recorded and subsidised the loss-making gigs, had just become problematic. One of the other things my music lawyer, John Kennedy, had mentioned to me at the time was that ATV Music was up for sale. One day, I got a phone call from Malcolm Buckland, who had been our go-to guy at ATV, to say he was going to lose his job as the company had been sold to Michael Jackson and the whole operation was to be administered by CBS Publishing, then based over in Rathbone Place, which was just across Oxford Street from their then-headquarters in Soho Square. Malcolm was a great friend and had been a vital help to us in those uncertain times.

By October 1985, I'd handed in my notice as a teacher, as I realised I needed complete freedom to do whatever was needed on behalf of the new enterprise. I remember walking up Bath Street during the October midterm holiday of 1985 to hand in my resignation letter to the education department. When I left the school a month or so later, the only two things people wanted to know were would I make a video, and would I be appearing on *Top of the Pops*? It would take fewer than eighteen months for the first to come true, and three years for the second.

In the meantime, I had no sooner assembled the first line-up than it became clear I needed to think a little harder about the band. In the January of 1986, we'd done a few shows under the name Ricky Ross and Deacon Blue, and my original publishing manager from ATV, Sally Perryman, had gone over to CBS to run the company as part of the wider CBS group. We asked for their support to go back into the studio to cut another demo. This time, we asked Bobby Patterson, the bass player with Love and Money, to produce two of the songs. Neither of the songs would make it on to the album, but this was the session where I learned we had to change to succeed. Bobby played bass and stamped his authority on the demos, which certainly made a difference, but also made me realise I needed people in the band who could make more impact on the sound we made rather than simply playing in a musicianly way.

I also knew they needed to be as committed as I was, and it became clear that Andy and Malcolm had study and work commitments they couldn't relinquish. Dougie, on the other hand, was as committed as ever. At that demo session, Bobby had asked if we knew any female backing singers. As it happened, Mhairi Gordon, my old friend from Dundee, was now singing back-up with my pal Andy Thornton's band in Glasgow. She sang with a young woman called Lorraine McIntosh, whose brother, John was also a pal who had sometimes provided guest vocals for my early chaotic solo shows. The second time we asked them, Mhairi couldn't make the date, but Lorraine came over to help finish the session. She was a revelation, because she adapted to the studio as if it was her best friend. It was almost as if the red light made her come alive, when in truth, it made many musicians I knew more nervous. The more we asked her to do, the better she became. She was a natural singer who had an incredible sense of harmony. As she was still with my pal's band at the time, and we had no real call for a female singer, we didn't really ask her to do much more at that point, but I realised that something magical happened that night in Park Lane, and we knew we'd found a special presence.

The demo itself had been expensive and caused my publishers to (justifiably) blanch at the cost. Without seeing any likely return, they were now paying out money on a regular basis to an act that another publisher had signed. How long could they keep doing this? At the same time, Dougie and I had found ourselves with no band. We needed to find some more musicians. Someone who came in at that time and made a huge impact was John Palmer who played rhythm guitar in Love and Money with Bobby Patterson. Bobby had recommended him when he produced our session. With a few rehearsals and one gig, we spent enough time with John to rejig the sound of Deacon Blue into what became the sound of the band.

Instead of playing the songs as if they were 'backing me up', suddenly it felt as if we were the owners of something unique, something all our own. Songs came and went almost as quickly as we could get together, and with the inspiration of new people around me, I wanted to write more. In a few short weeks, a lot of what became our first album emerged in our printer's basement off Buchanan Street. I was listening to what I'd always loved in roots music – Wilson Picket, Van Morrison, Willie Nelson, Bob Dylan, the Stones and Mahalia Jackson – but now putting it together with what we were all hearing from other bands who were a year or so ahead of us. Glasgow and Scotland were alive with rumours of new music. On a Thursday night on Radio Clyde, Billy Sloan was playing Aztec Camera, the Big Dish and the Blue Nile. We went to gigs by Lloyd Cole and the Commotions, the Bluebells, James King and the Lone Wolves, and we heard talk of a band from my home city called Spencer Tracey, who eventually were to become Danny Wilson. None of them were reinventing the wheel; they were simply telling stories through songs rooted in the music I recognised. In a sense, it was very straightforward: it was taking your record collection and handing it back, edited and augmented. Our reaction was that we should be part of that story too.

Although John was a great guitarist who knew what it took to put a song together, another vital person came on the scene via Park Lane Studios. Rab Andrew, who owned the studio, had become and remains a good ally. One day, he told me about a keyboard player he knew called Jim Prime who was looking to get more involved in a band again. He'd worked with lots of people, including completing tours for Altered Images and Hipsway, both of whom worked out of Park Lane Studio. Jim was around the same age as me, lived nearby and was a *real* keyboard player who owned his own gear and knew something about being in a band. Rab gave me his number and, like the entrance of Dougie many months before, our first conversation was memorable.

I could tell from the woman who answered the call that I'd picked a bad time. Jim had been expecting me, she told me, but currently he was on the street outside their house. An out-of-breath Jim eventually came on the line and started to explain that he'd gone outside after hearing a disturbance to see what all the noise was about. It had turned out a full-scale domestic argument was going on, in which Jim had intervened to try to 'stop a guy beating up his wife.' The strangeness of the conversation set the scene for the next thirty-five years.

Jim came down to rehearsal, I brought in the song 'Raintown', and something began to happen to make it sound like a band who had a direction. A lot of that 'something' was about what Jim brought to the arrangement.

We managed to get a gig at a little club on St Vincent Street called Midas, which was in the basement of a beautiful Georgian building near the centre of town. With Jim on keyboards, Dougie on drums and John Palmer on guitar, we only needed a bass player. I can't remember how we found him, but we met up with Raymond Docherty, who was then in the middle of making the debut album for the Big Dish on Virgin Records. We loved having someone who was a real musician doing proper, grown-up music stuff in our midst. Raymond was my kind of bass player: simple, with a pop sensibility that allowed space into the songs.

Our gig couldn't have gone any better. A scout appeared from CBS, and various Glasgow musical luminaries came up and told us how good we were. We even started to believe them. For five Glasgow minutes, we were almost cool.

Recently a tape surfaced of that show. It was instructive how many songs were played that went on to form the basis of our first album: 'Raintown', 'Chocolate Girl', 'Ragman', 'The Very Thing' and 'Dignity' were all in there.

Not long afterwards, John Palmer departed. He was beginning to be very busy with Love and Money, who at that time were the hottest band in Glasgow, and there were lots of stories of how much cash was being spent on their recording sessions and videos. It was understandable that John might want to leave, but already I knew of someone waiting to join the band. I'd met Gill Maxwell a few times – she was then managing another band in the city – and she'd mentioned that her then boyfriend, Graeme Kelling, might be interested. Graeme came over to my flat, and even in that first conversation, we found we had so much in common. Like me, he was a refugee from the Plymouth Brethren, but unlike me, Graeme had walked away early and had given himself over to all things rock 'n' roll. Graeme was *cool*. Pointedly smoking Marlboro Reds, which were always in the breast pocket of his denim jacket, he had all the time in the world to play music, and, in his words, had been spending the last ten years trying to get out of Glasgow. We decided to co-opt him on to the escape committee. Our first gig was to be back at the Fixx on Miller Street, where Dougie and I had lamely debuted the band a few months before.

With John gone, there was no natural harmony singer in the band, even though Jim and Dougie could both sing. I felt as if my own voice was never going to be strong enough without some help. The reasons we didn't ask Lorraine are a bit lost on me as I try to remember this now. Thinking back, I don't think I'd given the idea of a backing singer much thought until I bumped into Carol Moore on the May Bank Holiday on a visit to the MacKintosh House in Helensburgh to the north-west of Glasgow. I knew her to be a great singer, and spontaneously asked if she fancied doing some backing vocals with us for the upcoming gig. She agreed to try out some ideas with me, and ended up performing at a couple more shows we did in the late spring of 1986. Having another vocalist who lifted the songs into a higher place seemed to complete the sound of Deacon Blue.

At around the same time, I'd persuaded CBS – who were now looking after my writing – to allow us to record one more demo. They agreed to let us have three days in the studio, and not one penny was to be spent above the agreed budget. As luck would have it, a grand piano was left in the studio where Love and Money had been working for the previous few days, and no one was due to pick it up until our session was underway. As soon as we could, we cut three basic tracks, then got Jim to come in before his shift at the bank where he worked to put down the piano parts on the new song, 'Dignity'. Although the song had been around for a few months, it still hadn't been properly demoed. I always remember coming in to hear Jim's piano part and one of the staff at the studio saying, 'I'd forgotten how good he was.' In truth, it was Jim who made the sound of that song come alive. The piano part, almost identical to the one he would cut a few months later on 'Raintown' made the song; and the song gave us that thing we'd been needing – a reason to believe in Deacon Blue.

We recorded another song, 'The Very Thing', which would be arranged similarly on the album a few months later, as well as a song that was a bit too close to the sound of other bands who were around the city at the time. 'Just Like Boys' needed backing vocals, and this time it was Lorraine alone who layered the harmonies, quickly and fearlessly. Our fate rested upon the three songs on this demo tape.

None of us knew then how long 'Dignity' would remain with us, or how much it would be loved by everyone. Some of the parts that became integral to the later recording had yet to be improvised on stage, but that was coming. In the meantime, the demo was sent to London and our manager, Peter Felstead, who had come on the scene around this time, started to hawk the songs around to record companies.

The details elude me now, but I know that over the summer of 1986, we played the Fixx and Panama Jacks. By this time, Carol had come up with some arrangements on the demos I was recording at home, but – perhaps because she wasn't available – we asked Lorraine to do the gigs. There were now five people from the future final line-up onstage.

The demo tape we recorded at Park Lane found its way to Gordon Charlton, who, having been at CBS Records a couple of years back, was about to return in a more senior position. He had fallen in love with 'Dignity', and over the phone, the day after the Fixx gig, he spoke the magical words: 'I want to sign the band.'

By early August, we were hunched over a contract resting on a Cadillac bonnet underneath the Finnieston Crane, ready to make a record for one of the biggest entertainment companies in the world.

15

How Is He?

Here's my favourite Dad story:

He'd come off a train at Dundee station and bumped into an old friend, my best pal Doug's dad. They were in mid-conversation about life in their respective churches when a young man interrupted them to enquire about the whereabouts of a local hotel. Arriving home that night and seeing me heading out, we exchanged news and he revealed that his interaction had been with a member of the band I was about to see, the Clash, who were playing at the Caird Hall. I was going to see them with Doug, who met me having enjoyed a similarly garbled story from his own father.

True to form, my father never wasted a useful piece of social currency like this. After that, whenever Doug arrived, with his shortish hair and an oversized great coat that looked as if it might well have been purchased at an Oxfam shop, He'd look at me, shaking his head, and say: 'He looks like one of those . . .' He'd pause while he remembered the name, and then continue. '. . . Clash.'

I loved this about him. He got their name just wrong enough to maintain his 'dad' status, but he and I both got what he meant.

In my college years, I'd work for him over the summer, and we grew ever closer. Having me as a sounding board who knew and understood something of his business seemed to bring him a certain degree of confidence. He'd listen to my ideas and air his doubts on members of staff or decisions he was about to make.

He encouraged me to go my own way and never suggested I follow him, his father and his grandfather into the business. In my final degree years, we'd moved a little way out of town to a small village on the outskirts of Dundee. He'd often drop me off at college, as it wasn't far from the warehouse, and on mornings when I had exams and had been up all night cramming, he'd always offer a piece of token advice as I got out of the car. 'Read the question properly,' he'd implore, and on my walk into college, I'd laugh at how this middle-aged man, who'd left school at fifteen, felt able to bestow such wisdom upon someone whose academic career was far more advanced than anything he'd ever come close to experiencing. It was with a certain amount of irony, therefore, that on one of my final *finals*, I had to hurriedly retrace my steps in an essay because I realised I had wholly misread the question.

Leaving the car was to leave him to his world and me to mine. I'd disliked school, but enjoyed my life at college hugely. I'd found out who I was, what I was good at and what to avoid. Within a couple of years of graduation, I'd got caught up in the adventure of making music, and my attention was all focused on my own ambitions.

That was why, when the call came, it came as a complete shock to learn that my father had gone through some kind of nervous breakdown. The caller was an old friend of the family, one of Dad's fellow elders in the Assembly, who had gone over to visit him and found him in a state of distress mixed with severe paranoia that seemed to suggest a form of psychotic behaviour. My mother, for all the usual reasons, had thought it best not to worry her daughter and son, who were both eighty miles away, and so it befell the family friend to suggest I should try to see him as soon as possible.

By the time I got to Dundee that weekend, I'd had time to imagine what might have been troubling him. My parents had downsized and moved back to a beautiful spot near where we'd grown up, with a view of the river and intentions of imminent retirement. My father and his sister were actively encouraging possible new owners to consider buying the business, as none of the family intended to carry it on. Margaret's husband Peter had recently retired, and perhaps, I imagined, all this change had created a level of stress and anxiety that may have brought on my father's current state of mind.

It wasn't until I got to the house that I realised how ill he was and how much help he needed. Watching him in his distressed helplessness was not as bad an experience as I may have feared. I loved him, but was also fearful of his omnipotence, and seeing his vulnerability allowed me to feel close to him in a way I hadn't before.

He was able to get help and over the next few years, despite struggling on and off with depression, he managed to retire and even enjoy, for a short time, a new life in Glasgow, where he and my mother moved a few years before his death in the early nineties.

For fundamental Christians like my parents, a psychiatric illness is beset with problems. Given that the patient in question was used to singing choruses of 'Joy, joy, my heart is full of joy' or 'Life is wonderful', the actuality that life was not presently wonderful or anywhere close to joyful was problematic. How could a 'saved' person, one so in tune with God, become so weak, so uncertain and so fearful? These were questions that made matters worse for my father, though my mother was able to counsel and console him that this, like so many other ailments, was simply a period of ill health that had to be treated by experts. The word 'psychiatrist' was never used, and instead we were told that a 'specialist' was seeing my father. This seemed to help, despite there being periods when it all became too much for both of them. Even thirty years ago, relatively recently, there was a fear and shame surrounding mental health that made any healing more problematic.

The only time I remember him having to be admitted to hospital was well after I'd enjoyed some considerable success and been on the TV and the radio. My dad had enjoyed this, but nevertheless was currently in a ward in the main psychiatric wing when I drove up to see him. By the time I got there, any anxiety he'd been suffering had been countered by new medication that found him in a relaxed form of mind celebrating a newfound friendship with the chap in the next bed down.

'He's a lovely fellow,' my dad confided quietly. Then, leaning forward conspiratorially, he whispered (alluding to my recent fame), 'And he doesn't even know who I am.'

Who I was had become an interesting diversion for my father. My friends who knew him often enquired what he would make of his son giving up a safe teaching post to join the circus. I'd given this subject some thought myself, as I knew, for good reasons, he would have concerns. I told my friends he'd be happy once he saw me on *Top of the Pops*, and so it was. My father, despite everything, found a certain satisfaction in seeing his son enjoying success. It brought small bits of happiness where there was often unnecessary worry. It also gave him a distraction, which, I'm sure, was helpful in times of stress and despair for my mother, who, without any great deal of fuss, coped brilliantly with a husband who had been changed by ill health. My dad enjoyed my press cuttings, radio play and TV appearances, but also liked the challenge of getting albums sold. He'd visit local record retailers and satisfy himself that our recent releases were visibly racked at the front of the shelves. He'd enquire whether people had heard of us and extended this to Christian musicians he encountered at large-scale events, cornering them to ask them about their familiarity with our oeuvre.

'He was the pianist at the convention, so I asked if he'd ever heard of Deacon Blue,' he'd tell me. '"Oh yes," he said, "I know who they are." "Well," I said, "that's my son."'

Long after he died, I took one of my daughters to Visocchi's Café in Broughty Ferry, where the owner told me of my father's visits years before: 'We used to compare notes. I told him my son wanted to be a chartered accountant, and your father used to look fed up and tell me his son wanted to be a pop star!'

When he had finally seen us on the TV, my father decided to come along to a show when we played in Dundee. He seemed to enjoy it, but when he visited me in the dressing room afterwards, he asked why we hadn't performed our biggest hit at the time. I told him we had, and he seemed relatively consoled, as if it might have affected future sales and hastened a downturn in our fortunes. I introduced him to the other guys backstage.

'I hope you boys aren't smoking any of that marijuana?' he asked them.

'Well, not while you're around, Mr Ross,' Graeme inevitably replied.

When Lorraine and I got into our new house in 1990, I took him round on a grand tour. I'd assembled a small studio in a spare room on the top floor, where I'd put up a huge, almost life-sized framed poster of Springsteen I'd collected on my first visit to see him at Madison Square Gardens. My dad took a long look at it before asking, 'How is he?'

'Who?'

'Jim. Jim Prime.'

At this point, I realised my father believed I'd put a life-sized poster of a fellow band member on my studio wall.

This was just before he and my mother made the move to Glasgow, and soon he'd no longer have to make the eighty-mile journey to spend time with me or my sister. I remember how anxious he was to get home that day, despite it being high summer.

'We want to be back before nightfall,' he explained, as if there were unknown terrors waiting for him in the woods around the motorway.

Years later, and closer to the age he was then than I ever imagined I could be, I understand his enthusiasm for a swift return home. I enjoy visiting, but equally, I enjoy getting back to my own place in good time.

When my mother finally downsized to a more suitable retirement apartment after my father's death in 1994, she sifted through his old letters and papers and handed them on to the family. I took charge of a large file of old sermons and notes he'd collected. I held on to them for a further decade or so until my mother finally died in 2020. Leafing through them, I understood why my father had never been a preacher. He'd underlined verses and made various points of understanding what an apostle was saying here, or a prophet was pointing to there, but there was nothing of him that I didn't already know. I couldn't bear to imagine his papers drifting around on some waste ground, so I solemnly decided to commit them to a stately demise on a bonfire in the garden.

It was a mild spring day, and I remembered how, at each equinox, Dad had welcomed the coming of warmer times and lighter days with such a gladness of heart. As I grew older, I relished his embrace of the vernal months, knowing the winter was a long, dark time when your spirits find it hard to get through the days. I opened the big file of notes and committed each of them to the flames with a passing farewell and a gratitude for a faith that was never fully expressed in sermons or prayers, but lived in love and kindness.

What no one explains is the acute loss of familiarity at the death of a parent. Years later, there are events or questions or pieces of news that once would have given me the excuse to ring my father. He'd answer the phone, and I would see him in my mind's eye, standing in the kitchen or in the hall. I'd tell him some news and he'd be glad for me, and then he'd share a story of a school friend's mother who worked in a local shop, or tell me about the visit of some friends. He'd ask how everyone was, and he'd tell me of an old customer whose son liked my band too, and ask could I possibly sign something for their daughter?

I keep hold of these special memories, which grow rosier in the nostalgia of passing years. When my second daughter was born, I got home from the hospital in the early hours of the morning. It was summer, and there had only been a few hours of darkness, which had come and gone during the course of a long labour. As I closed the front door behind me and looked at the clock, I realised it was not so early that my father, who had always been a very early riser, would not be up and about. It was joyous to be able to call him with the news. It would be the last time I could make such a call, and I often replay these minutes in my imagination. I try to remember what was said and how the call unfolded, but the details are smudged in the soft focus of time, that golden light of memory.

Years later, I'd remember a story that had been told often at family gatherings. It was what my father was said to have exclaimed to his parents-in-law upon my arrival in December 1957 as he threw his hat into the air. Similarly, when our final child was born, our only son, I came home from the hospital in the middle of the night and scribbled a note to my mother, asleep with our daughters in another part of the house, echoing my father's words.

It simply read:

'It's a boy.'

Part Three

LONDON COMES ALIVE

16

Raintown

In late summer of 1986, it seemed as if we had been given the keys to the kingdom. Dougie, Jim, Graeme and I had signed the deal with CBS, and for the first time in all our lives, we received payment for doing something we'd all been happy doing for nothing, for as long as we could remember. On a personal note, as the eldest, I felt my dues had been well and truly served.

In the aftermath of the gig at Panama Jax, which finally sealed the deal, in a slightly drunken moment, Dougie asked Ewen Vernal if he wanted to join the band. Dougie and I had both played with Ewen briefly before we'd all gone separate ways, and was convinced it was the right time to ask him to hook up again. I think he prefaced it with, 'We're just about to sign a record deal.' Ewen was – and is – a brilliant bass player and a great singer, and we welcomed him into the fold.

From that moment on, I realised a dream I'd been having for years. All we needed to do in the morning was wake up and make music. We all received a wage based on what Jim had been earning in his job working at the bank, and the first thing I did was book three weeks to work on demos at Park Lane Studios on Glasgow's Southside, where we had always recorded everything we'd done.

It was a good studio and people made some fine records there under the aegis of their house engineer, Kenny MacDonald. Kenny was taciturn spilling over into monosyllabic, but a great recording engineer. In those few weeks, we put down fewer songs than we might have, as a good deal of time was spent trying out new instruments and falling down the odd rabbit hole, and we wasted some good hours flying frisbees . . . but essentially, we completed demos of the songs we hoped might make it on to an album. In many ways, we could have made our album there and then, except there was always a doubt about the band's ability with Kenny, and it led to us questioning our own skill. There were significant songs cut during that time; one demo of a song called 'Ribbons and Bows', which I'd always thought should have been more than a B-side, was better than the final version we cut later.

Our manager had booked gigs for us during that time too, and we headed down to play some support slots with Sandie Shaw; all of us riding with the gear·in the back of a Luton van. We watched in awe as we saw Sandie's 'luxurious' splitter bus pulling into the car park at Newcastle Poly one afternoon. How, we wondered, did we move up to that level?

As we returned to Glasgow, we listened again to the songs we'd been recording. As well as the ones we'd got together earlier in the spring, there were new songs emerging. I'd gone away on holiday over the summer and left my flat keys with Graeme and Jim to put some ideas down on the eight-track tape machine I'd bought with that first publishing advance. There were a lot of drunken ramblings on tape, and then an idea that immediately sounded brilliant. As I recall it, we listened to the tape and I started to sing along with the track, then wrote down the lyrics that spontaneously poured out. More than anything else, I think the song was really my own take on that first trip to London that Graeme, Dougie and I had made to talk to the labels who'd been interested in signing us. To me (to us), the opulence of London life was a complete contrast to the dull drudgery that made up so much of life in Glasgow. 'Loaded' was written pretty quickly. We rehearsed it and recorded it properly at Park Lane.

I only realise this now, many years on, but the months before an album is made is always the best time in any band. It's full of the possibility of songs and far removed from the harsh reality and outcomes of any new release. It's the time when everyone believes each new song is the best thing that's ever happened, and you suppose your common life is going to be changed for good, for ever. It was in these months we gathered our resources and plotted our conquests, defying the odds of triumph and failure. In a beautiful way, we also completely ignored the dim likelihood that this precarious new career would bring success. We assumed the world was waiting to hear our record, and it wasn't until the middle of the project when someone mentioned the word 'single' that my stomach lurched a little and I realised we hadn't really thought this whole music caper through very thoroughly. One of our greatest supporters in those days was my publisher, Sally Perryman, with whom I had placed a bet on our impending demise, so that, when the axe inevitably fell and our label didn't renew our contract, I could at least smugly say, 'I told you so,' as I collected the fifty quid. In retrospect, this was probably a twisted form of Calvinism.

Gordon Charlton, the A&R guy who'd signed us, liked what we were doing, and wisely counselled against us spending too much money, encouraging us to carry on recording at Park Lane. For me, this was the perfect world. I was twenty-eight years old; I'd left a full-time reasonably well-paid job to become a full-time musician. The only real annoyance I had was how late we started each day. Musicians would often roll in after lunchtime, and I'd think about how, as a teacher, I'd already have had a day's work done by this time. That aside, I was as happy as I ever could be. I would walk the autumn lanes through Strathbungo, past the park to the studio, and content myself that this was the life I had spent the last three or four years working towards.

•

Kenny MacDonald was formally contracted as producer, and we were to cut two master tracks. I'd been working on a darker, moodier song called 'Down in the Flood', which I was convinced was to be our pièce de résistance, the song that would change our world. It may have been, but Kenny persuaded us to use a drum machine and (as only he could programme the Linn drum), all of us became slowly disengaged and alienated from the project. There were moments of light relief when Dougie brought in some opera singers to sing backing vocals and we all drunkenly joined in, with mixed results, but as we moved on to more familiar ground with 'Dignity', the same endless programming and hanging around began to wear out all our spirits. At the end of the two weeks allocated to record the session, we hadn't really finished either song.

Gordon came up to hear it, and, in his defence, tried to explain to all of us how bad a job we were making of the process. I'd grown to trust Kenny, and probably felt Gordon was prejudging something that was not yet complete. There was a big discussion, and we agreed to listen again when it was finished.

In the meantime, we had a week of shows booked in and around London, including our prestigious first night at the Marquee, which was then in Wardour Street. In those days, there was a small twenty-four-track studio next door to the club, and CBS decided to tape the whole thing to multi-track too. The gig was probably the best thing we'd done since our early live adventures, and made all the more complete because Lorraine had come back to join us.

The Marquee show couldn't really have gone any better. We played a lot of the songs that would end up on the record and got some great press. Our label came down en masse to see the show. We encored with a song called 'Spanish Moon', which I'd loved ever since I'd seen Little Feat in Glasgow ten years before.

It was hard to explain, but over the course of that one show, we grew into a real band. I think that only happens when everyone knows what to expect of everyone else, and the playing starts to become seamless, relaxed but also vital. Over the course of around a dozen or so songs that night, we finally became Deacon Blue. Ewen and Lorraine – who were flatmates back in Glasgow – were with us, and looking into the audience, we began to feel the first flickering of belief coming back.

On our return, we were asked to play a couple of songs at a benefit gig for an Aids charity in Bennet's, Glasgow's most famous gay club at the time. Lloyd Cole was there, and others, probably including Craig Ferguson too. For whatever reason, those who saw our set almost didn't recognise us. We seemed to be a band who'd gone to London, and instead of taking a couple of years to find our groove, had done it all in a week. Like Gatsby, no one quite knew how we'd found our fortune.

Gordon had brought various producers along to some of the shows at London colleges and the Marquee. He'd sent out our demo tapes and was looking for reactions from some of those who'd listened. At one college show we were introduced to the producer Jon Kelly, who we were told was desperate to work with us. Jon was so quiet and unassuming, we all imagined a mistake had been made, or that Gordon was spinning us a story that wasn't true. It felt to us that Jon didn't think much of us at the show, and in any case, we wanted to finish what we'd started in Glasgow with Kenny. At least, I did.

Our manager Peter Felstead's office at the time was in Langholm Street, conveniently close to Radio 1 and CBS's office in Soho Square. For us, that square mile of west London would soon become our world. One particular afternoon, we were all sitting around Peter's office so we could properly listen back to our work at Park Lane. The previous night's champagne, which had been delivered to our dressing room courtesy of the label, had been consumed and the accompanying gift basket used in an early hours fruit-fight along the corridors of the Columbia Hotel.

Listening to the recording was sharply sobering. A rough mix had been put on to a cassette and Peter played it back to us. Our faces fell. Far from the spontaneity, ecstasy and joy of the night at the Marquee, the tape sounded like a different band. In fact, it was much worse than that; it didn't sound like a band at all.

It was then we decided we could do something better than we'd been recording at Park Lane. It was now late November, and the word came back from our A&R office that Jon Kelly would still like to work with us. We were slightly surprised to learn of his ongoing enthusiasm given how quiet he'd been after the gig where we'd met. Looking back now, I know this was just how Jon was in any social situation. What we were to discover was how much he would come alive in the studio.

Soon after this, Gordon arranged for Jon to come up to Glasgow to meet and arrange some songs. We brought him down to our basement and we played over some of the things we'd been hoping to cut sooner rather than later. Towards late afternoon, as we made plans to reassemble the following day, we asked Jon where he was staying. To our amazement and wonder (it still shocks me now) he was (courtesy of our label) flying home that evening and returning the next morning. We were never sure if he was simply keen to be with his family or if he was a little wary of spending the night in Glasgow.

The rehearsals were exactly what we needed. Although Lorraine wasn't there, as she was still not technically a full-time member, the rest of us went through the songs. It was 'Loaded', perhaps the newest song in our repertoire, which was finally to come alive. As it got to the second chorus, there had always been something missing.

'Key change?' Jon said.

We tried it, and suddenly the gearshift from D to F made the song explode. Even now, on any given night, it still sends shivers down my spine when it kicks in.

At the end of the day, when Jim had inevitably gone home early I suggested to Jon that there was one more number we should consider. It was the song we hadn't returned to since that first Deacon Blue demo with the old line-up, before Jim and Graeme had joined us. As luck would have it, though, Ewen had guested on that recording and knew the song. As Jim wasn't in the room, I played the song on piano and sang it. Jon liked it and suggested we cut 'When Will You Make My Telephone Ring?' along with the songs we'd been rehearsing that day.

'How are we going to play it, though?' I wanted to know

'Just the way you played it there,' came the simple answer.

We had been working so slowly at Park Lane that, by the time early December arrived, none of us expected to do any recording until the new year. It certainly hardly seemed worth starting anything in mid-December. However, Jon was keen. We were also shocked when he suggested we work in one of best facilities in London, which, as far as we were aware, was well beyond our budget. Nevertheless, such was the enthusiasm for the session from our manager and A&R that all budgetary objections were overcome, and we came down to London to begin the album properly. I was still sceptical about how much we could expect to get finished before Christmas. Jon was a little more sanguine when quizzed. 'About four songs,' he said.

I couldn't believe it. It seemed to us that, by definition, making records took forever – and if they didn't, it meant we were all doing something fundamentally wrong.

The studio Jon had picked was Air at Oxford Circus. From the lounge in Studio 1, where we would work for those first ten days, we could look down at the West End's festive lights four floors below. It seemed like the inhabitants of the entire capital city were bustling around Oxford Street and Regent Street, determinedly shopping their way to Christmas, while we looked down from our lofty perch, content to simply make music and allow the world to pass us by. Jon joked, cajoled and told us stories about sessions we'd only dreamed about: Kate Bush, Paul McCartney and Jimmy Webb. He took us to a pizza restaurant he recommended, and then he picked up the bill. This didn't happen in our lives in Glasgow. George Martin drifted in, and we all called home to share the news of this visiting royalty while spinning on the studio chairs in delight at the music that was emerging.

Because of Lorraine's session role within the band, she hadn't come down with the rest of us on that first flight, but Jon was keen to know what we were going to do about backing vocals. We'd expected he'd have wanted some exclusive studio singers on the session, so hadn't even told Lorraine what we were doing. When the subject came up, however, Jon suggested we call her and ask her to come down. Little did he know she had no phone. On a previous visit to her shared flat in Great Western Road, when Dougie and I had gone over to ask her to sing on a demo, Dougie had looked positively disturbed on his way back out of the close. They'd all been in the kitchen, and the main source of heat came from a gas cooker in the corner of the room. 'I didn't know people still lived like that,' Dougie had muttered, sounding not unlike a Dickensian commissioner to the poor house. Most musicians we knew at the time were unemployed, signing on for benefits and hoping for a regular piece of work to get them through the next few months.

We dispatched our manager in Glasgow, Gill Maxwell, to pop a note through Lorraine's door asking her to phone in. Within a couple of days, she was on a flight down and making her way to Oxford Circus to record some vocals. It was one of the best calls Jon could have made. After she started to record, he would turn around and say, 'That girl is brilliant.' In fact, he'd always say it three times: 'Brilliant, brilliant, brilliant.'

Deacon Blue was completed by her, and although she would be signed on a side deal at first, with CBS already imagining a separate career for her, it was clear to us we needed her in the band permanently. She sang on the songs we were recording at that time, 'Raintown', 'Loaded' and 'Ragman' but not the one we'd routined in our Buchanan Street basement, 'When Will You Make My Telephone Ring?'

At night, we'd all end up in the bar at the Columbia, and for some reason some of the guys met up with an American soul singer who was in town recording backing vocals on another record. As they played the rough of 'When Will You?', Wendell P. Morrison sang along with his idea. The next day, Jim told me about the encounter, and Jon arranged for the gospel singers who later became London Beat, but were then Paul Young's backing vocalists, to come into the studio. It was to be our final session before the holiday, and apart from our original track, George Chandler, Jimmy Helms and Jimmy Chambers became the only overdubs on the recording.

As we all came home for Christmas bearing gifts from our London adventures that holiday season, we played final mixes of two songs and roughs of two more. 'Loaded' and 'Raintown' had been mixed, and the others were finished but unmixed. We couldn't believe how quickly it all happened. I remember a huge smile across our manager, Peter's face as he came over that first night of tracking to hear 'Raintown' booming out of the big studio speakers. We monitored loud and we all loved hearing it back.

It was quickly decided that we all had fallen in love with Jon Kelly. Dougie recalls feeling completely disheartened during the Park Lane sessions, but suddenly feeling confident and refocused when we got to Air. We all felt the same. We'd found the perfect producer in the perfect place at exactly the right time. We came back to a London covered in snow on 2 January and, although we stepped out to perform two or three college shows at the end of the month, we didn't really leave Air until we had the mixes of our first album.

There were days and nights of confusion, drunkenness, discovery and lots of euphoria over the six weeks or so we took to finish off the project. We moved into Studio 2. Later, as we were moving out, Jon looked around wistfully and told Jim and I that there had been some great albums made in that space. He mentioned Stevie Wonder's *Talking Book*, and we were both glad he'd failed to mention it before we'd started.

Other bands came and went. Mark Knopfler was around, and Bob Clearmountain was along the corridor mixing a Bryan Adams record. I have a vague memory of the Proclaimers mixing their album at around that time too. But the real thrill was in Studio 3, where Steve Jackson was helping George Martin – Air's chairman and founder – digitise the Beatles' catalogue for CD release. At this point, they were on *Revolver*, and Steve, who we'd eventually work with on *Fellow Hoodlums*, invited us over to the control room when George had gone home. We got to randomly move the faders on one of the greatest albums of all time, giggling in delight to hear the boys' 'Happy Christmas' messages to the fans thrown in between perfect backing vocals. Had this been our only ever recording session, it might have all been just enough.

On one of the last nights of our mixing in Studio 4, the band were all down to hear the final album. Graeme and I had overseen the mixes until that point, but as the others joined us, the inevitable party started early. A drink was spilled on the console, and suddenly, like a scene from *Monsters, Inc.*, the engineers came in to dry out the desk. There was much relief it had only been tequila; no sugared mixer had gone into the equipment. Later that night, a couple of us dragged a drunken member of our team along the long corridor after he'd passed out on what remained of the carry-out. As his shoes bumped awkwardly against the carpet, we passed a member of an American band, who nodded sagely and offered, 'Mixing, huh?'

Before we finally cut the final record with CBS's mastering engineer, Tim Young, we needed to select the single and the B-side. 'Riches' is a song I still feel is one of my best, because I got close to saying something that felt true about the man to whom it was dedicated. Jim Punton had died the year before. He'd come into my life when I'd worked in youth work in Dundee, and he'd made sense of so much of what was streaming through my head at that time and for the years in between. My best pal, Doug, found a tape of him speaking, and we put a little extract of his voice on the seven-inch single B-side.

In those days, assembling an album involved cutting and splicing tape. Crossfades had to be recorded and edited in, with the gaps all counted by lengths of half-inch tape. It might have been a different record had Gordon Charlton not intervened. I can't remember where we had planned to start it, but he insisted it should begin with 'Born in a Storm'. 'Everyone starts their album with an up-tempo track,' he told us. 'You will be different.' He made his point strongly, and suddenly the album running order made sense. We had always known we wanted to finish with 'Town to be Blamed', and now we knew how it all began.

We played it back to family and friends at CBS studios, and came home with a test pressing in our luggage. I don't think I heard any of the tracks on the radio until one wet afternoon when I drove into our rehearsal space and assumed I was listening to the cassette of the album, only to realise that Johnnie

Walker was in fact playing 'Raintown' as part of his *Saturday Sequence* on Radio 1. My heart stopped. Suddenly, on a damp, dark Glasgow afternoon, my dream of escape, of setting off to rise up above the dark tenements, was being played back to me, and to (what seemed like) the whole world. It was wonderful.

17

A Short Tour of Some London Recording Studios

Occasionally, I'll find myself walking through Oxford Circus in London, on my way to catch the train home from Euston. I'll lift my head up, looking away from the commuters thronging round the underground entrances and catch a glimpse of the top floor of the corner building on the north-east side of the junction. When we first came to London to record, that was the home of Air Studios, perched high enough to look imperiously down Regent Street towards Piccadilly.

We'd get the Tube along the Central Line from Lancaster Gate, the nearest stop to the Columbia Hotel, and arrive every morning ready for a new adventure. Looking back on that record, it's hard not to describe it as one of the happiest times of my life. We got to go in and make our songs sound the way we'd always heard them in our head.

By the time we got round to thinking through the follow-up album, our world had changed. We were the people who'd made a record, been on the radio and played the Barrowlands. Our music had crossed continents to be played in Australia, America and (though we had to have a legal fight to stop it) South Africa. It's hard not to let all of that affect the way you see the world, and I suspect my own head had been turned in a number of ways by the time we came back to record our next album.

For that one, we decided to move away from London and record in the countryside. We did come back to the city to finish the thing off in time for a release schedule that was very tight. We stayed at a hotel at the top of Tottenham Court Road, and would be picked up by our producer, Warne Livesey, every morning to go and record final vocals in a studio called Mayfair in Primrose Hill. It was January, freezing, and I have no happy memories of this time at all. By early afternoon, the tape would be whipped off the machine and Lorraine, Warne and I would go down to Whitfield Street, home of the CBS Records 'Hit Factory', where Bob Clearmountain was to mix our recordings into a final album. This was also where we assembled to hear the whole thing back. As I walked along towards the studio that day, I bumped into the legendary Muff Winwood, head of A&R at CBS. He was heading towards the studios with some sandwiches in his hand. 'I'm just bringing my lunch,' he told us. I loved this world-respected record guy not realising his label had laid on a five-star buffet for us all.

In the same building worked Tim Young. Tim was the king of the cut. This was where the half-inch master tape – now DAT – would be turned into a production master for vinyl, tape and CD. On a good day, you'd go in the morning and leave by late afternoon with a twelve-inch test pressing in your hand. On a bad one, you might have to wait for the postman. Tim mastered every record I made until 2019, when I discovered, having called up his new home at Metropolis, that he'd finally retired.

Metropolis in Chiswick is one of the last of the big studios in London. So many other fine places have gone. Air moved from Oxford Circus some years ago; Abbey Road is still there, but the record label that once owned the home of the Beatles and so many other great recording rooms has now disappeared too. In 1990, we recorded the string arrangements for our *Four Bacharach & David Songs* EP in Studio 1 there. Later in the evening, we threw up a couple of mics and recorded Eddi Reader busking her way through an old folk song for a charity album I was making for the Oscar Marzaroli Trust.

When the Beatles weren't at Abbey Road, they'd assemble in Barnes at Olympic. The first time I ever went there, I was coming back from one of three nights we were playing at Hammersmith Odeon in 1989. We'd been assigned an A&R man from Columbia in New York called Jovan Mrvos. We all loved Jovan, and on my first-ever visit to New York, a year before, he'd been my guide and inspiration. As part of his trip, he was officially the record label guy for the Rolling Stones and, as the bus made its way from Hammersmith back towards Kensington, he asked if anyone wanted to join him as he dropped in to see the band in the studio. I was the only one who said, 'Yes,' and we must have walked or hitched a cab to cross the river and head over to Barnes, where they were working with Chris Kimsey at Olympic.

It was nearly midnight when we arrived and joined the party. Everything was in full swing. Ronnie and Keith were both there as Kimsey tried to keep the whole thing rolling. It seemed the guitarists would only work at night and Mick would only come in during the day, so the producer needed to be there the whole time.

It was the only time I was ever in the same room as any of the Rolling Stones. They were both so welcoming and charming. For years afterwards, I carried around two smudgy Polaroids of my late-night visit.

We recorded a few tracks at Olympic with Chris Kimsey ourselves in the mid-nineties, and upstairs were Eric Clapton and his band. As we toiled away for the full ten-hour day, the late Richie Hayward (Little Feat's genius drummer) would pop his head in to say hello to Chris on his way out.

'Are you finished for the day?' Chris would ask. It was four o'clock in the afternoon, and they'd assembled in the upstairs cafeteria around noon.

'Yes.' Richie would nod sagely. 'All done for today.'

I imagined a world where you arrived so late and left so early, but I've never yet experienced it.

I went back to Mayfair up in Primrose Hill in the early part of 2001 to mix a Deacon Blue album. Again, I remember it as a less than heart-warming experience. Mixing is one of those things others do, but you have to approve. It's a bit like a haircut: there's no way you can do it yourself, but it's only your opinion that really matters. So, you walk the streets or go the movies until the time comes for you to drop in at the studio and hear everything back. I've stopped doing this in recent years, and now enjoy playing mixes on my phone in the car. I remember a drive up to Loch Lomond a couple of years ago, where I batted mixes back and forward with the engineer as he tried to get closer to what I was looking for. Listening beside one of the most beautiful backdrops in the world seemed to help.

In the intervening years, I've only had a passing acquaintance with London's studios. A day at Abbey Road recording strings, a session at Britannia Row, an interesting experience with my Big Bruvaz friends at the Dairy in Brixton, an album mix at Eden in Acton, and a couple of days at the Town House are about the size of it.

There is, of course, one studio that hasn't changed much in the seventy-odd years it's been there. Maida Vale, the BBC's trustworthy recording base, has hosted them all. Big bands, Bing Crosby, Peel sessions and, on my last visit there, a Radio 2 away-day where the entire available staff deliberated about what they were doing right and wrong. I was the guest turn at the end of the session, which was a mixed blessing. There was some relief among the assembled producers and content editors at being spared any more exercises in navel gazing, but I sensed an equal measure of awareness that when my song ended, the bar would open. I kept it short.

So, when I'm passing Oxford Circus, or remembering that ride on the Central Line from Lancaster Gate, I think of the days when we'd imagine what being in a band with a record in the shops would feel like. It's February 2020 as I write this, and I wonder where those thirty-three and a third years have gone.

18

Springsteen

I have tried to write this chapter in so many ways, stopped, then started all over, again and again. Reflecting on this process, I realise it echoes everything about following the lifelong career of an artist. We fall in love, we feel we're losing them, or they are losing us; we lose interest, then suddenly we're back on it, as if nothing in this world could possibly be as important.

In my shallower moments I could kid on that Springsteen is just another singer I have enjoyed along the way. 'I like *Nebraska*,' I might intone casually, as if the other records, the raps, the band, the camaraderie, the voice, the fun, the pathos and the melancholy, lonely ache don't matter. But it does. With Springsteen, it all matters – and it really matters to me.

In 1975, I was looking for something. Music had become almost everything in my life, and listening to it loudly, watching people play it live, and haltingly, hesitantly, playing it with pals had started to take over my teenage life. I was finding out about everything, without any sense that something huge was missing from all I'd heard until that point. I didn't even know that I was looking for that missing something, until Bruce Springsteen arrived in my life and I found it.

It's lunchtime, and we're heading back to work after our break. My dad is driving and, somehow, he's letting me listen to Johnnie Walker's show on Radio 1. Suddenly, the man I'd heard about but not yet heard comes on the radio. Bruce Springsteen and 'Born to Run'. I could probably take you to the exact spot where the music started playing on a medium-wave radio at *Dad*-volume; it's summer and we're driving along the Arbroath Road. As buildings get higher or we go under bridges, the signal goes in and out – and the signal is not that strong to begin with. Nevertheless, it's a glorious three and half minutes of sheer rock exuberance. It seems dense, exciting, and slightly out of control, and Springsteen sounds as if he's fighting to be heard over this tumult of noise – but he also sounds magnificent. The song ends and Johnnie reflects, 'He sounds like he's singing through a pile of old socks.' I'm disappointed in Johnnie's reaction, but what does he know?

For me, it was a small epiphany.

Within a couple of weeks, the album was out. I was on my way home from college, which I'd opted to attend instead of sixth year at school. I'd walk down the hill towards Reform Street and stop in at Bruce's Record Shop. On that afternoon, *Born to Run* was playing from beginning to end, then all over again. I hung around the shop for as long as I could, thumbing through everything I could possibly browse, until it came time for me to head, reluctantly, towards the bus stop. I had heard the album I now needed to own, but on that day I had no means to buy it with. When some pocket money arrived, I asked a friend who was going into town to buy it for me on the following Saturday. I still remember the smell of the album as it came out of the Bruce's bag.

I had met up with another friend who played guitar he had a sunburst Les Paul copy. He told me about music I'd never heard, and he and his brother had a fantastic record collection between them. He'd come round, and we'd play Neil Young songs together and imagine what it would be like to be in a band. We would talk about the music we dreamed about, and somehow, we realised

Springsteen had been that *thing* we'd all been looking for. To me, his music was urban and seemed to have no knowledge of any kind of life beyond the city limits. It was dusty, noisy and troubled in all the right ways. He was *Born to Run*, but seemed to have nowhere to go, even though his car was parked and ready. On the cover of the album was a black dude who looked about the coolest guy you could ever imagine. If we'd seen Clarence Clemons walking down the street in the city centre, we'd have asked him to join our band before even hearing him play a note.

The record itself had an arc and flow of epic proportions. Towards the end, the two songs 'Meeting Across the River' and 'Jungleland' felt like the finale to everything. How could anyone follow that? My guitar-playing pal also played football, and one Monday he came into college to tell me excitedly that he'd been playing against a team with a full-back called 'Eddie Mann' – a lyric from 'Meeting Across the River'. We had, it seemed, become obsessed.

On *The Old Grey Whistle Test*, Bob Harris invited on a music journalist who had seen Bruce Springsteen and the E Street Band live. There was no footage available, so we had to endure a review that kicked the whole mythology up another level.

'The light show is incredible. The set goes on for hours. There will be one gig here, but you'll never get a ticket.'

He was right about the last bit. Springsteen played two nights at Hammersmith Odeon, then headed back to the States for the next six years. Six years!

By the time he did come back, I'd moved on, cooled down, heated up, gone cold and then suddenly become red-hot again. It was the bootlegs that worked their magic. I met some musician pals who became lifelong friends who slipped me a C90 cassette of a gig from the *Darkness Tour*, which confirmed everything I'd suspected years before. He was better, the show was bigger, and the music trumped everything else I was listening to. He went into old songs, he told stories and people were booing . . . oh, no, wait. They were simply shouting, 'BROOOOOCE!'

I was going out with a girl who turned up at my flat with the double album of *The River*, and when I'd met up with her during the summer, I'd found a pin badge on a railway platform that simply said, 'I Love Bruce Springsteen'. I realised it was love or nothing at all. The bootleg pals camped out and got tickets to see him in Edinburgh in 1981, when I really should have shown more willing and gone camping too. The reports confirmed what I feared: I should have been there. In 1984, I made the dire decision not to go with a lot of friends to Newcastle to see him there, because I was terrified I'd just want to ape the whole show when I got my own band together. Who was I kidding? Like I could!

In the meantime, he'd released an album that I was finding hard to bond with. *Nebraska* was a dark folk record of bitter stories about the downside of the American dream. The optimism of Kitty, Wendy and that working man whose freedom came when he walked out with his pay packet on a Friday to be 'Out in the Streets' was gone, and the dull, deadly certainty of the rest of life was now being laid bare. 'At the end of every hard-earned day, people find some reason to believe' – wasn't that the truth?

I was teaching in Maryhill, and I felt like the record was talking to everything I knew. However, a lot of it felt as if it was in the same key, the same tempo. It seemed the whole feel was being limited by the acoustic guitar, voice and harp minimalism. Then one night, I heard the woman who would become my wife sing 'Open All Night' with her brother at a party, and I knew I had to listen all over again. It was dark, minimal and narrowly focused, but it was also truly great.

A couple of years later, in Air Studios in London, I'd play piano as Lorraine sang a version of 'Used Cars' and again, the lyrics would floor me. There was Arthur Miller, Steinbeck and the detail of Joni Mitchell, all in these few lines.

> Now my ma she fingers her wedding band
> And watches the salesman stare at my old man's hands
> He's tellin' us all 'bout the break he'd give us if he could
>   but he just can't

I ignored the hype of *Born in the USA* and kept hold of my love for *Nebraska* and the earlier albums as I awaited the next adventure. That came quickly after we'd signed our record deal with CBS Records, the very home of Springsteen. Suddenly, I felt I was within touching distance – or, in reality, that I might be able to get my hands on any missing back catalogue and perhaps even some early future releases. In 1986, this involved our A&R man arriving with freshly printed boxed sets of the *Live 1975–85* album before a gig in Glasgow. I felt it was so precious, I didn't want to leave my copy in the dressing room for fear it would be stolen when we went on stage.

Then came pay dirt: it was 1987, and there were rumours of a new Springsteen album that was without the E Street Band, and might even be a bit 'country'. One of these things was true, and though Springsteen would now be seen as an essential writer of country and Americana songs, and his catalogue is plundered in depth by artists from that world, *Tunnel of Love* was no country album. Instead, it was the most personal record of his career, a window into the private doubts and loves of the man himself at his most vulnerable. He'd not long been married, but this was not some honeymoon record, but rather a troubled twelve-song explanation of why he wasn't really ready to settle down. I loved every syllable on every song. We had the album on cassette, vinyl and CD, and so many copies have been worn out or damaged and replaced that I can't remember what or where the original is.

At the end of that year, I got even closer to the myth when we hired Springsteen's mixing maestro Bob Clearmountain to record a new version of our first single, 'Dignity'. We'd only wanted Bob to remix the track, but in agreeing to re-cut it, we ended up spending more time with him than I'd ever imagined. I told Bob how much I'd enjoyed *Tunnel of Love*, and we bonded over our delight with the album. When he'd originally been sent the album, Bob's first question to Springsteen was, 'Has Julie [Springsteen's then-wife of a couple of years] heard these songs?'

A few months later, I'd managed to get myself to New York on the basis that a couple of songs were being remixed there. For me, the exciting part was that Springsteen's *Tunnel of Love Express Tour* was to be at Madison Square Gardens all that week, and if I got it right, I could go to at least one of the shows. On the first day there, I went into CBS Records and picked up two tickets for the Garden. Our A&R man, Gordon Charlton, was with me, and his jetlag kicked in before the encore, so on this epic first night I walked back to my uptown hotel alone. As I wandered up 7th Avenue, through Hell's Kitchen, I looked around to find myself the only member of the audience still walking at eleven at night through what was then a fairly tough area of the city. Sensing it wasn't the wisest thing to be doing, I quickly jumped in a cab. Back at the hotel, on my first-ever night in America, in New York and having finally been at a Springsteen show, I slept soundly. It was raining too; I was already feeling at home.

I walked the whole length of E Street, and went back to see him later that week in New York. Then I caught the show in Sheffield when it came to Europe, by which time the whole gig was a little more relaxed, as it had become clear that Bruce and Patti were now an item, and these protracted looks of longing that had so fascinated everyone in New York had been explained by subsequent events. All of this was immaterial to the second set in Sheffield, when the Boss 'ripped up the set list' and played a blinding final ninety minutes or so, with 'Because the Night' making the two-hour wait to exit the mud-strewn car park worth every minute.

Within a year of that show in Sheffield, we would we be on our first-ever American tour, heading west to east across the continent, hurtling towards two shows at New York City's Bottom Line, the venue where Bruce had played for five consecutive nights in 1975 on the *Born to Run* tour.

I'd read and heard about (and listened to tapes from) the Bottom Line for years. I'd had no idea where it was or where the Village was located, but I'd imagined this wonderful place in my head since reading about the New York folk scene of the sixties around a decade after the events. My way into that scene was by finding a cut-price compilation album featuring the music of John Prine, Arlo Guthrie, Bette Midler, Van Morrison and others, called *The Bitter End Years*.

I imagined there to be a 'scene' where all the folk singers hung out, swapping songs and stories as magical happenings evolved on smoke-filled nights. The two clubs always mentioned were the Bitter End and the Bottom Line. The Bottom Line had hosted the mid-seventies run of Dylan shows featuring Patti Smith, which were feverishly reported in the music papers back in the UK. I was so excited about Patti Smith that I imagined running away to London just to catch her. In a parallel world, this was what Mike Scott actually did! That probably sums me up more clearly than anything I could explain. All the rock 'n' roll, all the longing, all the posturing and the escapism only happened in my head. In reality, my feet were planted in Dundee, and I was never going to take that train to London – not then. That would come later.

·

And then later came, and in 1989 we were in a stench-filled New York City in August, where they were just recovering from the first heatwave of the year. The streets were exploding with garbage, and our tiny hotel rooms were made smaller by the air conditioning units blasting out cold air. We arrived from Philadelphia to play a show at the Bottom Line, but also, for most of us, to drink in everything we could about New York City. It was dirty, foul-smelling and rude. We loved it.

We'd gone from the UK to Australia, and were now on the third leg of our first 'world tour'. We'd gone through San Francisco, Los Angeles and Chicago on the way, and we were now to play our first-ever date in New York. It was only on the day, or shortly before, that someone explained the Bottom Line expected us to perform two shows on the one night. There was an early evening show, and then the audience would be cleared before a second house arrived at nine, hoping to see us do it all over again. This information notwithstanding, we approached both performances as if our lives depended upon it. I can't remember much about the detail, other than it was one of our best ever nights. It was so all absorbing, I seemed to be the only person who didn't clock Rod Stewart in the audience watching us.

At the end of the evening, the assorted heads of label and various friends gathered round for a drink. The new heads of CBS were all there, and pictures were taken just in case it turned out we were going to be big news, so the bosses could frame them to display in their Manhattan corner offices. I was being snapped with a couple of the portly execs when my eye fell upon a man I desperately wanted to meet: Jon Landau, journalist, manager to Bruce Springsteen and co-producer of some of some of the seventies' most seminal records. He was standing just feet away. I started to make my excuses and found myself explaining that I must shake the hand of the man who had produced some of my favourite albums. Walter Yetnekov (then CBS Chairman) looked bemused, then started to laugh as he gently let me drift away. It was then he intoned the immortal phrase, 'You think Landau produced these records?'

I didn't really care. The fact was that on the sleeves of *Born to Run, Darkness on the Edge of Town* and Jackson Browne's *The Pretender*, the name Jon Landau was credited, and I wanted to meet him. As it turns out, I can't remember much of the conversation, but the next day, the woman who had made the introductions, our publicist Marilyn Laverty, called to say Mr Landau would like us to join him the following Sunday at his wife's birthday party in the Hamptons. So, on the day, Lorraine and I clambered into a minivan, along with her brother John and his wife Lynsey, and a couple of strangers, to be taken on the long drive out to Long Island. Early nerves were extinguished by the other couple passing round an enormous joint as the four country cousins gawked out the windows on their way to their first (and possibly last) showbiz bash.

No sooner had we arrived and been welcomed than Landau himself loudly declared, 'I'm off to pick up Bruce and Patti from the heliport.' It was enough to make the four of us scamper in fear into the garden in search of more grass and nicotine. At this point, seeing the nervous Scots cowering in a corner under the decking, Marilyn came to check on us. Discovering that we were all terrified of meeting our hero, Bruce, she cast us a withering look and a deep sigh at our display of teenage adulation.

Within minutes, it was obvious that Bruce and Patti had joined the company. There weren't that many of us to begin with, and we dutifully sang 'Happy Birthday' to Mrs Landau, wondering all the while why we'd ever been invited. The party then moved on to a more serious footing and a new location at the local country club where the Landaus' neighbours were to join us. Soon we'd be making small talk with the singer from Foreigner (at the time, I didn't really know what he looked like or even what he was called), Jan Wenner and Billy Joel. As we found a quiet table in the corner, we were aware of Billy Joel drifting our way. It was at this point my brother-in-law John took matters into his own hands. He stood up, proffered a hand towards the Piano Man and memorably declared: 'Billy. Big fan.' Billy took this with great grace and made himself available to us all. The trouble was, as we reminded John later, we'd not been aware of John's fandom of the Joel oeuvre until this point, and though I now would consider him to be a truly brilliant artist on every level, I was thoroughly side-tracked by the looming presence of the big Boss in the room.

We were, of course, all Springsteen fans. Of the four of us, I might even have been the least obsessed, such was the level of Brooce devotion in our group. Our intention, on this trip to the Big Apple was to cross over to Jersey and head down to Asbury Park to drink in the E Street Kool-Aid. A year earlier, on that first visit to New York, I'd not only seen the show twice, but I'd also visited the New York office of our record company and asked everyone I met if they could give me any Springsteen bootlegs. I'd left with my case stuffed with copied cassette tapes. On the morning of the Bottom Line show, my old bootleg pal Craig, had sent me a cassette tape called *The Other Bottom Line Show*, which was a C90 tape of one of the gigs from Springsteen's five-night seventies run there.

Bruce was front and centre of every move we made. That he was at the party we'd been invited to was beyond all our expectations. Eventually, the inevitable happened, and he came over to hang with the mad superfans sitting in the corner. I got the conversation all wrong, even asking if he'd ever consider putting together a new band. I really don't know what I was thinking, but it's still true that, for every reason, you shouldn't meet your heroes. Bruce lived up to and beyond all expectations, even when we met again a few years later. However, the real spark was between his wife and mine. They connected in such a way that by the time I joined their conversation, Patti was writing down her phone number and inviting us over to New Jersey for a barbecue later in the week. (The knowing look as she slowly enunciated 'Patti S . . . p . . . r . . . i . . . n . . . g . . . s . . . t . . . e . . . e . . . n' was a particular joy.) As we were leaving the party and crossed the room to bid farewell to Bruce, he reminded us we were meant to be coming over to the house later in the week.

'You know we're not going, don't you?' Lorraine informed me on our return to the city. The next day, it was my job to call and explain to someone who answered the phone at the Springsteen house that we couldn't make it. In our desire to keep hero and friendship separated, we'd driven to Canada to make it impossible to meet our social obligation.

I have no regrets about not socialising. I wanted to be and remain a fan.

I've loved and watched and intently listened to Springsteen for the thirty years since that meeting took place. I'm not big on seeing artists multiple times. I've seen Neil Young four times . . . possibly once too many, if I'm honest. I've seen Dylan three times, and McCartney once. There's plenty of folk I love whom I've never seen, and, as a gig is still a bit of a busman's holiday, there are many invitations I'll happily pass on. When it comes to Springsteen, however, I've seen him more than any other artist by a long measure. In Edinburgh, Glasgow, London, and one great time in Manchester, when it all came together and the bootlegger Craig and I drove down on a gorgeous summer evening to witness 'Meeting Across the Water' segue into 'Jungleland' as the sun came down over Old Trafford cricket ground. Perhaps the most joyous thing was taking almost my entire family for an E Street experience at Hampden Park a few years ago. Three kids ranging from twelve to twenty-one stood for four hours, enjoying and absorbing every moment. I was, and remain, a proud dad of Springsteen fans.

Years later, in a different world, we had a rather clumsy encounter with Tony and Cherie Blair. It had been going well, until I blurted out that we'd lost faith in Labour and voted SNP in the recent 1997 election. Cherie got quite sniffy at this point, but Tony, to his eternal credit, took it all in his stride. There was an awkward silence for a couple of seconds, until Lorraine remembered that he'd requested Springsteen's '4th of July, Asbury Park' on his recent spot on *Desert Island Discs*. We had both loved it. The conversation had been saved and we carried on talking about music quite happily. As we chatted, we were keen to know if they'd met Bruce. Sadly, they confessed they had not.

'Have you?' Britain's new prime minister enquired.

'Oh yes,' we said. 'We've met Bruce.'

Part Four

YOU CAN HAVE IT ALL

19

Paris

For a while after our initial success, we got to do what we wanted. We followed our hearts in making the records we made, pursued the side projects we favoured and managed to avoid too much interference from those who would be expected to be guiding our career. It was only possible to do this because people bought our records and came to our gigs. For both of these things, we remain wholly grateful.

From 1988 until 1990, Deacon Blue enjoyed a purple patch of successful singles, chart-topping albums and increasing international recognition. We played in bigger venues to thousands of people, toured Australia and the US for the first time, and in 1990 played to a record-breaking crowd on Glasgow Green at the Big Day. The success we enjoyed allowed us to consider what we wanted to do next, and we all knew we wanted to go back to where we'd started and work with the man with whom we'd loved making our debut album.

As *Raintown* was joyful, in almost every way, so *When the World Knows Your Name* became, for me, the difficult second album. Almost all the difficulties were of my own making, however, and in retrospect, it all could have been so much easier.

The great thing about that second album, though, was it bought us success and real freedom to do what we wanted. For me, that meant the ability to really imagine an album and allow the creativity of the band to flow. We'd finally arrived at a place where we were entirely happy in each other's company and I wanted to make something much more organic than we had on the second album. On that, I'd already experienced too much programming and not nearly enough spontaneity. All the people in Deacon Blue could play and sing, so I needed to write something that would allow that to happen more naturally.

In the early days of 1990, Lorraine's father died very suddenly. Although I'd only known him for a few years at most, I'd become very fond of him. His death was a complete shock as he was still relatively young. For Lorraine, it was a dreadful blow, as she had lost her mother aged eleven and was now without either parent aged only twenty-five. As a dad of three girls all beyond that age, I have some idea of how young that really is. In the aftermath of his death, I wrote the first of a bunch of songs that reflected upon his passing and, in particular, on dealing with grief. It was the first time anyone very close had died prematurely and music had been the balm that brought comfort for us both. Often, we allowed ourselves to listen to the saddest songs possible. Somehow, all music in and around that time seemed connected to loss.

'Your Swaying Arms' was the first new song to come from this time. Whether it was written before or after that sad event, I can't now recall, but essentially the song started out with the story of a man who wanted to read everything his lost partner had ever committed to paper. The main character wants to know who she loved, where she travelled, and if, in some unknown way, it was possible they had passed by each other before they'd met. I've always been intrigued by the idea of ghostly meetings or faint interactions between people who didn't yet know each other years before they became close. Within the song, there is a deep longing for an afterlife, which is imagined as the beautiful tree-lined road running through Kelvingrove Park. Kelvin Way is one of the most scenic routes in Glasgow's West End, taking you from the cloisters of the university to the grandeur of Kelvingrove Art Gallery and Museum, the river shadowing you every step of the way. It seemed to me to be as close to an image of heaven as I could imagine.

As the song came early, it set a template for those to come. Having travelled the world in the eighteen months since the last album, I now felt more drawn to writing about anything and everything if the action remained set within the place I knew best, Glasgow. Although Glasgow had formed the backdrop to most of our songs up to this point, with occasional diversions to other places, I'd never fully formed a picture of the city being the theatre in which all the business of each story happened. Until now.

We were looking for a studio to record the new record towards the end of 1990, and we were interested in finding a place that wouldn't be too far from home, but would be awkward enough to get to for anyone on the record label to be put off dropping by. It was suggested we take a look at Guillaume Tell in western Paris. In the madness of these times, Dougie and I took a flight there to check out the studio and didn't even stay overnight, leaving ourselves no time to even stop and have something to eat . . . in Paris! I always remember the awful decision that we could just pick up a McDonald's or have nothing. It would sound better if I told you we chose nothing, but we didn't.

Studio Guillaume Tell in the village of Suresnes was an old cinema with a huge live room, as well as a spacious control room. It would be perfect for what we wanted to do. We approved the studio that day and made plans to return in early 1991 to commence making a record that was already taking shape in my head. Rather than the usual procedure of recording lots of things and piecing the album together – a lifelong habit – I'd felt strongly that the songs on this album already had a narrative flow that would make it seem like a more cohesive project. Though the recording would take place away from home, I saw Glasgow laid out like a map on which the stories would all take place. As a band, we were keen to bring as much work as we could back to Scotland, for many different reasons. It meant that conversations were easier and simpler, and we felt bound to support other creative people in our own neck of the woods. We'd found a graphic design company in Edinburgh who understood what we were about, and some artists in Finnieston who might design the next sleeve. We also enjoyed working in our local studio in Glasgow, CAVA, where we were to finish the recording session after Paris. Time off and new priorities had changed where we all lived, however. Graeme had married and joined his new wife in New York, while Jim had moved to Ayrshire and Dougie was living part-time in London, so recording was a way of bringing us all together. Choosing to record it somewhere abroad meant we would all be together, without distractions, for the time we were tracking the record.

Before heading to Paris, we had booked a small studio in the Merchant City in Glasgow where we could rehearse and also record anything if we wanted to put a rough idea down. I can't remember if this was any use, as the main takeaway was our casual visit to a nearby pet shop where Lorraine wanted me to look at a kitten. We came home with two. Had it not been for Gill, our manager, who lived nearby, I don't know what we would have done, as we really had no plan for how to look after them for the month or so we were about to spend in France.

The real joy of this time for me was a sense that we were all celebrating what we did best. There was freedom for me to sing about the stories I wanted to tell, and with Jon at the helm, we knew we would be trusted to follow our musical hearts. Songs had come together and occasionally found their way into the set over the last year. Older songs were being looked at and new songs were written in the months preceding the recording sessions.

The first real burst of creativity, however, had been a few months earlier, when we'd had to come off the road in Germany due to Lorraine contracting acute appendicitis on the morning after a show in Bonn. She was taken to hospital for an emergency appendectomy, and I stayed on with her, travelling back and forth between the hotel and the ward, up and down a steep hill that ran between them. On the morning after her emergency operation, when the tour had been cancelled, the nuns of St Marien Hospital looked a little shocked to see a troop of road crew in black tour gear and a varied stylings of hair, beards, tattoos and jewellery pay their respects to the patient before they got back on the bus to go home. If the nuns found it unusual, the other patients in Lorraine's room – three other elderly ladies – looked terrified.

As visiting time was limited, I spent the rest of my days thinking up ideas for new songs on a guitar I'd asked the nun-scarers to leave with me. It was there 'Twist and Shout', 'I Will See You Tomorrow' and a few songs that never quite made the cut started to come together. The real narrative for me was this underlying sense of grief, as this all happened only a few weeks after the death of Lorraine's father.

On one visit to the hospital, I brought some photographs I'd managed to get developed from a roll of film in my camera. There were lots of shots of family and friends, socialising and occasionally laughing . . . all in rather formal dress. I had taken the shots to commemorate the day we'd come together to remember Davie McIntosh, Lorraine's father, who was such a great character. In the midst of the sadness and sense of loss, there had, inevitably, been times of helpless laughter. As the older German ladies in the ward took an interest, Lorraine had to explain, to their clear surprise, that these prints were not of a family celebration, but had been taken at the buffet after her father's funeral.

On our return from this tour, when it was clear we couldn't be back on the road for some time, Jim and I hatched the plan to record the *Four Bacharach & David Songs* EP. No sooner had we discussed it than we brought Jon Kelly into the proposal and asked if he'd come up to Glasgow to record it with us. It was this experience that confirmed for us that Jon was the right producer for whatever we were going to do next.

The pleasant surprise of a hit single from that EP – which was really just a side project we completed for fun – again bought us freedom to write and record the next album the way we had always intended. I also felt a freedom to write songs about the places and people I knew closer to home.

One morning, Dougie and I were in a taxi from the airport after an early flight into Glasgow. The taxi driver looked at the two of us in the rear-view mirror and, quickly surmising we were a little weary from the night before, suggested he could take us 'up to the Budgie for a wee livener'. I had no idea where the Budgie was, but it transpired it was the pub where all the early workers would go after their shift at the fruit market. We didn't take up the offer, but I kept the idea, for a song called, 'The Day That Jackie Jumped the Jail' and it became part of the story of an escaped Barlinnie prisoner who keeps thinking about the day he'd been arrested, and how he just wanted to spend the last few minutes of his free time with the woman he loves. Whether that woman is still there for him is a moot point in the lyrics. I liked what this song became, as it allowed me to roam across the city. I even brought in the previous New Year's Eve, when we'd been visiting family on Hogmanay only to be shocked by an enormous explosion of fireworks lighting up the sky as the new decade was welcomed in style.

One Saturday afternoon, I'd been in the city centre near the Stirling library (now GoMa), and I'd seen an old-school street evangelist shouting over the shoppers, helped only by a sidekick with an accordion. The wind blew away most of what he was trying to say, so we were only left with the visual clue of his apparent anger at the would-be converts passing by. I kept the story in mind until I went to see Jim one day in the rehearsal space, where he was leading the others through an idea for a song. It came together as 'A Brighter Star Than You Will Shine' and still feels to me to be at the heart of *Fellow Hoodlums*. The title track itself came from an article I'd read about a newly appointed mayor of a US City (probably Chicago) beginning his acceptance speech by declaring, 'Fellow Hoodlums, thank you for electing me.' I liked the raw, if uncomfortable, honesty in the statement. Perhaps it was that sense of looking at ourselves for who we really are that was behind the title. Now I can't remember, but I wanted the themes to say something about people I knew and understood rather than trying to imagine people I'd never met.

For the last leg of touring we completed before we began the album, we'd been in Spain, and we'd used the soundchecks to try out some new songs. Jim started playing this beautiful chord progression, and it quickly emerged into a song we pulled together in a loose arrangement as 'The Wildness'. We'd always have a DAT player at the front-of-house mixing desk, and Dave Pringle (still our FOH engineer) knew when to hit record. 'The Wildness' cradled all the elements that gave us our true identity at that time. Most of the arrangement came from that sound-check in Spain, and when we came to put the song together, we simply listened back to the recording and repeated what we had done spontaneously on that afternoon.

In a strange quirk of fate, the number fifty-nine bus route ran from where I had lived when I first came to Glasgow to where

Lorraine and I had just bought our first house together. In some ways, that route told my own story, showing how much my life had changed in a few short years. In 'The Wildness' it became the journey travelled by someone so obsessed they needed to stand outside their lover's home to feel close to them again. It's a song of forbidden love and the fear that, despite all our efforts, there is nothing that can extinguish desire when we have been rejected in some way, no longer able to connect with the person we want the most. The lyrics were really me remembering a girl I'd once known who broke up a young relationship. For months after, and perhaps longer, not even knowing why, I'd try to drive past the place where she'd worked, just so I could catch a glimpse of her again. I never wanted to re-engage – at least, I don't think I did – I was just troubled by our break-up and wanted to see her, just once. I never did. She contracted an illness and died very young, and it was a mutual friend who told me the news. Recently, I received a lovely correspondence from her son, now a writer, who it seemed had heard we'd once gone out together and remembered stories about my visits to see his mother. It was a beautiful reconciliation of a lost relationship that had slipped away without my ever making sense of what it had all meant. I knew it was never to be, but valued the fact that, after all this time, I'd found out that it had meant more to her than I'd ever imagined.

By the time the Christmas holidays had passed, we had a strong idea of the twelve or so songs we wanted to track in Paris. For us, it felt as if this was the best of times. We had beautiful accommodation in catered flats on George V Avenue, just round the corner from Fouquet's brasserie, and we made our way to the studio each morning through the Bois de Boulogne on cold, bright January days that were free of tourists. The only cloud on the horizon was the impending Gulf War, which had been threatened over the course of the last few months since Iraq's invasion of Kuwait. It meant that security around American franchises was stepped up, and there was clear anxiety in and around the city and on the twenty-four-hour news we were getting from home. As we got back from the studio on 17 January, we watched in horror as the allied attack began on Baghdad. Needless to say, in the long Ross tradition of support for lost causes, I was against the war, and we joined a fairly muted Parisian protest down by the Seine that weekend. However, we were all focused on making the record we'd been preparing to make for some time, and we knew what we were there to do.

Jon had brought in Steve Jackson, an old Air graduate, to engineer, and for the first time we recorded on a new digital forty-eight track. It meant we experienced the possibilities of digital editing for the first time, back before it became something anyone can now do on their phone. The studio was huge, and it allowed us all space to have our own sound, so we could keep everything we wanted but still overdub what we needed. A lot of the best bits of the record happened in those few weeks in Paris before we returned to Glasgow to overdub and finish off recording at CAVA.

One of the beautiful ideas Jim had come up with was a short hymn, to which I'd then added lyrics about a fictional working man being mourned. It doesn't take much imagination to know this was based around Lorraine's father. We'd met – and continue to meet – folk who would tell us stories about him. Often the tales were madcap and hilarious, but there was also a real love and respect. Thirty years later, we were walking through Cumnock in Ayrshire, where he had lived, when we were stopped by a man who had been a colleague and wanted to tell Lorraine about the time her dad had built him a sledge. He started to laugh, remembering how he'd insisted on his own preferred colour scheme. It seemed Davie had still delivered the sledge, despite the man's insistence that it be decked out in the colours of the Glasgow Rangers. 'Goodnight Jamsie' became the song, and an echo of the melody was written, by Jim, into the string lines of the opening song, 'James Joyce Soles', in the final recording session a few weeks later at the Hit Factory in London.

'James Joyce Soles' (a fictionalised name) came from an idea I'd seen in a BBC film by Peter McDougall featuring Harvey Keitel. *Down Where the Buffalo Go* was the story of an American military man posted to the Holy Loch as part of the US submarine base some thirty-five miles or so from the centre of Glasgow. Inspired by the drama, I came up with the story of a serviceman who had died a long way from home. In my head, the song was obviously written in the voice of his male partner. These days, there's nothing about that story that really surprises the listener, but back then it was still illegal to be a gay member of the military, both here and in the US. It was a time of discrimination against gay people, for all the usual historic reasons, but with added venom attached due to the Aids crisis. I hadn't really seen this as a protest song until I came to introduce it one night on the subsequent tour, and heard a heckler shouting something homophobic towards the stage. For gay people, and for heterosexual folk too, there was still a long way to travel.

One night my old friend David Heavenor dropped by the house, and I played him some of the things we'd been working on. They were either demos or rough mixes, and I could see the surprise in his face.

'What have you been listening to? Folk music?' he enquired.

In fact, he'd got to the heart of the thing very quickly. I'd really gone in the opposite direction to whatever was happening in modern music at the time, and had instead tried to listen to as much traditional music as I could, so I'd understand where our songs had all really come from. There was a little shop near the Trongate that specialised in folk music, and I'd picked up cassettes of various things I wanted to know about, including Jean Redpath singing Burns songs, along with Dick Gaughan, early Dylan (the *Bootleg Series* had just emerged) and Richard and Linda Thompson, whose music I kept returning to.

I loved hearing each instrument or voice in these recordings. It seemed digital recording and eighties album projects had allowed everyone to add as much as they could. When we'd first worked with Bob Clearmountain, he'd told me he was going on to mix something for Tears for Fears from seventy-two tracks. He was already daunted before he'd started. The more I thought about what I wanted to hear, the less I wanted to expand the number of tracks we had. I sometimes wished – still wish – we had to make the same choices the Beatles had to make back in the day: 'You want a tambourine? OK, you can put it on the vocal track – but only in the gaps!'

So, it came to pass there were mainly drums, bass, guitar, piano/organ and some voices on the record, with fewer over-dubs. During the work on one song, 'Cover From the Sky', Jim and I went back to Glasgow to launch the Marzaroli Trust album *The Bird and the Bell and the Fish and the Tree*, leaving the others in Paris. By the time we were back, most of the song had been cut by the other four. Jim added Hammond, and one of my oldest songs, first written some seven years before, had finally found a home with the obvious decision that it would be Lorraine's voice as the lead vocal.

The record ended with a theme I would come back to about thirty years later. During a writing period defined by the Covid-19 lockdown in 2020. 'One Day I'll Go Walking' is a song of movement and energy where the whole thrust of the music is propelled by the sense of being outside, driven by the elements. I guess it's a promise I made to myself about that vague idea of the afterlife I'd touched on earlier in the album. In this song, it's the simplicity of walking free, of abandonment to that which allows us to lose the fetters of lifelong responsibility and care. Instead of fearing what's to come there is a sense of welcoming the inevitable. On my better, more optimistic days, I still run with that hope.

After Paris and Glasgow, we headed to New York, where Michael Brauer was to mix the album at Quad Studio near Times Square. Michael surprised us all by completing mixes in four or five hours, and slightly ruining our plans to sightsee while he fiddled with the controls. We'd no sooner have decided to skive for the day than he was calling us back to the studio to hear a finished track. We'd worked together before; on my first-ever visit to the city, he had mixed two songs from *Raintown* for radio releases.

In America, our career was taking a while to get going, and we felt we wanted to use the chance of our presence near the epicentre of the Sony empire to bring the label on board. Our management duly corralled a few of the key people down from uptown to hear a playback, and we sat there while they took in the whole thing. In fairness, I can't imagine how difficult a procedure this must be for people who work at record labels, though equally I can't ever imagine working at a record label. My only recollection of the whole afternoon was one of the marketing guys looking up after the full chaotic six minutes and twelve seconds of 'Closing Time' and smiling goofily. 'Wow . . . that's a wild ride.'

New York was still New York, however. We took in a play off Broadway, went down to a jazz gig at the Blue Note, and got our photographs taken by the legendary and elderly David Gahr, whose main interaction with us was to insult us as loudly as he could shout over the city traffic. 'Smile, you stupid Scottish bastards,' was used more than once. His house was a vault of photographs from the previous four decades. He was, in fact, a lovely man, who made a point of giving me two New York shots he'd taken of Dylan and John Lennon. I treasure them both.

The final task in New York was to go to Sterling Sound to master the album with another legend, Greg Calbi, whom Brauer used on all his finished albums. We were happy with the cut – until Tim Young, our regular mastering engineer, requested he should, at least, submit his own version. In the end, we recognised that it was Tim's sound we liked best, and it is Tim who cut everything else we made until very recently.

Making *Fellow Hoodlums* had been the most perfect experience for all of us. We loved working together, and we found in that incarnation, a unity of purpose we probably never had again. Towards the end of the mixing process, when we had to select a single, I was hit by the dawning reality that we probably didn't have that killer track that everyone hoped would lift us to another level. I'm not sure I cared too much, and reflecting on it now, there's very little I would have done differently with the songs or the production. To be making music, to have the freedom to write and record songs and put all that together into an album, and to see it go out into the world is as good as it gets.

20

I Intend to Shoot Each Member of the Band Individually

Imagine it's 1993 and you are at home in Spain watching your favourite Saturday night variety show on television. It's Ant and Dec meets the Generation Game and Noel's House Party . . . on ice. There's music, comedy, dancing and a grand finale. I imagine by now you'll be used to this part. You'll know the plimsoll-wearing host with the tuxedo and the designer stubble, and you will also recognise his younger, glamorous female co-presenter. I'd imagine the sixteen-strong line of Brazilian dancing girls won't cause you much surprise, either. As you look along the line, however, a small cloud might cross your consciousness, as you see an uncomfortable-looking, pale, thirty-something guy trying to keep up with what has now become a conga. That thirty-something guy is me. It seems that, when asked in broken English if I would be happy to join in with the 'poom, poom, poom that normally ends the show', I had unwittingly volunteered for ritual humiliation on a grand scale, live on Spain's biggest network.

It was TV. I should have known.

It had always been the same. To promote a single, an album or just ourselves, we had to become part of a world to which none of us had ever aspired. It involved hanging around studios for hours, long trips abroad, staying up late drinking, being taken to some fabulous restaurants, and conversing exhaustively on every subject we could all talk about – and a dozen more we couldn't. Heck – we loved it.

Spain seemed to host the most chaotic television events for Deacon Blue. We'd be stuck in a studio with some mics pushed in front of us while people ran around, shouting and smoking incessantly. A researcher would arrive in your dressing room to prep the questions for the interview after the performance.

'How do you feel about being number one in Spain?'

'We're not number one in Spain.'

(Muttered discussion between TV researcher, management and record label.)

'Yes, you are.'

'Oh. We're . . . delighted!'

For a while, we did a lot of this. There was the time we were somewhere in the middle of a line-up involving Boy George, the New York Gay Men's Choir and a live crocodile in Berlin. There was a chaotic cable channel interview in Chicago, where none of us was sure if it was them interviewing us or vice versa. Then there was the time we became friends with Jimmy Boyle in Belfast, or the Christmas show we did in Germany when Ewen's hired bass guitar strap was elasticated, giving the performance that extra sparkle the snow-filled grotto hadn't quite achieved on its own. 'You're lucky,' our international label rep informed us. 'When I was here with Paul Young, they'd arranged singing Christmas trees.'

My first brush with TV was on *Reporting Scotland*, a nightly news programme on the BBC. They wanted to run an item about up-and-coming bands who were currently 'doing something'. What we were doing or not doing was almost nothing, but that first incarnation of Deacon Blue must have attracted enough interest for the show to feature an interview with me and a short clip of a song. This was 1985, and we were all gathered after soundcheck, craning our heads above the bar to see the report on the telly.

Our first proper TV break happened a couple of years later. We were looking through prints at Oscar Marzaroli's studio, high above Park Gardens, when our manager called and said we were to go down to London to be on TV that weekend. This was to promote our first-ever single, 'Dignity' which was released in March 1987, and though it would be wonderful to tell you the show in question was some great late-night music programme, the truth was there were very few music shows on TV at that time. *The Tube* had stopped by then, and *The Old Grey Whistle Test* was on its last run. The show we had secured was on hideously early on ITV and called *Wide Awake Club*. It was aimed at preschool children who watched early on a Saturday morning while their hungover parents dozed in front of the telly, or, more likely, went back to bed.

None of us had been up that early for many years, but we duly went through the motions and mimed our way through the transmission. I don't think they really 'got' the song entirely (they'd put a map of the Turkish coast behind us, I assume because of the word 'raki') but it was a TV show, after all, and it was suggested that one or two parents might just have taken a bit of notice. A month or two later, I was asked back to do an interview, as they showed the video to our single 'Loaded'. I also had to join in with a spot of home baking – something involving bananas, I recall – and had the pleasure of hanging around the canteen with the late comic genius Richard Briers, who was also a guest on the show.

None of these appearances involved us playing live on the box. That didn't happen until a little later that summer, when we performed on a German TV show that went out from Munich to a live audience who had no idea who we were. The TV show, however, recorded us playing a good chunk of our live show, including a version of Van Morrison's 'Angelou', a song that suited almost everything we were about at that time. It was romantic, full of ebb and flow and sexual chemistry, and loose enough for everyone to express themselves within the music. Ewen pegged the whole thing down, Jim played the melodic line and Graeme could happily sit on a groove all day. Dougie was at his best in songs like this too as he listened to what the vocals were doing and followed every interplay Lorraine and I made. If the audience didn't know what was in front of them, we were lucky that the cameras kept turning and the tapes kept rolling. Finally, someone had caught what we were truly about on film.

A few years later, we were playing a festival with Van Morrison, and the promoter asked if we'd like to say hello to him. I was nervous and agreed, but Lorraine was too shy and took the wise approach of 'never meeting your heroes'. The meeting went well, and I felt as if I could go back and see my pals in the pub and say, 'I met Van, he was lovely, and I've no need to ever do that again.' Before I left his tented sanctuary, he said, 'You do one of my songs.' At which point, my mouth went dry, and I wanted to say, 'Van, we do them all . . . we rip everything we can.' He was talking about 'Angelou' of course, and seemed to be suggesting he approved of our version. I left walking on air.

The only other time around those early days when we were filmed for TV was at the ITV studios on the South Bank, where they hosted a big event for the new Night Network on London Weekend Television (TV up to that point stopped just around midnight). We were filmed performing a couple of songs, before the fans of the other band on the show, Pop Will Eat Itself (it was a fairly eclectic line-up) invaded their stage at the other end of the studio, and the whole evening dissolved into chaos. I think we enjoyed the performance and the chaos, as most of the TV we'd done up to that point had been fairly well ordered.

Getting on TV was what record companies wanted at the time, as it reached the mass audience radio was never going to cover. We were getting very minimal radio play at this point; we weren't having much luck at Radio 1 in terms of daytime play, although we'd started to get some evening spins and a radio session or two. This was despite our radio plugger telling Dougie how much he'd loved the record. 'I went home and put on the album,' he confided. 'Don't tell anyone in the company this but I lit a big spliff and I said, "Blow me away." Do you know what, Dougie? It did.'

The first serious TV that changed our lives came from a show we recorded for BBC Scotland early the following year, in which we performed the usual tracks from *Raintown*, but also threw in a song that still hadn't been properly recorded or released. We'd been including 'Circus Lights' in our live shows over the last few months. I had written the song during the *Raintown* sessions at Air, overlooking Oxford Circus, and Jon Kelly had suggested they record it on a quarter-inch tape while I played it at the piano. That slightly tentative recording morphed into a full-on band version that was broadcast on TV a little while before we played at the Barrowlands in Glasgow for the first time. If you hear the tape that was recorded of the show that night, you can hear my genuine shock and delight as the audience sang along to an unreleased track, all on the basis of having seen us play it on TV. It was a beautiful moment for us – and for the audience, who recognised our joy at their collaboration.

The main TV plugger at CBS then was a lovely guy called Nick Fiveash, with whom we eventually struck up a great friendship. In the early days, however, our relationship had got off on the wrong foot. Lorraine and I had been asked to attend a spring record label conference to talk up the album with the sales reps and promotion teams. This involved sitting through presentations of new products coming out over the next few months. It fell to Nick to make the case for Dolly Parton's new album. Lorraine and I are and always have been huge fans of Dolly's music, and especially her songwriting. Watching someone give a crude send-up of her art based around a slideshow of various people with drawn-on enlarged breasts was too much to stomach. We made a point of making our way out of the room very sharply. It's said people should never witness how sausages or laws are made. Recording artists should probably avoid witnessing how records are promoted too.

The next time we encountered Nick, he had booked us on another children's TV Saturday morning show, which was broadcasting to a big audience. These Saturday shows were the ones everyone wanted. On the best days, they could be fun; you'd meet some famous folk, and all your pals and family would get to see you on the telly. This particular show was to be filmed at a castle near Aberdeen somewhere, on a weekend when the rain showed no signs of letting up. Unfortunately, it coincided precisely with the point in my career when I had begun to take myself far too seriously. It was a perfect storm. As we got to the location for the camera rehearsal the day before the show went out, we were shown the plan, which involved all us being spread across the castle forecourt, with others in turrets or ramparts high on the walls. (I seem to remember a particularly unbecoming placement of the keyboards behind a section of battlements.) It was all too much for my prickly, artistic sensibility, and I threw a tantrum. Perhaps I naively believed the music business to be something that it never was and never would be – or I, mistakenly, thought the entertainment world should be taking us as seriously as I took myself – but for whatever reason, the castle, the ramparts, the fakery of miming in the dreich drizzle, all got too much and, frankly, I lost it.

Driving back in the car after that 'rehearsal', there was a dead silence as I fumed and the others stared at their shoes. The driver was a gentle rural type, happy to be doing something different for the day. As Graeme always recalled it, he quietly broke the ice by staring up into the smir of rain, which was still showing no sign of letting up. There was a long intake of breath, then a resigned: 'Aye . . . steedy.'

Back at the hotel, Nick was trying to rescue our career – and, no doubt, allowing his thoughts to drift off towards his own prospects. I was lying on the bed, still in a filthy mood, when the phone rang. It was Nick. In one beautiful sentence, he sorted it all out and managed to extinguish all my pomp and fury with a very simple, 'Darling, we've got to talk.' The TV show was done with no more fuss, and Nick became one of our best allies at the label.

The TV show that everyone wanted to be on was *Top of the Pops*. It had been running since the sixties, and it simply defined what was and wasn't successful in terms of chart singles for most people not concerned with the finer nuances of an artist's career. If you were on *Top of the Pops*, you'd reach the kind of people who didn't bother to read music papers or rummage around record shops – but, strangely enough, artists, music-business people and anyone connected with pop music would also watch it or, at the very least, would know who was due to appear on any given week. As the chart was printed each Monday in *Music Week*, the acts selected to appear on that week's *Top of the Pops* were noted in a sidebar. Two things had to happen to get on the show. At the bottom line, the song had to breach the top thirty. Secondly, the song had to be going up the charts. You wouldn't get on again unless you had a huge climb in two weeks' time, as successive appearances were only permitted to number-one acts.

In early 1988, we were still nowhere close to getting on *Top of the Pops*, despite having a great new record plugger in Amanda Beale, who in the following years was instrumental in getting almost every single we released on to the Radio 1 playlist. However, our new single, a re-recorded version of 'Dignity' had still only scraped in at number thirty-one, and so didn't meet the

Top of the Pops baseline requirement. We did, however, get on another show – and that, single-handedly, broke our career wide open to the British public. Terry Wogan hosted a chat show in the early evening on BBC1 three nights a week. The show lasted half an hour and there was a music slot that, although mimed, seemed instrumental in breaking new acts. Even established artists would see their releases pushed further up the chart after appearing on the programme.

On Monday 15 February 1988, we made our first appearance on *Wogan*, a show on which we were to feature more times than I can now recall. Terry Wogan was a genial host, who we never actually met until much later when he hosted his Sunday show on the radio. I suspect many people didn't see the best of Terry on the television show, despite its popularity, as his real genius was as a radio host. On the radio, Terry was king of all he surveyed. No one did it any better; no one had more ease, charm or wit. The TV show, on the other hand, seemed very much like all TV shows of that kind at that time: slightly bland, free of controversy and populated with people like us, keen to promote their new product. However, in our case, we were the 'turn' who were there to break up the monotony of the chat, and, for reasons we'll never fully know, the audience liked us. I often think it was our appearances on that show that brought our music to a much wider audience. We are all still grateful.

Over the next few years, we'd make the trip to London to hang around all day, before getting the all-clear to rush to Heathrow to make the last flight home. The only time we nearly screwed it up was when we discovered Hue and Cry were also doing the show that evening, and we decided to go to the pub with them. As we were only miming, I seemed to have thought it would be OK to join the general carousing with the guys over the course of the afternoon, leading to my insistence that before we took to the stage for the live performance, we should borrow the coloured blazers of Terry's house band, The Harry Stoneham Five. The very patient, long-suffering – and, in this case, career-saving – Nick Fiveash brought reason to the room, and though the performance was fuelled by slightly more than natural enthusiasm, we wore our own clothes throughout.

Television, for all its ability to offer instant recognition and promotion, could also bring opportunities that, in retrospect, might have been best avoided. Video was still king in the eighties and the budget for any one promo clip for a single was astronomical. As rumours spread about the budgets comparative acts were getting to make their videos in ever more exotic locations, so too our own ambition increased. We wanted to make more substantial pieces of film as promos for our 45s. The trouble is, as I reflected many years and thousands of pounds later, we didn't get into all of this to make videos. We really only ever wanted to make a record or two, and, counting it up afterwards, I often wondered whether we'd all have been better off blowing the money on some fancy holidays or high-end leather jackets with 'Rock 'em and roll 'em' inscribed on the back. Actually, thinking back, we did buy the latter.

With each successive release, the single would be sent out to various video directors to come up with a treatment. They were usually selected on the artistic basis that the last couple of promos they'd made had been hits. We'd then go through interminable pitches about how the director was going to turn these five drab Scotsmen and a photogenic female into international rock stars. The script often opened with the immortal words, 'I intend to shoot each member of the band individually.'

The first video we ever made has never surfaced. It was produced by two guys who'd decided they wanted to move into video, having been, up to that point, a successful graphic design company. They promised they could deliver something on a trial basis should the band cooperate with their vision. This involved two days of hanging around a film studio where the dry ice was provided by a bee-gun to simulate smoke. In fact, it was actual smoke. Not only did it break every health and safety convention going, but it also caused nose bleeds in various members of the band. In the end, we left them to edit the takes together, optimistically hoping the outcome couldn't possibly be as bad as it had felt on the shoot.

We were right. It was so much worse.

To say the premier was something of a disappointment is akin to describing *Heaven's Gate* as a little over budget. We were met at the edit suite somewhere near Covent Garden by the two 'auteurs', who'd clearly been up all night trying to stitch their masterpiece together.

'Hope you like it,' the less weary of the duo implored. 'We've been here all weekend and our wives may be about to divorce us.'

All of us tensed a little at this preface, as none of us had come away from the shoot feeling we were in the hands of a new Oliver Stone. Sadly, this proved to be correct. In the silence that greeted that first screening, I took the coward's route out. I may have made the excuse of looking for the restrooms, but quickly ran out of the building and never came back. Before I exited, my last memory was of the shocked hush as the screen went blank at the end of the song, and our manager breaking the silence with a tactful, 'Maybe we can see that again?'

After that, there were videos produced by a succession of people I can't really remember, though I do recall the odd moment, such as this, on the way to a video shoot for an early video:

Leather-jacketed and head-scarfed director: 'Have you guys ever been to Cornwall?'
Us: Collective shaking of heads.

Leather-jacketed and head-scarfed director: 'There's some really funky kids there.'

Video director with oversized turn-ups on baggy 501s, pointing to the only props on the set: 'Do you want the ladders?'
Me: 'Not really.'
VDWOTOB501s: 'Well, just fucking perform.'

Scene: A desolate field in southern Spain. A member of the film crew is erecting a large cross in the middle of the field.
Me: 'What's that for?'
Video director: 'That's for the final shot. You're going to be singing on the cross.'

There was one director who became a trusted ally and friend. Don Coutts managed to make 'I'll Never Fall in Love Again' our most successful promo/video ever by dint of us all going on holiday and not actually appearing in it. That the budget was the cheapest, the band never appeared in the film and the song went on achieve our highest ever chart placing can't all just be coincidence. This spate of non-appearance even extended to a decision *not* to go on *Top of the Pops* if it was available – a slightly foolhardy estimation of our own career status, in all honesty.

Top Of The Pops remained the holy grail of TV shows, even in the new MTV generation. It took until October 1988, and our first-ever entry into the top thirty, for the dam to be breached, and we were invited to perform on the show the next week. My only memory of that first appearance was saying quietly to Ewen as we waited for the cameras to turn round to us, 'Let's enjoy this, as it may well be our last time.' We ended up playing on the show a lot in the first incarnation of Deacon Blue, but in the gap between our first split and our miraculous resurrection, the music world changed so much that when we came back to releasing singles again, not only had music formats changed fundamentally, but *Top of the Pops*, perhaps the biggest institution in the British music scene, had ceased to exist. It is still a hugely popular show, as evidenced by BBC Four's regular placing of old episodes to fill up their Friday night schedules. On occasion, we'll see our younger selves again, and recall for a second the excitement that was being on the biggest TV pop programme in Europe.

In the sixties, we'd watched the show with our parents and grandparents, often facing their howls of derision and outright hostility at the presenters (the criminal, Jimmy Savile was the most regular host) and the performers. It was, however, only ever able to reflect the chart of the week preceding the broadcast, and the older generation were quickly pacified when Clive Dunn came on with 'Grandad', soothing them after their outrage at T-Rex singing 'Ride a White Swan'.

It's always interesting to talk to American musicians, who are amused by our eclectic taste in music made possible by shows like *Top of the Pops*, where the appearance of Tammy Wynette could easily be preceded by the Tams, Donna Summer or Disco-Tex and the Sex-O-Lettes.

It was a show that paid almost no respect to musicians or songs other than to signify where they were on the chart. In some ways, this was its USP, and when it did try to become more 'musical', it somehow lost its mojo and became just another show. It was the bad juxtapositions of artists, the awful dancing and clothes of the audience, and the banality of the presenters that made it so unique.

I can't really separate my memories of one experience of being on it from the next. It was often pre-recorded on a Wednesday; then there came a time when they put the whole show out live on a Thursday evening, which was good for us, as there were no retakes, and we could speed our way back to

Heathrow and be home in time to order a curry in the West End of Glasgow.

What telly, and especially *Top of the Pops*, did for us was to make us, for a few short years, relatively famous. It was now less possible to shop, go to the football or visit a pub without being noticed. The good bits were occasional episodes of over-polite assistants when carrying out Christmas shopping in Frasers. Fame was something that only concerned us at home; in London, no one is famous. When you can see the Queen or the Prime Minister driving by of a weekday, there's no need to turn your head for an act you may have glanced at on the telly. For me, the first and only time some kind of fame came in handy was at the football, when I went to see Dundee United play at Ibrox. Instead of being in a terrified minority, I was happily signing programmes for bears in blue scarves who were smiling at me.

TV shows were rarely enjoyable affairs. There has always been, as Charlie Watts famously said, a lot of hanging about. In the first few months of getting serious radio play in 1988, Lorraine and I often found ourselves diverted from the others at different times so we could go on some programme or other to promote a particular single.

At one point, we had been booked to be interviewed on a Saturday morning kids' show while the rest of the band were travelling by coach to play at a festival in France. We were grateful to miss the bus ride and the ferry crossing, but had to be flown to the festival in a tiny plane with a pilot whose Brylcream-boy demeanour seemed too stereotypical to be true. As we taxied away from the terminal, a harassed-looking woman ran towards us as the engines revved up, the wind blowing huge sheets of paper around in her hand. The pilot opened up his side window and grabbed the papers gratefully, then turned round to us. 'Nearly forgot the maps!' He delighted in telling us there were drinks and snacks in a cool box, and his was the gin and tonic. As we reached Tours to land, and I could see nothing but fog closing round our tiny cockpit, he casually asked me to look out for lights on the runway.

'As soon as you see them shout, "Lights!" . . . By the way, Mick Jagger was sitting where you are last week.'

I began to pine for the tour bus.

There were many diversions to appear on telly, as it was always seen as the biggest factor in breaking a record. We were on tour in Spain for the first time, and about to enjoy a day off in Barcelona, only to be whisked back to appear on a music show coming out of Borders ITV in Carlisle in a bleak February. I remember too making my way, on my own and at an unearthly hour, to Milan airport so I could be interviewed on some show or other for five minutes back in London. The taxi was playing the local music channel, with all the usual combustible babble of Italian DJs, jingles, adverts and occasional pieces of pop. Suddenly, a familiar voice: 'This is Paul McCartney and you're listening to . . .' We'd done a million of these idents for radio stations, and I smiled wistfully at actually hearing one being used. On that cold January morning in Milan, my mind went back to LA the year before, when we'd sat on the grass in some dead time, recording hundreds of idents for American radio stations in places we'd never visit.

Whenever I'm in the Garden State, I'm tuned to WDNG . . .

You're tuned to the Top Thirty's Best Friend in Tulsa . . .

Hey Mike, thanks for playing Deacon Blue on Wenachee's best Mix.

In 1990, there came our appearance at the biggest and best Glasgow gig ever. The Big Day started with a letter from our friends, Don Coutts and Stuart Cosgrove, who wrote to me to explain their vision.

Glasgow was to be the European City of Culture in 1990, and throughout the year there were to be many cultural events, right across the spectrum of the arts. Stuart and Don had started an independent TV production company, and they were noticing the lack of a central, big event in the middle of the year. Their idea was to have the city centre taken over by music for one day of the summer and film it all for a continuous broadcast. They wanted to invite international artists and also celebrate the new music that had been synonymous with Glasgow over the last few years. They needed a headline act who would commit to the idea, and wrote a letter to me that I remember receiving in the dressing room at the SECC in Glasgow when we were there to perform two shows at the end of our tour in December 1989. It was these two shows too which were to be filmed for our first-ever long-form video release the following year. The letter suggested we should perform as the headline act on the final concert of the day at Glasgow Green, in front of as many people as possible. The two worrying aspects of the proposal were that this was all to happen outdoors, in what everyone knows to be one of the wettest cities in the UK, and, perhaps even more unsettling, that there was to be no ticketing. It was going to be a free concert.

The other aspect of the day was to highlight Glasgow's ongoing homelessness problem, and a good deal of the TV coverage was to tell stories around people's experiences of homelessness and to highlight the importance of helping people find permanent accommodation. Given the social aspect of the day, we bought into the proposal strongly, but were nervous about the weather and the unknown element of a free gig. Even if it was sunny, there would be no way of knowing how many would come.

Stuart and Don's proposal for the day had been well researched. They picked the driest weekend on the calendar over the previous twenty-five years or so, and the event went ahead on 3 June 1990. It was held across four different stages, including George Square and Glasgow Green, and it was called the Big Day.

We had gone down to the Green earlier in the afternoon when the crowds were elsewhere to soundcheck for our performance. The weather was perfect. Sunny, dry and as warm as you could expect it to be in early June in Scotland. Everything seemed to be going to plan. The only cloud on the horizon was whether people would opt to come to there in the evening, given so much free music had already been available during the day. We were nervous.

However, as our little bus made its way from the West End towards the Broomielaw that evening, then east towards the venue, we began to feel the excitement build. People were moving in the direction of Glasgow Green, and by the time we parked up behind the stage and took a look out to the audience, the organisers were making estimates that around a quarter of a million people were stretching back for ever in front of the stage. The helicopter above the city centre caught the scale of the crowd in all its glory. It was simply the biggest gathering to have assembled for any concert in Scotland, ever. In reality, it's unlikely such an event could ever happen again, for lots of reasons, so we often still look back with gladness at the night when it felt we were playing to the whole city, as well as an audience of millions watching on TV across the UK. If we were going to be on the television, it was perfect that we were caught doing the thing we did best; playing our own set to our own audience in our own city.

We played five songs or so. It was our only gig in central Scotland that year. Onstage, I expressed all my anger and disappointment at the performance of the Labour Party in Scotland at the time. It's not a speech I would make now – though you never know – but I still believe I was expressing a frustration so many people in Scotland were experiencing around that time. I wish I was still as certain as I appear on the clip when I look at it again, but I remind myself that getting angry with society is often the way change happens. The 'rant' (that's really what it was) was all to introduce a song called 'Orphans'. In the last two years, we'd travelled the world and found ourselves trying to explain who we were to all sorts of people. The song opens, 'I now describe my country as if to strangers.' On the Big Day, it felt as if a quarter of a million folk on Glasgow Green understood perfectly. I suspect those watching at home on the telly may have been less sympathetic.

At the end of Deacon Blue's first life in 1994, we all went separate ways. Given our rather fragile relationship with the medium, it's ironic that two of us ended up having successful careers in television. Dougie went on to become a natural broadcaster, hosting factual shows on everything from sport, farming and outdoor activities to cookery. Lorraine became an actor and starred in BBC Scotland's first soap opera for a five-year period. Graeme met a beautiful woman called Julie Smith towards the end of our time together. Julie was a successful TV producer who made great music shows, and before he became ill, Graeme had found a niche writing and recording theme music for television. I have made the odd TV show, but have always felt the others were better at understanding and appearing on screen than I could ever be.

Outsiders always ask the same question of bands. I've checked this with fellow musicians, and it seems everyone is keen to know whether any given music group hang out together when they are not working. Invariably, we all reply negatively. All of us spent so many days hanging around TV studios, waiting for our three-minute slot, that we used up every conversation, joke and game we knew. When we got home, everyone needed to see other people.

We seemed to waste the most time – and have the best time – on TV in Spain. I remember being on a bus coming back through Galicia, having spent three days to make a two-song appearance on some big telly show for which we didn't even have to play or sing, as it was all mimed to track. It had been us, some Spanish band and a very drunk Joe Cocker, who had tried to cadge some cigarettes from our party the night before the show, while telling us stories of two pigs he'd been bought by Jane Fonda. I suspect I'm remembering this through a slight haze of alcohol myself. Joe wasn't on the coach as it passed through the little village famous for its local wine on the way to catch the flight back to Madrid. It was an early departure, and we were already running late by the time the bus came to a halt in a dusty car park outside a small *cantina*. Everyone started to get out of the bus. Our tour manager began to point to her watch anxiously, gesturing to the shrugging driver, who had been told by the Spanish travellers that this was a compulsory stop. Although we were slightly hungover, we too were aware there was a flight to catch, and expressed our curiosity to the Spanish musicians, who were, by now, hurriedly exiting the coach and entering the bar. One of the party turned, and as if he were telling us the Earth was round, explained: 'We need to drink the Albariño.'

So, at ten in the morning in a dusty roadside bar, we did just that. It was the most beautiful white wine I'd ever tasted too. It would be another twenty years before Albariño found its way on to supermarket shelves in the UK; when that happened, we bought it up and enjoyed it all over again. That morning, however, in the Galician sunshine, we took our time, drank a glass or two and quietly acceded to the Spanish sense of prioritising what was and wasn't important. When we enquired gingerly about the flight we were all meant to be making back to Madrid, our fellow traveller shrugged and smiled.

'It will wait.'

21

The Final

It took me about twenty-five years to really understand why being in a band – being in *my* band – was important to me. Most musicians have a rather detached view of band membership. Sometimes it feels like an exclusive club, but often too it feels like you are fenced in and removed from whatever else is going on.

It was that feeling that did for Deacon Blue 1.0. We had spent eight intense years together, making music, travelling, doing gigs and TV shows, listening to each other's opinions on everything, and hanging around on buses, on planes, at airports, and in hotels, studio green rooms, dressing rooms and catering rooms. There was no subject untouched. We never fully fell out, although I finally lost the plot with Graeme before the last tour and both of us had to be coaxed back into rehearsal to ensure we could finally breast the finishing line.

It's hard to understand now, but in 1994, all I wanted to do was to leave Deacon Blue. I really don't know about anyone else; I suspect I wasn't alone, although Lorraine didn't feel as strongly as I did. I was deeply unhappy, for reasons that now seem to be fairly inconsequential. If I understood it better, I'd probably have managed it all a bit more carefully and made it easier on all of us. What I didn't understand then, and what I know now, is how much I value what we have, and how it now feels central to my own identity. I guess I'm proud that we survived, and that people still value what we do.

•

Trying to write as honestly as I can about our break-up that year, I can't believe how I let something so good slip away so easily. My only defence is I think I felt under enormous pressure to keep feeding the machine that was Deacon Blue. By that, I mean the sense that there were six people needing to make a living and fulfil their own artistic ambitions, as well as management, crew and various other folk who more or less earned their living based around what we did.

A neutral observer might conclude that this makes a more compelling reason for keeping going. However, I think I had that feeling of responsibility for a couple of years before the final break-up, and it all became too much of a burden to carry. I also felt, as I explained at the time, that we no longer knew what to do when left to our own devices. It seemed we needed someone else to come in and help shape how we should sound. Quite reasonably, the others might reflect that I too had lost whatever it was that drove the band on in its earlier days. I do remember writing and demoing songs that lurched all over the place stylistically, and when I played some tracks to producer Chris Kimsey, who'd been asked to record some extra songs for the forthcoming *Our Town: The Greatest Hits* compilation, he commented that we sounded like a band who didn't know what to do next. He was right, up to a point. I, however, felt I did know – I wanted the chance to work alone or with some different people for a while.

What I should have done was listen more to my manager and other wise voices, who counselled that I could easily take a break, make a solo record and pick up with the others in a year or so. I was far too obstinate and pig-headed for that advice, and, scrambling to recall my own feelings around that time, I probably felt I didn't want the deadline of a band waiting for me to come up with something when I'd ceased my wandering. That we truly found our way back over the last dozen years or so is a great credit to their patience and commitment. I am forever grateful.

By the time 1994 arrived, it was pretty certain the tour we'd cancelled the previous autumn and rescheduled for the coming spring would be our last outing together.

It was to prove to be the most momentous year for a variety of reasons. My father's health was failing, Lorraine and I were expecting our second child in the November, and we were planning to move house, to the home where we still live and where our children have all grown up.

There was one more factor that became a handy explainer of my emotional state. After years of turning up at losing finals, the football team I supported with my dad would finally win their first-ever Scottish Cup.

Towards the end of the sixties, I discovered football. It was my cousins, who were at boarding school in England and had come for the Easter holidays, who started it off. They wanted to go to a football match, any match, when they came to spend their holidays with us.

From their boarding school near the coast in Lancashire, they regularly went to see Manchester United and Everton. They would tell me stories of what it was like at their football grounds as we leafed through the *Topical Times Football Annual*. My mum didn't want me to go to a real match for fear I'd be stabbed or have a bottle broken over my head. This, she insisted, was a regular occurrence at football games when Celtic or Rangers came to town.

My cousins persuaded her that their seniority and worldly experience could alleviate her worst fears, and a midweek match wouldn't be high risk. We went to see the only fixture playing that week, which involved Dundee United, the local team most people didn't favour, playing Aberdeen. United beat them five–nil, with our star player, Davie Wilson, ex of Rangers and Scotland, scoring a hat trick. I have never witnessed such a cuffing of our oldest rivals since, but that night I took it for granted that this was how the land lay, and made up my mind to be a United supporter.

In 1970, the club changed their colours from black and white to tangerine and black. The following Christmas, my great aunt Jessie, who'd always liked to create something with her own hands, gifted me a home-knitted Dundee United scarf. The only problem, which was impossible to amend, was the tangerine was a little more pink than orange – but times being what they were, and scarves being a luxury that couldn't be taken for granted, the scarf had to be worn.

I was seriously put off in the mid-seventies when it seemed violence and general aggravation and hooliganism had become too much of a factor when it came to going to, watching and getting home from the game. There was no segregation between fans, and skirmishes and battles would annotate every football occasion. On one Saturday, our fans were singing a fairly bawdy song, which involved serious violence being visited on the away support, when the police moved in to eject the troublemakers. I was quietly minding my own business, but was clearly near enough to the protagonists for the bobbies to huckle me out of the ground. I protested my innocence, only for matters to collapse into full-scale humiliation when the ejecting police officers took one look at my scarf before they asked, 'Are you some kind of poof?' Auntie Jessie's scarf had to go, but in a strange old way, so too did football.

I stopped going to matches as regularly, although I'd make the odd exception. Between that day and leaving the city, I always followed the results and attended some of the bigger games, but overall it had lost its appeal.

My dad's own interest had been one of the things that kept us both focused on the game. He would take me and pay me in if I offered to go for pies before half-time to avoid the queue. We'd sit in the stand, and we'd listen to all the post-match radio reports in the car on the way home. My dad loved the game, and had been a regular Dundee supporter when he was growing up, continuing a habit his own father had instituted of watching both Dundee and Dundee United, but supporting one. We went to see Dundee sometimes, and I would love to see if they could beat Celtic or Rangers, but also quietly rejoiced if they were brought down by a team at the lowly end of the league. Dundee were a good side in those days, while Dundee United were the plucky newcomers. As time moved on, though, United became the bigger team, and when I finally moved away to Glasgow, I was persuaded by my best pal (a fellow Dundee exile in the west) to take in more away games by a United side that was now making waves. We were going great guns in Europe, and a year and a half after I left the city, we won the league . . . which, to this day, in all truth, is still one of my greatest days ever.

Getting into music and moving to Glasgow brought different football joy. I loved being near to Hampden, where I could see Scotland play, even though it was a place that brought very little reward for Dundee United fans. I went to all six losing Scottish Cup finals we played there before 1994, and numerous semi-final and League Cup disasters. In 1991, however, United were again in a semi-final for the Scottish Cup. I was in New York without any access to the radio, so I phoned up my father to get an update on our match against St Johnstone. He answered the phone by telling me we were winning, but that there was only a short time to go, and immediately put the receiver down by the radio so I could hear – or better, so he could listen without interruption from me. We won, and for the first time since our

first losing final in 1974, I made plans to take my father with me
to the final.

It was the 'family final'. To the neutral, it is still the gold
standard for such matches. A four–three thriller going into extra
time, and the teams managed by two brothers from the football-
ing McLean family. Sadly, it was four–three to Motherwell, and
throughout the tussle I did begin to wonder about the strength
of my father's heart.

By the time the next serious Cup run came together, my father
was in a different place. He'd crashed his car one Sunday morning, blacking out behind the wheel, and his general health had
deteriorated significantly in the weeks he'd been in the hospital.
In the last few years, my father had suffered from depression
and, although it had occurred once before as a younger man, it
seemed to hit him harder in his senior years. It coincided with
retirement, and eventually my parents moved from Dundee to be
near me and my sister in Glasgow. He still followed the football,
and in the years when some fame had allowed me more access
to the club, Dundee United, and Jim McLean in particular, had
been good to our family. My father loved being able to glean
some backstage gossip from the club, and we took in games
again together, re-establishing our old routine.

On that next Cup run, Deacon Blue would be on our final tour.
Having decided to stop being a band, we went out on one last
outing, culminating in two nights at the Barrowlands Ballroom
on 19 and 20 May 1994. Perhaps it's because of what happened
next that I forget almost everything else about that time. The
argument with Graeme had been typical of all the stupid fallings-
out that can happen at rehearsal, except this one time, I took
out all my frustration on him alone. Correctly, he decided he
had taken enough, and promptly walked out. It was Dougie who

called us both to the pub that night so we could sort it out in the grand old Scottish musical tradition: with fags and booze.

Other than that incident, I recall almost nothing from that period. There was much discussion about whether – and how – we would let people know these were to be our final shows. There was the constant backdrop of my father's ill health, but balancing this was my awareness that the pressure I'd been feeling as the leader of a travelling band was about to ease. As I looked ahead into the coming months, I could only see a time when I could start to think about working on my own, in a direction I'd choose myself.

As we rehearsed for the tour in early April, I was going back and forth to see my father in hospital. Although we'd been told about his weak heart, we were all relatively relaxed about visiting him, without any sense that these were his final days.

It was a Tuesday evening, and Dundee United had been in the semi-final of the Scottish Cup on the Saturday before. A draw against Aberdeen meant a replay at Hampden Park that evening. The stadium was a short walk from the hospital where my father was, and I had decided to go in to see my dad, make sure his radio was tuned to listen in, then join my friends at the semi-final replay at Hampden.

I can clearly remember looking in the fridge for a yogurt and checking its sell-by date so I could give it to give my young daughter at teatime that evening, just as the phone went. It was my mother. She was in a clear state of panic. The hospital had called saying she should go over right away, as my dad had taken a turn for the worse. She made her way with my sister from their home in the Southside, and I drove over from the West End to join them. By the time we all gathered at the hospital, my father had died.

All of us were in a state of shock at this sudden turn of events. The previous evening, we'd gathered round his bed, with nearly all the grandchildren there, including my then twenty-month-old daughter. My sister had brought in her wedding album for him to look through, and it had been a magical time, although none of us had expected it to be our last night together.

By the time we'd said our farewells to my father and gone back to my sister's house to comfort my mother, then finally to our own home, I was completely drained. The most natural thing to do was to pick up the remote for the TV and let anything it offered drift over me. As the picture came to life, I remembered where I should have been that evening. The football highlights were being shown, and Jim McInally was toeing the ball across the line to take Dundee United to their seventh Scottish Cup Final. With or without my dad, I'd gone to six previous ones, where we had lost each time. I offered up a rough, ironic laugh that I would have to endure this next one without his presence or his consoling words in inevitable defeat.

It turned out the game itself was to be played on 21 May, the day following Deacon Blue's 'final' concert at the Barrowlands. Lorraine and I made a plan to go to the final with our two great friends, Doug and Linda, with whom I'd watched that league win eleven years earlier. In fact, I may well have been at all the Cup finals with these two pals, apart from the first in 1974. Then, I'd gone with my father, his brother Tom and my cousin Colin. We'd been roundly beaten by Celtic, and my lingering memory is of my father's shock at the rows of Catholic clergy refusing to stand for the national anthem before the game, and my own team's lame capitulation on the day.

The previous night's show, our 'last' as Deacon Blue, had gone from joy to sadness back to joy before inevitable farce. After playing at the Barrowlands, we'd gone back to King Tuts for a party, then had all been thrown out on the street by the local police as the club had no late licence. It was a perfect ending. Exhausted by everything and badly hungover, we nevertheless made our way to Hampden for a 3pm Cup final against an all-conquering Rangers side. Our team were barely that. A mixed bag of old faithfuls, some misfits who wouldn't really ever play again and a couple of youngsters who were destined to go on to new clubs. Rangers, on the other hand, were one game away from winning a treble on a journey that would take them to nine league wins in a row three years later. No one gave us an earthly chance.

When the goal went in, it came as a result of a complete breakdown in the Rangers defence. Our centre forward, the immortalised Craig Brewster, tapped the ball into the net. I missed the whole thing as I held my place in the pie queue. I couldn't have cared less; it was enough to know we'd scored. I only wanted the twenty-year misery of lost finals to end.

It did.

A photographer I knew brought Dave Bowman – still coaching the club now – to celebrate. In my favourite ever photograph, I am pictured hugging Bo while three senior policemen threaten to arrest me. I had my defence prepared. What court could convict a man for exuberant celebrations knowing the pain and misery he'd suffered at all those losing finals?

Although I had spent the last few years coming to public occasions, if not wholly in disguise, then certainly dressed down, as I left Hampden that day, I answered every person who called my name, not only admitting that I was in fact the big singer out of Deacon Blue, but also hugging them and their children in a manner that would have been more appropriate for reunited long lost relatives. We bought two flags, which were ceremoniously hoisted through the sunroof of the car – until a mixture of common sense and police aggravation brought them back inside.

As we drove through Langside, we passed the Victoria Infirmary where my father had died just five weeks before; five weeks that had taken me round the country saying goodbye to thousands of people. My father had gone without so much as a wave from the stage and, after all our trips, waiting and hoping, United had won the Scottish Cup without him even listening at home on the radio.

22

Glasgow

As life has taken different twists and turns, home remains a constant – and Glasgow is at the centre of all of that. Through all the changing times, it has provided the stories and emotional currency I've used in writing the songs I've performed, both alone and with Deacon Blue.

Michael Marra, who always had a deep well of stories, understood Glasgow perfectly. It was an outsider's take on a place that, ironically, has been invented by outsiders. His song, 'Mother Glasgow', affectionately gets to the heart of the matter.

> In the second city of the Empire
> Mother Glasgow nurses aw her weans
> Trying hard to feed her little starlings
> Unconsciously she clips their little wings
>
> Mother Glasgow's succour is perpetual
> Nestling the Billy and the Tim
> I dreamt I took a dander with St. Mungo
> To try to catch a fish that couldnae swim

I remember him telling an audience about a Polish man who used to work beside him at the Caledon shipyard in Dundee, who pronounced the city 'Glasgov'. I kind of liked that.

It could be so many peoples' city. There are big Polish, Lithuanian, Pakistani, Irish, Italian, Romanian and Chinese communities. Seen through any of these lenses, Glasgow becomes a place of refuge or authority, welcome or alienation, and perhaps a mixture of all these things. For many Gaels too it became the city where they found work or education during the second phase of the Highland Clearances. The wide tunnel taking Argyle Street below Central Station is still known by many as the Hielanman's Umbrella – the gathering point, free of rain, where many would meet to share news or opportunities of work. To young people from smaller places across Scotland, Glasgow is the place where they got a chance to find identity and self-expression; to make mistakes, and maybe even make a name for themselves.

My first memory of driving through Glasgow was with my sister in the back of our family car. We must have been going through to visit an aunt and uncle who lived in Mansewood at the time. My sister wanted my dad to stop so she could stand on the street and hear the people speaking in Glasgow accents. My father and mother were quick to pour cold water on her idea before I could join in.

My other memory is of driving through the city to pick up an old uncle who was returning from Canada to Prestwick. We were to meet him very early in the morning and bring him back to Dundee with the promise we'd stop for 'breakfast' at the Five Ways restaurant near Stirling on the return journey. Although this was an exciting break from the mundane, the adventure was tempered by the knowledge that Dundee United were playing Celtic in Glasgow the same Saturday, and we were unable to see the match. The tenements looked dark and foreboding as we skirted the city, unaware of which area we were passing through.

Glasgow was big and gloomy, and seemed always to carry some threat of violence in my understanding and imagination. Glaswegians could be comedians, like my childhood heroes Francie and Josie, or villains, who carried knives but dressed sharply. Frankie Vaughan had come to Easterhouse to encourage the gangs to hand their weapons in, and the stories of Celtic or Rangers supporters coming by their thousands to the games at Dens or Tannadice had led to my mother's conviction that football games involved random violence being visited upon innocent Dundonians. Glasgow's reputation loomed large.

My father's younger brother, Tom, was a civil engineer who ended up managing a successful firm in the city from their plush offices in Park Circus. He'd temporarily moved his family back to Dundee while going through a divorce in the early seventies. It was really his spin on the place that began to completely change my understanding of Glasgow. He made it seem like the centre of the world. He bought expensive suits and fashionable ties with European designer labels, which, when discarded, would be passed on to my grateful father. He rode around the city in a Jaguar, smoking Rothmans King Size. 'I've travelled fifty miles today,' he told my mother once, 'and I haven't left Glasgow.' Travel fifty miles from Dundee, and you'd be more than halfway *to* Glasgow.

He worshipped Jock Stein's Celtic, seeing them as the team who played real football in the city. He'd grown up going to Dens Park with his father, but his move west had coincided with the great Stein team of the sixties, and he'd grown fond of European nights at Parkhead, when eleven men from within a short radius of the city would take on and defeat the aristocrats of world football. It was that sense of belief, pride and sheer audacity that became the Glasgow I grew to know.

We'd go to Hampden to watch a semi-final, or later to see Scotland. Finally, there came the day we saw my own team, Dundee United, play against Celtic in their first-ever Cup Final in 1974. We came away with nothing.

'No spunk, that's their trouble,' was Uncle Tom's verdict to my father as we disconsolately made our way back to the car. My cousin and I sniggered at the double entendre.

My sister went to university in Glasgow, and would write letters home and occasionally bring back friends to stay over the weekend: male students with long hair and beards, or girls with kaftans and beads. They all lived off University Avenue, and she'd pin up posters of the Citizens Theatre or the GFT. I was intrigued by the names like Benny Lynch and Charles Rennie Mackintosh, and also by a place called the Danish Centre, where sandwiches were served 'open' and called *smørrebrød*. In my final year at school, I came to stay with her in Hyndland, and spent days on end just leafing through the vinyl in all the record shops. I'd walk over to see a pal from Dundee, who was staying at Maclay Halls in Kelvingrove, then head down Woodlands Road to Sauchiehall Street and the joys of the big city.

Years later, in 2007, I remember working with the late Nanci Griffith, who I'd met in Nashville earlier in the year, who was over to record a song we had been writing together. It was shortly after the terrorist attack at Glasgow airport, and there had been a good deal of nerves around travel between the UK and the US. Explaining how the incident had been unofficially policed by a passing baggage handler on a smoke break, I could see Nanci's intrigue at the news reports. She particularly relished the testimony of John Smeaton, the baggage handler, who declared: 'Me and other folk were just trying to get the boot in and some other guy banjoed him.' Until that point, Nanci's understanding of the banjo was as an instrument much loved in country music. Needless to say, 'Smeato' became a local hero whose fame spread across the world.

A few days later, I went to BBC Scotland to record a programme, and one of the security staff apologised for the rigorous checks that were now having to be enforced before we were allowed into the main part of the building.

'Sorry about this, Ricky. It's because of all that carry-on at the airport.'

That is Glasgow. Never upstaged. You can send in your top terrorists for some plot that has all of Western Europe in a mild panic, but it will still be dismissed as a 'carry-on' by the locals.

The other group of people who will remain firmly combobulated when those around are fully discombobulated are the gentlemen of the official taxi service. Glasgow, like its sister city Edinburgh, has always kept to the tradition of the black Hackney carriage. Over the years, this affectation has been slightly more loosely interpreted with the advent of bigger vehicles, but a true first visit to Scotland's first city would be incomplete without at least one ride in a 'fast black'. Stories are legion, and rides in the older vehicles were/are often mildly more uncomfortable than being pulled in a rickshaw. Corners will be cut, remarks will be made, and the driver may well reserve the right to explain his views on politics, religion, guitarists, singers or opposition footballers. On a bumpy trip across the West End many years ago, an exiled Glaswegian pal now living in Liverpool pulled himself back on to the flip-down rear-facing seat after a particularly brutal swerve and enquired of our driver if he hadn't noticed him from an older episode of *Daktari*.

Celtic had been taken apart on a European tie during their time in the doldrums of the late eighties and early nineties Rangers' dominance. The morning after, on my way to the airport, the taxi driver talked me through a full post-mortem of the game. The main striker who'd put them to the sword seemed to have been Egyptian.

'My old man was over there during the war, Ricky. I'm thinking if he'd just got his aim right, that wee fella wouldn't have even been on the park last night.'

Then there was the time my wife got into a cab in town, only for the driver to insist on finishing his bagpipe practice, the music for which was pinned to the sun visor. My own favourite experience came on a journey travelling south across the Kingston Bridge, when the cab came to a halt behind a car stalled at the following set of traffic lights. As they changed from red to green, the driver in front managed to start the ignition, jump two or three yards, then stall abruptly as the lights switched back to red again. Noticing the 'P' sign on the rear end of the vehicle, my taxi driver looked over at me with a heavy sigh, pointing to the offending Nissan Micra now causing a tailback of some considerable length.

'What do you think that "P" stands fur?' he asked.

The lights changed. The car lurched and stopped, and the lights changed back to red again.

'I'm thinking they'd be better off with a "C".'

Glaswegians do travel, of course. A pal once told me the story of a friend who had finally encouraged his mother to join him on holiday in Rome. She had been worried about making the trip for fear that she wouldn't understand the language, and that the locals wouldn't understand her. He told her not to worry, and said the best way was to speak slowly and clearly in English. Given the number of tourists in the city, the chances were she'd always be understood.

They were passing a watermelon stand when she expressed an interest in buying a slice or two to take away. Remembering her son's advice, she decided to engage the vendor.

'Excuse me, son. How much would the likes of wan o' them come in at?'

When I first started teaching, there were still bits of Glasgow patois I didn't fully understand myself. 'Cybees' – for spring onions – dry rolls and ginger were all strange concepts. My sister, who had become a social worker after university, had been impressed by the Glaswegians' penchant for 'ginger', until she realised it was the generic term for lemonade.

Similarly, I hadn't quite twigged how polarised colours were in the city until I brought in an old tin of paint to brighten up my very dull classroom. Having asked permission from my boss, John Lawson, a kindly head of department who would do any-thing to make the place more attractive, I painted some of the old desks in the classroom with the cheeriest hue I had left over from my house. Later, at a staff meeting, he joked with the other members of the department that I'd 'only gone and painted the desks Hun blue'. I suspect if the school had been on the other side of the religious fence, green desks might have caused more of an uproar.

All these aspects to the city only strengthen my affections. It was, and still remains, a welcoming place, despite the stories of violence that bedevil any large urban area. In recent years, one of the most noble organisations has been the Violence Reduction Unit, founded by an ex-policeman, John Carnochan, which has tackled violent crime head-on and sought paths out of violence for those who have been caught up in it. On visits to Barlinnie or other prisons in and around the west of Scotland, it is always clear that so many people who have ended up there have had a childhood of poverty and associated social exclusion. Glasgow's 'no mean city' reputation was established almost a century ago in times of crippling unemployment, squalid and overcrowded living conditions and a scarcity of social mobility. Where these conditions still apply, violence still occurs.

On one visit to Barlinnie many years ago, I was with a group that included Celtic's legendary ex-captain and manager Billy McNeil. Billy was a warm, kind man about whom no one spoke a bad word. He would later suffer dementia and an early death that was mourned by the whole city. That day in the jail, however, he was still the legend for at least half the inmates at the time. As he was spotted crossing the main hall, there was an eruption of joy and general shouts of 'Hail Caesar!', the old moniker from his playing days. I loved the passionate welcome he received, and was envious of how him simply walking through the door could lift downcast men from their imprisoned gloom to a state of sheer joy. It was Glasgow responding to one of their own true sons, and it was great just to feel the love, even on such an unlikely occasion.

In the year of lockdown, 2020, Lorraine and I would go on long walks in different directions across the city. We'd pass through Shawlands, Govanhill and the Gorbals, and retrace the steps her mother and aunts had taken when they first came from Donegal looking for work in the late 1950s and early 1960s. Some of the streets are gone now, but there are still tenement flats where their friends were welcomed into already crowded accommodation.

Now the new Glaswegians are arriving in these same places and spreading outwards from there as they make their way into new lives in a strange land. There are tensions, but there are also great success stories of people who've been exiled from their homeland now becoming part of the fabric of public life in this city. In the 1980s, Glasgow based its renaissance around a slogan that advertised its friendliness but also its perceived self-improvement. 'Glasgow's Miles Better' was a campaign that seemed to resonate with citizens and visitors alike. The current mantra, imagined at around the time of the Commonwealth Games being hosted there in 2014 seems to be more accurate: 'People Make Glasgow'. To me, this is a better, truer description of a city that requires you to stop and spend a little time before you dismiss it as just another post-industrial sprawl.

A few years ago, Deacon Blue were playing a concert right in the heart of Glasgow for Hogmanay. It had been freezing cold over Christmas, and George Square was covered with ice when we arrived for soundcheck that afternoon, on the last day of the year. In those circumstances, it's always best to get things done as quickly as possible and it's usually the case that we'll go through songs we're less familiar with rather than ones we know backwards. As we looked around from the stage, the council workers on shift had been sent out to break up the ice on the paving stones where the audience would be standing in a few hours' time. The men working had been diverted from their regular shift as refuse collectors on the bin lorries. As we tuned up and plugged in, one of them looked up to the stage and, looking straight at me, said, 'Do "Dignity".'

How could we refuse?

Suddenly, at that moment, on that day, in the middle of our hometown, it felt we were performing the version of the song all of us had waited thirty years to witness. A passer-by, leaning on the perimeter fence of the improvised auditorium, filmed it all on a phone. It's not difficult to find the footage on YouTube. If you do, watch until the end as the anonymous cameraman gives an instant critique.

'Fucking magic.'

I don't think we could have summed it up any better.

23

Isn't That Our Jeffrey?

With Deacon Blue no longer in existence, I wanted to make a differ-
ent kind of record with new musicians. In the spring and summer
of 1995 I went, with my family, to spend a summer in California
making my debut solo album.

The album *Our Town*, which was a collection of Deacon Blue's
greatest hits, had been released just before that final tour in
1994. Even as the band went our separate ways, the record continued to sell very well and our label, Sony, offered me a new
solo recording contract on the Epic label. It was a clean sheet,
both artistically and financially, and I used most of the next year
to write songs and experiment with new musicians. With hindsight, all that freedom was probably a bad thing, and the lack of
a clear steer from my then-record company became problematic.
Frustrated at my lack of progress, I looked up some of my favourite records at the time to see who had produced them. It was in
this way I happened upon the Robb brothers, a trio of studio
owning producers based in Los Angeles.

Bernie, my A&R man, was dispatched with the task of con-
tacting the brothers and asking if they'd like to work with me.
I got the news in an excited phone call a couple of weeks later.
A career in the music business can never be achieved without
harnessing a certain amount of hyperbole into one's working
lexicon. 'I've just heard back from the Robbs,' said a breathless
Bernie. 'They're turning cartwheels about your demos.'

The other major axiom of the music business is as critical as the above for day-to-day survival. An artist must always go with the hype.

So, I found myself recording in West Hollywood by early summer. We – Lorraine, our two young daughters and my older daughter, destined to join when school term finished – decamped to a house in the hills for recording to commence. I'd had a frantic two-song try-out with the Robbs a couple of months previously, and we'd all got along famously. I'd brought over my guitar-playing buddy from Glasgow the first time, and the brothers had suggested we compliment Mick's playing with a rhythm guitarist they would find from the LA scene. We were excited to meet him. Sadly, it was not quite what we'd hoped.

Despite having good credentials, there is a fatal misunderstanding among Americans about the thin line separating punk and dire heavy metal. Dan (if that was his name) and his guitar knew little about that line, and he had to go. When we broached the decision with the producing brothers, they understood all too easily. To make it clear, I'd thrown a few other things that had annoyed me about his input in the session.

'Do you want me to call him up and sack him again?' Bruce Robb asked joyously.

Who would we get in instead? A list was drawn up and there was much 'Oh, he's on tour . . . Oh, dear, didn't he move to Nashville? . . . Is he even still alive?' as we pondered the possibilities. The mood was gloomy. Then Bruce picked up and looked around nervously to the other brothers. 'There's always Jeffrey?'

Jeff 'Skunk' Baxter was a living myth. A founding member of Steely Dan, he'd gone on to join the Doobie Brothers, where, as well as playing lead guitar, he'd also made his name as a great pedal steel player. He also had a reputation for being slightly eccentric.

On the next morning, we met Jeffrey. His massive eight-litre-engine truck coughed its way into the parking lot, and then he popped his head into the control room and took in the view. 'You're all under arrest,' came the voice, from under a very large walrus moustache.

'These fellas are from Scotland,' said Dee, the leading Rob.

Immediately, the Skunk rolled into a five-minute mono-logue of second-hand Billy Connolly jokes in what, he clearly imagined was a pitch-perfect Glasgow accent. We were stunned. It turned out he'd produced Nazareth ('great bunch of guys') in the late seventies, and he'd kept hold of everything they'd taught him. If this wasn't disarming enough, the conversation then drifted to what Jeff had been up to the night before. He had, it seemed, been out on patrol. Formerly a heavy drug user, he had now turned from poacher into gamekeeper: a card-carrying, gun-using conservative, the Skunk had formed a strong alliance with the Los Angeles PD, who were in the habit of taking him on drug busts and similar excursions. It was rumoured his favourite calling card was: 'I'm your worst nightmare. A hippy with a badge.'

'We were in Compton last night till late . . .' Jeff wiped his eyes and patted my leg, then looked knowingly round the room. 'We'll need to get Rick out in the black and white.'

There's always a good time to stop talking and start making music, and this seemed an ideal point. Either that or lunch. To Jeffrey's eternal credit, the truck found its way back to that parking lot for the next ten days or so. We tracked the songs with Jeff and he soloed with ease and taste. It was a surreal time, but here's what I remember:

When Lorraine visited the studio one night, and Jeff planted his bottleneck slide between her bare legs (to keep it warm) as she sat cross-legged on the sofa.

When we had a debate about a snare drum pattern, and Jeff assured us it was perfect, as it was the kind of part played on the soundtrack over every US battleground scene.

When we asked him to play something close to part of 'Papa Was A Rollin' Stone' and he claimed to have played on the original. There was no internet, so we couldn't check.

When he showed us his police badge. Bruce: 'Did you notice the mouse ears?'

Or, the best one, when Jeff told us about his weekend plans. In all the time he'd been with us, we'd loved his input, his stories, but most of all, his ridiculously great playing. I'd done a deal with the producers, however. Jeffrey had a horrible nineties electronic effects board made by Boss. I'd asked that we take a dual feed so Jeff could hear the effects pedals, but we could get a clean signal to a warm valve amp. That Friday, when weekend plans were being discussed, he pointed to the offending board. 'Going out on manoeuvres with the US Navy. Same shit that went into this thing goes into missile launching. We're going out to see how it works.'

How we all laughed. Many years later, a friend sent me an article in the *Times* that seemed to verify the whole story.

On the 4th of July, we took a day off making the record. The brothers had a rather large boat moored at Long Beach harbour. For these occasions, they invited almost everyone they knew, including their elderly father, Dave Robb, who looked as close to a salty old sea dog as one could imagine. He'd regularly come into the studio and tell us how he hoped to make it back to the old country some day: 'I want to go to . . . these places where they sell beer . . . pubs. And get into fights.'

As well as Dave, Jeffrey's parents came along for the cruise too. The two dads were overheard having a chat about passing themselves off as visiting professors.

'What if they ask what our subject is?'

'We'll tell them to mind their own god-damned business.'

We took off into the blue Pacific, a happy crew of musicians, relatives and nautical people. As the fireworks exploded from *The Queen Mary*, I realised it was more than likely none of the crew or passengers was sober enough to steer us home. Somehow, we all made it back in one piece, with one of the producers' sisters-in-law taking a soaking when she missed the gangplank altogether. The radio played as everyone enjoyed their barbecue of barracuda, beef and beer. Steely Dan came on the air, playing 'Reelin in the Years' and the senior Baxters, Jeffrey's mom and pop, were seen lifting their heads from their plates.

One looked at the other and they both smiled wistfully as the guitar solo played on. 'Isn't that our Jeffrey?'

24

Mr Love, the Piano Tuner

December is the cruellest month. December 1996 was perhaps the most difficult of my life. I'd got used to the idea that my solo recording career was not working out as planned. In all honesty, I'd not given it nearly enough thought, and had approached making my first solo album in a slightly cavalier manner. I was so happy to leave behind the gloomy last years of the Deacon Blue experience, rejoicing in working with new people on new songs, that I'd quite forgotten that some people were expected to buy it, otherwise it would all be over. Now, it was really, really over.

I'd gathered some musicians together to record a final session that might change the label's mind about renewing my deal. The trouble was, no matter how good the session or the song, the die had been cast. Epic Records had looked around and quite rightly realised that no one was terribly interested in my career at that point. The music business, as it often does, had moved along, and its attention was elsewhere. It was Britpop time, and there was no one more out of step than I was.

It was also Blair time. I had no real love of Tony Blair or the 'cool Britannia' that seemed to be in the ether. The excitement of the Tories finally being bundled out of power in 1997 was lost on me, because by that time, my mind was made up that I wanted to see an independent Scotland and the restructuring of the UK was less of a priority for me. Looking back, although I still broadly agree with my sentiments from that time, I do have a great admiration for what those in that first Labour government for eighteen years were trying to do. Much of it (Scottish devolution) is still with us and, although they were slightly ridiculed in my mind and those of others I knew for not being socialist enough, they were (as history has proved) as good as we'd get for a long time to come. (We can talk about the Gulf War another time.)

In every sense, then, I was out of step with public opinion, fashion and taste. I felt I had to start to reconnect with what had made me want to write songs and sing them in the first place.

It was now that I started to follow my heart again, but before all that came the pain of a farewell to the life I had known for ten years. A few days before Christmas, I managed to submit the tracks we'd been working on in Park Lane Studios to my manager, who was to take them to Rob Stringer at Epic to see if he would extend my recording contract and the life of my first solo record. Rob was a good friend, but also a realistic business person, who would go on to run Sony in the UK and the US, and he knew that giving me more time wasn't really going to sort out my career at that point. However, for these last ten years, I had only known the life of having a major publisher and a major record label behind me. As it happened, my publishing contract (a very generous one) was due for renewal, and the company that owned my catalogue was the same one who was now deciding my recording future. Everything was up for discussion, and the answer that came back, just a couple of days before Christmas, was a firm 'No.'

I can't remember why it was this day I had engaged a piano tuner. He was probably one of the ones who would just phone and suggest he popped by as the piano was overdue a tuning, like a persistent dental hygienist, but instead of putting him off,

I had acquiesced to his visit. He was at full tilt on the piano when the call came in from my manager. I remember being in the kitchen, taking the call and hearing the inevitable news that my life was about to hit the worst of times, at the worst time of year.

After the message came through, it was time to pay Mr Love (for that was his name). I stood in what is now my home studio but was then a dining room, with cheque book in hand, willing him to finish as he marched, waltzed and calypso'd his way up and down the keyboard. He'd get almost to the final cadence before looking up gleefully and modulatingly violently into a polka or some ghastly version of a standard as he demonstrated his finished task. I've never wanted to kill a man so urgently; in retrospect, it's probably a good thing that there were few blunt instruments available, and at that moment my six-foot Kawai was the most tangible asset I could really claim with any pride from my run in the charts.

Mr Love always wore a sports jacket and a shirt and tie (musical notation featured on the tie). He was a large man with a heavy, booming voice that could drown out even his loudest piano performances.

'Listen to this, Ricky,' he'd say, as he murdered some song I'd been fairly equivocal about up until that point, his banana fingers greasily pounding my pride and joy.

'Thanks . . . but I've really . . .'

'And listen to it up here, now.' Off he'd go into medley number five, before triumphantly returning to the original song until at last the chords announced (what I hoped would be) the grand finale. There was no stopping him.

On that awful December day, when the phone call that put my working life on hold came in. On that day, it seemed Mr Love would never stop.

I can't remember much more about that Christmas. I had three young daughters, and it probably passed like so many before and after, happily and joyfully, with food, drink, pantomimes and various gatherings. In the year that followed, I went back to the thing I'd wanted to go back to so many times before: the simplicity of a song and a voice.

I started working through my old songs, and even wrote one or two new ones, where I just played piano and elementary guitar. I was starting to put together a live solo show, something I'd done many years before Deacon Blue existed. I realised that playing on my own, with only an audience for company, although deeply terrifying at points, was also one of the best experiences I'd ever had of playing music.

At this point, in early 1997, I hadn't played a solo show for thirteen years or so, and really had to start all over again. Songs I'd written had been forgotten, and some Deacon Blue songs had been so quickly worked up and performed by the others, I barely knew what key they were in. For a few months, it was enough to just sit myself behind a piano or guitar and try to learn enough to put on some kind of show. That 'show' became two very intimate nights at Glasgow's Tramway Theatre in the spring of 1997. I got a lot wrong on both of these nights, but did enough to convince myself that, somewhere in that ninety minutes or so, enough magic happened to make me feel it was worth doing again.

I carried on by engaging in some of the most ill-booked shows of my life. My agent at the time had wanted to forget the whole idea. He liked what I'd been doing with my solo band and was keen for me to reassemble that and get back on the road as soon as possible. I decided instead against all of that and embarked on a haphazard solo adventure, which would have been a disaster were it not for one magical evening in Dublin.

The city of Dublin, though one of my favourite places on earth, had never been a great place for Deacon Blue shows. Despite a favourable start, shows there had either been too noisy or (often) we'd played there for opening tour nights and let ourselves down by not quite being in top gear. Often, we'd reach Belfast the next evening and wonder how it could have got so much better in the course of a day – but it frequently did. On this night in Dublin, I was ready to give up. I'd played a couple of shows in England and one particular evening in Manchester, where I'd been booked into a small rock club, which was all wrong for everything I wanted to do. I came away feeling at my lowest point ever. All the promise of the spring shows in Glasgow had disappeared in the fog of a smoke-filled rock club on a damp night. Now, Dublin.

For some reason, everything that could have gone well did go well that night in Dublin. I met two young Spaniards who became lifelong friends, Angel and Mercedes. They happened to be in the city learning English and were big fans of our music. They couldn't believe that I would be appearing there during their visit when I bumped into them in the bar of the Mean Fiddler. Perhaps it was their enthusiasm, or the fact that the venue was perfect for what I wanted to do, and that the audience were there to listen, but, for whatever reason, I felt I had undergone some kind of spiritual awakening during the time I was onstage. I phoned home and told Lorraine that, somehow, my life had been saved. Everything was going to be OK again. Nothing had really changed, and yet I knew, sipping my Guinness after that show, that there was something in creating songs and singing them in their most simple form that was always going to have a potency for any audience. At my best, and alone, this was something I'd always be able to do. Just me. Just an audience of a hundred-odd folk would do for now. But it could happen, and it could be as transcendent an experience for me – and for them – as anything we'd ever hoped to do in a football stadium or arena with thousands of people. It paid less, but I was fine with that. And so, about nine months after falling out of the music business, I felt I had taken one shaky but optimistic step back into being part of it all again.

Part Five

WANDERING THE WORLD

US tour, 1989.

Mixing *Fellow Hoodlums*, NYC, 1991.

Recording at The Manor, Oxfordshire, 1992.

Final photo shoot, 1993.

The Final Show, Barrowlands, 1994.

Barrowlands Dressing Room after that 'last' show, May 1994.

The day after.
Dundee United win
the cup and a pitch
invasion ensues.

Solo, 2005.

Performing alone.

On the radio,
2000s.

McIntosh Ross.
For *The Great Lakes*
album, 2009.

In Nashville.

At The Bluebird Café, Nashville with Gregor Philp.

North Coast 500
road trip, 2017.

Bukavu, DRC,
January, 2020.

East Neuk with the
extended family:
Collin, Lorraine,
Caitlin, Seamus,
RR, Georgia, Fergus,
Emer, Gez and
Alf the dog in
summer, 2021.

Deacon Blue
Cities of Love
tour, '21.
The Campfire Set.

The last summer
with my mother,
Catherine Ross.
1928–2020.

25

Brazil

In the years after Deacon Blue broke up, I found myself open and
available to new adventures. I spent time co-writing, recording
acoustic solo projects, completing theatre and film commissions
and, occasionally, just occasionally, saying 'yes' to ideas that would
take me beyond any experience I'd encountered so far.

I was in my damp-infested studio one cold day in 1998 when the
phone rang. It was my friend Eildon, who worked for the charity
Christian Aid. 'Would you be interested in coming to Brazil?' she
enquired.

I tried to sound non-committal, but my heart was beating
very fast. I'd never been to South America, and the idea of somewhere that wasn't Glasgow, somewhere that had associations of
sunshine on this dark, nothing day, was too attractive to ignore.

A month or so later, we were on our way. I'd been experiencing terrible back pain, which had caused me to get out of bed
and spend more than a few nights on the floor, so although I
was looking forward to experiencing Brazil, part of me dreaded
the journey. We were going economy, of course, and I feared the
worst for my back. It was my first time flying long-haul without
children in a long time, though, and I rejoiced in the freedom to
drink, sleep, sober up and drink again.

We stayed for one blessed, civilised night in a small hotel
in São Paolo before travelling for around eight hours in a very
uncomfortable minibus into the rural part of São Paolo state.

Our second night was spent on a concrete bed in a disused village radio station; what chance had my back really got?

The purpose of this trip was to see and report back as best I could on the *Movimento dos Trabalhadores Sem Terra*, or MST – the movement of the landless people. Millions of Brazilians need their own land, despite there being an excess amount of unused free countryside available. The landless people are a social movement that organises occupations of land until an agreement is reached with the absentee landlords to allow for the establishment of new communities. We were staying in a village that had been established along these lines ten years before.

To someone from Scotland, it looked like paradise. In a few square miles of fertile ground, which had once been overgrown scrub, the little community of Promisao (promised land) had built houses, a refectory, a pharmacy and a school, having lived in tarpaulin shacks in the first few months of the occupancy. It was a joy to be in their company and they made us feel so welcome.

The only cloud on the horizon was our guide, who often made life a little more difficult than it needed to be. There were a few times we were left wondering about his suitability to be the general factotum for the trip. On our first night sleeping in the radio shack, he'd taken it upon himself to open all the windows, leaving us, in turn, open to a swarm of Brazilian bugs, which, as first light hit, were alighting in great number in and around my sleeping bag. On another occasion, he was anxious to show us what happened when a land occupation took place, and assembled all the men of an encampment in a tent bearing every blunt instrument they could muster. On the way to the occupation, he seemed to delight in the fact that the owners of the land were readying themselves with guns. At this point, I made it clear I had a young family at home, and wasn't interested in his staging mini revolutions for our benefit.

Later in the visit, we realised he was even more of a liability than we'd feared. Acting as a translator, he explained to me that the woman sitting beside the priest we were interviewing was the priest's wife. I expressed some surprise that, in this strongly Catholic country, priests would be allowed to marry, but he shrugged it off confidently, explaining that things were different in Brazil. It was only on our return to the city and double-checking his translation that we realised his grasp of Portuguese was a little short of sure. The priest's 'wife' had, in fact, been an acquaintance from the parish.

It was some relief to know it was very unlikely I'd ever meet him again. I still remember his final translating duty, as he introduced us to one of the officials of the MST based in São Paolo. 'This is Delvechio Mattheus,' he told us. 'Or Derek Matthews, if you prefer.'

Our translator aside, it was an amazing trip. Eildon is one of my dearest, oldest friends. She is immersed in development work, and was brilliant at finding the people I needed to meet and getting alongside anyone we happened upon. We encountered some amazing families whose stories were, in general, good news. The folks we met had gone from homelessness to having small farms with healthy crops and a reasonable standard of living within a few years. Their children were able to be educated, and they were also free from the crime and exploitation so prevalent in the favelas we witnessed in the city.

On some days on that November trip, I saw small glimpses of heaven through the eyes of the people whose stories we heard. We'd be up at five to try to make the most of the coolest part of the day, spending time with farmers on their fields or meeting others still working on sugar plantations, who were mulling over the possibility of joining a land occupation. The contrast between those who were still working for others and paying high rent for their properties and the freedom and joy we experienced in Promisao was visceral.

The reality of being the guest on these trips is that the locals often wonder at the presence of someone who seems – and really is – of no earthly use to them. The folk from the charity can be charmed to plough in more money, and journalists or photographers can be relied upon to relay their stories, but a singer? As often as I was asked, I gave the excuse that, there being no piano present, I couldn't perform anything for them at the time. I would play them some things on the mini-disk player I had with me, but I was aware that I could have been playing them the Beatles and they'd be none the wiser.

On the last night in Promisao, there was a big social gathering involving lots of performances, dancing and songs by the villagers, and I could feel pressure building to sing for my supper. Again, I shrugged off the demands by pointing to the lack of instrumentation until, through the double doors, one of the young men arrived, triumphantly beaming as he bore aloft a two-foot, battery-powered Casio keyboard. The villagers clapped and cheered with delight; there was no way out. That night, I gave a faltering, slightly limited, but ultimately heart-felt version of 'Dignity'. I also told them I would dedicate the song to them when I next played it live, and I kept my word. As I played the song, the faces of those I'd met, those who had helped me recalculate my own priorities and values, would flash before me. I will always be grateful to the MST people from Promisao for that.

As for me? Well, not only did the trip *not* cripple my back beyond repair, but since that time, I've suffered none of the chronic discomfort I experienced in the lead-up to the trip. I never slept on the floor again.

But more importantly, something happened in Brazil that connected with where my heart was way before deciding I wanted to be in a band and be successful. I realised something about happiness and joy that I was to discover again and again over the next twenty-odd years. There really is something about being bonded with others, being happy in your own space and feeling you are needed. When someone needs us and values who we are, we immediately forget about ourselves and find our satisfaction and our joy, our deep joy, in helping the person next to us. I saw this in Brazil, and I discovered it in myself again. I came home comfortably unsettled, but aware too that I had everything I'd ever need.

It came at a perfect time for us. Our lives had been turned upside down by losing all our potential earning from publishing and recording almost two years before, and yet, as we reached the end of 1998, walking along Princes Street carrying a doll's house for our daughter's Christmas present, we reflected that this had been one of the happiest years of our lives.

26

The Further North You Go

Brazil was one of several one-off experiences that came together as part of that interim period when the certainties of life within the confines of a band had all drained away. Sometimes I ended up in South America, and sometimes South America came to me.

At around the time when I felt my career was going backwards, I got a call asking if I'd take part in a benefit show in London. I never get asked to do benefit shows in London, and it is rare to be invited into a show that actually sounds like the kind of thing you might want to go to yourself.

Long before I knew anything about politics, back in 1973, the CIA-backed military in Chile had removed the democratically elected left-wing government in a violent coup. Mass arrests ensued and many were tortured and killed, including the folk singer Victor Jara.

I was blissfully unaware of all of this as a teenager, until the Scottish football team proposed to tour South America before the World Cup in 1978. They were scheduled to play in the Santiago Stadium, where the political prisoners had been held. In Victor Jara's case, the torture had been brutal. His hands had been mutilated before he was tortured and killed, and his body was dumped in the street.

After the coup, thousands of Chileans left the country, and many ended up in the UK, which, with a Labour government in place, offered a safe haven. There are many great stories of how the trade union movement stopped arms and repairs to British fighter jets that were being used by the *junta*, headed by the notorious General Pinochet.

It was in this context that a Chilean support group organised an annual celebration of music and poetry. In 1998, they decided to make a bigger splash, commemorating twenty-five years since the coup. This was made all the more memorable as Pinochet had gone and Chile was then experiencing a time of democratic and cultural freedom. In fact, the Chilean Embassy in London, so long a target for protest and boycotts, supported the event, and invited all the performers over for a cocktail party the following evening. So relaxed was the atmosphere that we seemed to be able to wander in and literally leave our coats in the bedroom.

It seems someone had seen me perform with Scottish folk group Capercaillie on my first-ever solo tour the previous year, and now they asked if I could come back and do something with Karen and Donald Shaw from the band. As they were now good friends of mine, this seemed like a creative way to help a cause I supported. We'd all met Chilean refugees, and there were many stories of exile familiar to people from all parts of the UK. In all parts of Scotland too Chilean exiles had been welcomed as new citizens who had much to offer.

As well as performing a couple of songs on my own, I suggested to Karen we could sing the beautiful song written about Victor by the poet Adrian Mitchell and Arlo Guthrie, simply called 'Victor Jara of Chile'. What we hadn't realised was that Joan Jara, Victor's English-born wife, and her daughter would be guests of honour and sitting just in front of the stage. The refrain of the song is very simple: 'His hands were gentle, and his hands were strong.' It's a beautiful song, which I'd learned from my old friend, Dick Gaughan, and I have only ever sung it that night.

However, to look down at this woman, who'd lost her husband in the cruellest fashion, and see his daughter sitting beside her, quietly listening, made the performance one of the most poignant moments I've ever experienced.

Emma Thompson hosted the whole event and had persuaded Sony Publishing, with whom she had some connection, to sponsor it. Their contribution was a chartered boat, moored off the quay at the Festival Hall, which took the contributors and a few favoured guests down the river for a late summer sail. It was only the second time I'd ever sailed down the Thames, and this time we went east towards the estuary, heading in the opposite direction to the journey I'd made to Kew on my first London visit with my family thirty years earlier. At one point, I passed through the lower deck, where people were sitting at tables having a drink. I was stopped by Alan Rickman and his partner Rima Horton, who had been at the show. He was at pains to tell me how much he'd enjoyed one of the songs I'd performed.

It was a song called 'The Further North You Go', and it seemed to be appropriate for the evening, as the lyrics are essentially a conversation between an unassuming young man from my home city of Dundee and an enthusiastic, if slightly misguided, student from St Andrews University. Though I'm never sure if everyone sees the song in the same way I do, it involves the student wanting to hear about all the important landmarks she should look out for. There's clearly a language gap between the two, as he speaks in curt, terse sentences and she effectively gushes. In the original version, Lorraine and I sang the respective roles. It's a song about disconnection. It's not a song glorifying the beauty of the north over the south, as I suspect some might assume, but rather about how, so often, we can't really explain ourselves adequately. The final twist is her desperate desire to be of use to people who have never asked for any help. As much as anything,

I'm trying to examine my own background here. When facing a problem of some kind, somehow I have assumed I can help fix it, when, in fact, people are capable of doing so much of that themselves if they are given the freedom and resources they need to manage change.

> The further north you go
> The buildings grow, the trees don't show
> The people seem to let you know they're only saying, 'No.'
> If there's a place for me it's here
> It's where I feel I'm really needed
> You're really needed the further north you go

As Alan Rickman enthused over the song, I experienced that nagging feeling that has often gone through me, and which inspired the song: that it must be difficult to understand Scots' discontent with their life if you are an outsider looking in.

One of the hardest things for most countries seems to be finding the right way to celebrate national pride without it spilling over into jingoistic hubris. I suspect we are all more acutely aware of this when it affects our own place of birth rather than a foreign country. Britain and Scotland both seem a little awkward with this kind of celebration, and both forms of nationalism can make me feel a little queasy.

Experiencing the joy and pride of two thousand exiled Chileans that night, singing songs from home and celebrating their own culture, seemed a more appropriate level of festivity than the kind of mawkish events we tend to put on at home. Not only that, but there was the distinct feeling that in this general air of revelry, there was a warm sense of inclusion for anyone who wanted to join in. That they listened to and applauded my songs was typical of that openness. That spirit, ironically, reaffirmed some of the basic tenets behind the lyrics of 'The Further North You Go'.

The song itself has been pulled out on a few occasions, and it seems like one that could be sung in lots of contexts. The audience spoke of nothing else but her after my daughter, Georgia, deputised one night for her mum when we performed it at a benefit gig. And on another night, in the upstairs part of the same venue, Oran Mor in Glasgow, Lorraine and I performed it again at a Burns Supper where the late Jimmy Reid and ex-First Minister, Alex Salmond, outdid each other in terms of sexism and general inebriation, before we had to sing it on a piano that had decided to stop working. It killed off the idea of ever performing it again in such circumstances.

The real background to my experience was sharing a train through Fife one day in the company of St Andrews students, who all seemed to be ultra-reactionary and ultra-loud; always a bad combination. At that time, the university was – and probably still is – a breeding ground for Conservative Party hopefuls who, certainly at that time, would outdo each other for who might become the next Julia Hartley-Brewer. Famously, they held events to which adherents sported 'Hang Nelson Mandela' T-shirts – and worse. It was high Thatcher era, and no one had yet suggested they might be seen as the 'nasty party'.

I'd put that memory together with one from my childhood. On a warm July day, I'd caught a special train with my grandfather from Dundee to Blackpool. My parents had taken my sister, cousin and grandmother in the car to Lytham St Annes, and my grandpa had volunteered to take me by the scenic route as there was no more room in the family Corsair. On the way through Fife, we'd shared a carriage with a young man who struck up a conversation with my grandpa about football and lots of other points of common interest. The only thing I remember him telling us was about the ash pitches he'd experienced in Glasgow, and how you could get easily injured. All this, as we

looked out the window on a glorious summer day on our way to
our holiday. I went back to the story many years later in a song
called 'On Love', which dotted around between recollections of
childhood and adolescent romance.

> Just before the decade changed, he took a long rail journey
> into England
> It was early August and he went with his grandfather to join
> his family on holiday
> The slow summer train wound its way south over the Tay and
> Forth valleys
> As they got talking to a traveller about life in other parts,
> The traveller told them about playing football in Glasgow and
> hurting his skin on the ashes and the red blaes
> As the carriage got warmer, his head hurt and he stopped
> talking with his grandfather
> He tried to cheer the boy up and after a while the boy felt bad
> about ignoring the old man.

Out on the river after the benefit show at the Festival Hall, as
the boat slowly turned round at the flood barriers and we made
our way back to the South Bank, I looked out at the view on either
side of one of the world's great cities. Slowly, the familiar sites
came into shot: St Paul's, the Tower, Tower Bridge, and, along the
Embankment, the magnificent mansions of the capital city. It was
and is a wonderful metropolis. I have never lived there, and have
no desire to ever be a Londoner, but I am always enthralled and
uplifted by the surge of possibilities London still affords.

It would be convenient to believe all things get better, kinder
and more absolute the further north you go. But they don't. The
world is full of wonderful places and amazing, diverse people,
who can be good, bad and indifferent. The secret is to make the
place you are as good as it can be. In London town that night, it
felt as good as it gets.

27

Nashville

I always imagined Nashville in my head, having heard so many stories of how music was written and imagined there. I couldn't understand how this hick-sounding town could be such a big part of the music business. It really loomed into my consciousness in 1985, when I received the embossed contract for my first music publishing agreement. Across the top of the letterhead were the main offices of ATV Music, in London, New York, LA and Nashville.

Of the three US cities, it was Nashville that intrigued me most. Was it like a cowboy town from the westerns seen on TV? Did the people there only love country music? And why was it so important to songwriters?

When I was without a publishing deal for a couple of years in the late 1990s, I'd met up with an old friend, now working at EMI, who offered to send me to Nashville to write. It never happened, and though my manager had encouraged me to just go ahead and co-write there, I was nervous about launching into that world as a complete unknown. Our US career had fizzled out pretty quickly, and I felt I needed some kind of calling card to introduce myself to possible collaborators.

In 1999, I signed a new publishing contract with Warner Chappell Music, and the main intention was to co-write songs with a view to getting them recorded by other artists. What I never knew about the songwriting world was it bore almost no relation to the music business I had known up to that point.

Songwriters are a group apart, with their own rules, priorities and pecking order. In that world, I was a novice and a complete outsider. I could only imagine this feeling being amplified ten times more by trying to make sense of it in America. So it was I rolled up my sleeves and went to work trying to write songs or co-write songs with other artists here before even attempting it there.

Having spent a good decade in this world, I'm not sure I know more or am any better equipped to make sense of it. The kings and queens of songwriting are often names the general public wouldn't recognise, and, as the years have gone by, the number of writers on hit songs has increased so considerably that it often seems to make no commercial sense to attempt to be one of the ten co-authors on a minor pop hit. However, from around the start of the millennium, and over the next ten years or so, travelling to write or hosting sessions in my own home studio became my main working life. There was some touring and recording too but I began to think of myself primarily as a songwriter. In many ways, it was a return to what I had first wished for when I'd stepped into ATV's offices some fifteen years earlier.

The life of a songwriter can be, perhaps should be, good fun. Sometimes I felt I was more upbeat about the whole business of the co-write than those with whom I'd come to work. Older, wiser, writers would often lift their eyebrows in despair or cynicism at the task set before us. (On a writers' retreat, I offered up that the collective noun for us was an un-recoupment.) Publishers liked to throw out the possibility of an artist 'looking for a song' (or really a next single) as a starting point for a session. The experienced writers often knew that there was little chance of our song being listened to, let alone recorded, without some kind of collaboration with the artist in question. In time, this proved to be true and all of us, as a community of writers, worked towards the days when we'd be put together with artists who wanted to co-write. There were many such days for me. I'd set off to another city with a laptop and a guitar, and find myself on different forms of transport, dragging assorted baggage to dusty studios, programming rooms or occasionally fine houses and smart, upmarket recording facilities, before trying to write a song in the five or six hours given to us. There were many days when I felt I was getting nowhere, and, in retrospect, any success I enjoyed was often simply a case of being in the right place at the right time.

One day in London effectively changed my luck – and my life – as a co-writer. I'd already worked with a young unsigned artist called James Blount (soon to be Blunt) at my house in Glasgow. It was 2003, and he had not long left the army. He'd been introduced to me by my publisher, who was hoping her bosses at Warner Chappell would sign him. As it happened, they never made an offer, and his publishing went over to EMI. We wrote a few things together and, as time moved on, I heard he'd signed a record deal, but heard no more about him for a long while. One morning, my phone rang. It was James.

'That song we wrote, "High", is coming out,' he told me. 'It's going to be my first single.'

He had gone to America and recorded his album, including the song we had written, and it had been chosen as the lead track for the project. As most people in the world now know, however, the second single, 'You're Beautiful' eclipsed that first track, and 'High' was slotted to be re-released as the follow-up to one of the biggest-selling singles of that decade. As the months passed, I watched in disbelief as sales went through the roof for the debut album of a young army captain I'd first met on his lunchbreak from working with the horses at Hyde Park Barracks. Not only was the single and the album a success here, but there was huge success in almost every country in the world. No song

I'd written has ever come close to the sales and plays of 'High' and, for that afternoon spent at James's flat in Fulham when we got the song together, I'm eternally grateful.

By the time he came to tour on the back of the initial success, he was selling out a 2,500-seater venue and was on his way to filling out the arena along the road for his next visit. I took one of my daughters and her friend to the show and went backstage to thank him after the gig. I'd told James I'd managed to put off buying my kids a pony by telling them his album had to break the million mark before we could even consider it. It broke over ten times that number, and Reilly, our dearly beloved horse, became a good four-legged friend to our girls for the years they were in secondary school.

Having a hit song that people knew changed my mind about Nashville. Encouraged to go and write there, I asked my publisher to arrange a visit with the help of Warner Chappell on Music Row. It was the spring of 2007, and I pulled up outside the Hampton Inn on West End Avenue on a Saturday evening. As I was unloading my luggage and my guitar from the rental car, there were two rustic-looking characters checking in at the same time, and they politely enquired if I was a musician. I was so used to Scottish sarcasm I couldn't quite believe they were genuine, but eventually I affirmed my troubadour status. This seemed to bring them a pleasure that matched my own at finally coming to the place they call Twang Town.

I had spent a part of almost every year over my previous twenty in the music business visiting America. We'd been over to record, mix, promote and tour. We'd come back for family holidays, and we had lifelong friends in California. So, there was nothing particularly alien about flying over to work there for a couple of weeks. However, apart from a short family holiday to Florida, I had never been to the South. That it was different to all the cities and states I had encountered in America was a huge understatement. Despite so many people telling me how much had changed in Nashville in recent times, the town I encountered in 2007 was still a place apart from the America I had known up until that point.

Like so many Europeans, I have always loved the chance to get up close to everything we've ever seen on TV and in the movies, and the South, it seemed to me, could only amplify this feeling. Like other places with a history of turbulence and unrest, Nashville, even with the arch conservatism of the surrounding areas of Tennessee, was a place where visitors are made to feel at home. It wasn't simply the community of songwriters and musicians who populated my visit that made me think this way. It was waitresses and hotel staff, fellow travellers at the bar in the evening, and almost anyone else you happened to meet.

There is, of course, a socio-political back story. Some of the bloodiest battles of the Civil War took place here, and signposts and tours still mark out the sites of the conflict for visitors retracing the steps of the thousands who died during the conflict. One hundred years after that event, Nashville was still witnessing the struggle for racial equality. Some of the Civil Rights Movement's biggest demonstrations in the 1960s took place within the city limits. Racial equality is the story of American politics, and Nashville will give you as good a primer as any other city if you're willing to look and listen. From there, you can travel in any direction to keep following the story.

On that first visit, Nashville was not the small western town of my teenage imagination, but neither was it the metropolis it was to become in the following decade, when house prices soared as it started to welcome new residents in their thousands to what was becoming America's new 'it city'. The downside of this was the limited consumer choice at that time. Eating out was a simple affair, and there was the sense that things moved a little more slowly, with fashion and style slightly behind the curve. All of that has changed utterly. Any visitor to Nash Vegas these days will not be short of choice for anything. Restaurants, shops and high-end urban living have all become part of a city that has changed almost beyond recognition in the last fifteen years or so.

One drawback to this is the city fathers' lack of concern for the music heritage so closely associated with the area. Buildings on Music Row that once housed famous events and sessions are regularly pulled down without any concern that the culture so many come to witness is being destroyed just as quickly as the malls and hotels are going up. When the *Nashville* TV series became popular, downtown became a magnet for bachelor and bachelorette weekends away. Broadway, which had a noisy hum before, suddenly felt like a year-round, seaside Spring Break destination. In a way that many stars of Music Row can relate to, fame and its aftershocks proved to be a difficult concept for the city of Nashville.

Though very few of the musicians I encountered on my early trips had grown up there, many of them had settled there and adopted Nashville as their natural home. It was a place where musicians, tired of an itinerant existence, seemed to find a welcome refuge. Back in 1995, when I was recording in LA with the Robb brothers, many of our requests for session musicians were answered with, 'He used to be here, but he's moved to Nashville.' Los Angeles had suffered following the riots of 1992 and the earthquake of 1994, and, as recording became digitised and pop music no longer required those state-of-the-art recording spaces, the musicians who relied on session work started moving east.

In Nashville it was, and perhaps still is, possible for session musicians to find regular work. What I found there, however, was a group of talented people who did *everything*. The writers all sang and performed and played a number of instruments. When they weren't on 'a write', they were on the road or in the studio. After a couple of visits, you would imagine you had some sense of the scale of the place, and then you'd open up the credits on a country album and realise that, even with this much knowledge, you still didn't recognise any of the names. What was clear, however, was that in this town, the songwriters were not at the bottom of the creative pile in the way they were at home. The Nashville songwriters were organised and had campaigned as a group on a number of issues regarding their own craft. On country music TV channels, for example, all the writers were credited on each video shown.

No visit to the city was complete without going to the Bluebird Café. It's a chance to witness songwriters play the songs you might know from hearing a well-known record, but here you get to listen to the raw songwriter's take. It's a magical space, with four writers in the centre of the room surrounded by a pin-drop silence, with an incredibly well-informed and responsive audience, and some very subtle food and drinks servers who know when to and when not to pour a beer and serve the fries.

On my first night there in 2007 I saw four writers I came to know very well over the next dozen years or so: Gretchen Peters, Bill Lloyd, Tia Sillers and her late, great songwriter husband Mark Otis Selby (Mos to his pals). Performing in the round involves taking a song in turn, and it's now a great tradition of songwriters' performances. Towards the end of the second set, the group all started to play songs they'd written for Trisha Yearwood, and, as it finally came to Gretchen and she played her epic song 'On a Bus to St Cloud,' the tears rolled down my face. They were tears of homesickness, joy and recognition. Recognition of the sentiment of the song – someone has gone and they're not coming back – and recognition that I'd found myself in a place where songs were being listened to, adored and revered as they ought to be. It felt like coming home.

The writing sessions were varied and plentiful. On any given day, the songwriters will be writing with someone for something or other. Sometimes they will be getting together for their own projects or at the suggestion of their publishers to write a song for another artist who is looking for something new, or, as in my case, to see what might happen. Should you consider the song you might be about to write has a route towards being recorded for a major release, the publisher's and songwriter's doors, once seemingly locked and bolted, will miraculously swing open.

It was the first time I'd gone somewhere other than Glasgow and imagined I could live there. There is something about Nashville that made me feel at home in a way London, New York or Los Angeles never could. All are great songwriting centres, though New York is no longer the place for writers it once was in the days of Tin Pan Alley and the Brill Building. Nashville, however, holds the attraction of being a little provincial, and therefore never takes itself quite as seriously as the others. It also successfully micromanages an entire – and significantly large – sector of the entertainment business: country music. The record labels and management companies on Music Row control the creative output of a huge percentage of the music consumed in America. Nashville itself is the epicentre of all of that, but the consumption happens right across North America and now, increasingly, around the world.

And yet – and this is what I still love about the town – you walk the long streets of 16th and 17th Avenues south, and you pass suburban houses that have become publishing companies, their homemade banners advertising the latest radio success from their writers. Then you see the cars heading home in the late afternoon sunshine so people can be back for family supper by early evening, and you reflect that this contrasts, in almost every way, with the music business you have come to know everywhere else.

There's an accessibility and a camaraderie here not really present in other outposts of the industry. I remember sitting around the green room in a writing session when someone introduced me to the man whose publishing company we were working in. Suddenly, I was having a conversation with Major Bob Doyle, the manager of Garth Brooks, whose career over the last thirty years or so has been nothing short of sensational. Brooks is actually the highest-selling album artist in the US since Nielsen SoundScan began tracking sales in 1991. Equally, he could probably walk along Oxford Street with barely a head (other than those of American tourists) turning.

On my first day writing on Music Row, I wrote with Phil Madeira, who has since become a good friend. I loved the fact that it took me until mid-afternoon to notice that I hadn't removed the plastic label stuck to my new chinos, purchased the previous day at the mall at Green Hills. Phil had noticed it but had said nothing, assuming it was some kind of fashion statement.

Nothing major happened that first week, other than me finding my way around town and making connections as to who was who. No one wanted to work over the weekend, so I drove down to Memphis, listening to the radio. Minutes on to Highway 40, and I heard Patty Loveless singing 'Blame it on Your Heart'. I knew country had taken a firm hold on me then. A weekend of Lorraine Motel, Stax and Elvis only gave me more time to think about how all this music came together. Driving back to Nashville late on Sunday evening, I realised how much my heart was rejoicing at my quick return.

•

A mutual friend back in the UK, Edwina Hayes, who'd been out on a solo tour with me a couple of years earlier, recommended me to Nanci Griffith. I'd been a huge fan of Nanci's since I first heard her music back in 1988. On first encountering it, I'd gone out and bought all her back catalogue in Echo on Byres Road, an old-school Glasgow record store that sold new and second-hand albums. I had kept up with Nanci since that time, but she had undergone some fairly major health issues in the intervening twenty years or so.

She was someone who wasn't afraid to speak out. Driving around Hillsboro, where she lived, and looking out for the house, I noticed a large placard staked into the front lawn, which stood out in this relatively conservative neck of the woods. It read 'Impeach George W Bush'. I knew I'd found Nanci's house.

I enjoyed the day at Nanci's. I'd taken along an idea for a song, which we worked on and completed that day. My only real worry was that everything she talked or sang about seemed to be part of her general rage at the Iraq War, and every lyric was twisted into an attack on Bush's handling of it. I was as dismayed with Bush and Blair's war mongering as anyone, but was also keen to write a song that had a wider target market than the protest song she seemed keen to deliver. In fairness, I should have known. In her emails to me, she had declared: 'I can't write any songs just now. I'm too angry at George Bush.'

That the song was written and recorded, I am thankful. I had, on my first visit to the town, managed to get a cut. Since that time, I only saw Nanci a few more times, as she slowly withdrew from public life. I was, perhaps, less surprised than most when she died in the summer of 2021. The last time I'd seen her had not been a great experience, and her fragile state of mind and poor physical health told its own story. Sometimes I'd pass her house on my way through Nashville's west end and see her truck parked in the driveway, and I'd remember that magical day we wrote a song together. I'd asked her, back then, why she drove a pick-up truck.

'I'm a Texas girl,' she'd teased. 'I gotta drive a truck.'

She made some wonderful recordings, and it was mesmerising to see her live. Somehow, I always felt sad whenever I passed that big house, or thought of Nanci alone inside. Passing it also reminded me about the great thing that still happens in that town: you go to meet someone you've never met, and might never meet again, and you write a song together. And sometimes – enough times to make it still worthwhile – the song gets sung and recorded and begins to make its way across the world. To carry that thought with you as your car pulls up another drive and you press the bell of some house in a strange but welcoming sunlit street is always a powerful reminder.

Since that time, I've made many more writing trips to Nashville, and in recent years have combined the visits with picking up long interviews and special features for my BBC radio show, *Another Country*. I've made friends and new discoveries, enjoyed magical nights at hidden honky-tonks and driven miles around town, just listening to medium-wave radio and the voice of my favourite ever presenter, Eddie Stubbs. I can't fully tell why I love the city so much, unless I use the analogy an old musician friend, Fingaz, used when telling me why he, a Ugandan who was a hip-hop producer and beats-driven songwriter, loved country music. 'It's the stories,' he explained.

I love the stories too. The history of the city is steeped in legends of how songs came to be, how famous records got made, and how it affected everything we know and love about pop music. Rodney Crowell told me once that to love country music was to love a ghost story, and I suspect that's very close to the truth. In my early days there, I would rejoice in my isolation, and pick up books and albums from Ernest Tubbs' record store on Broadway, devouring all the information as I dined alone in a booth at a dimly lit restaurant. That I knew no one and no one knew me was perhaps the greatest freedom I'd ever experienced. One story would lead to another, the days would be open, and once the sessions had finished, I realised I could drive as far as I wanted, and no one would miss me. Thirty minutes north and I'd be in Kentucky, while if I drove east, the signs said Chattanooga. Head south via Franklin and through the little Amish town of Ethridge, and suddenly you are crossing the state line into Alabama, towards the music haven that is Muscle Shoals. Keep driving west, and before long, you're in Tupelo Mississippi – and the myths roll on and on.

The best stories were never on the road, however; they were told to me by the writers in the writing rooms. At first, we'd gather on Music Row in anodyne lounges with pianos and sofas meant to encourage creativity. Next door would be another session, and along the corridor, you could hear the strains of harmony as a song was created out of thin air. As time went on, I began to be invited to writers' homes out in the suburbs. So many of these contained state-of-the-art studios adorned with gold discs and trophies of success: Grammys, BMI and ASCAP awards, CMAs, ACMs and BMI certificates. They'd tell you how the song that made them famous came about; how no one wanted to hear it and it travelled back and forward between the manager, the label and the publisher. They'd explain that they too were outsiders from Missouri or Louisiana, exiles from the north or escapees from California. We'd talk over cities we had in common.

I once shared that I'd always enjoyed LA more than San Francisco.

'Correct,' a suntanned beach type replied. He'd tired of the West Coast and, like many before and after him, had found

Music City offered more bang for his buck when it came to buying real estate. 'San Francisco's too . . . communist.'

Sometimes I wanted to explain I came from Red Clydeside, and really, they hadn't seen anything yet, but mostly I just enjoyed the conversation, wallowed in the musicality and learned to listen as I immersed myself in the Nashville way.

There were days when I'd come back to my hotel room and wonder if there was any point in trying, so steep were the odds of having any success there. One day, I returned to my room and started to look for flights home, feeling desolate at the writing experience I'd just endured. I was twenty-five years into my career, and the morning I'd just spent in the Orbison Building had made me believe I could no longer write a song. The next day, I worked with a legend of Music Row, one of the biggest, most successful writers of all time, Bob De Piero, who, in a few short hours of working together, brought me back from the brink and made me believe I had something worthwhile to give. Years later, I met up with him, and thanked him from the bottom of my heart.

Something keeps drawing me back to Music City. It's nothing special to look at; the Cumberland River winds slowly through the centre of town, but there is almost none of the 'river life' that you might expect in other cities across the world. Though the hills and small towns around Tennessee are cute, and the fields, farms and main streets of the country towns can charm on an early summer evening, they are no more endearing than the rolling fields of many of the other eastern states. In the city itself, east Nashville's boho outlets and quirky shops are a great distraction, and the west end offers the allure and patronage of Vanderbilt and its stately campus, but still, like my home city of Glasgow, I suspect the real magic is all behind doors closed to visitors. It's in the writing rooms, the control rooms and the studio floors, the back porches on Music Row and the houses in Belle Mead, Brentwood and Berry Hill where the real action occurs. Oh, to be a fly on the wall when the stars tell their heartbreak stories and the writers of the Row translate those tears into verses, killer choruses and hummable hooks. If Tennessee could package that experience, I suspect the beer trams carrying bachelorette parties might well lose some of their appeal. Meanwhile, Broadway goes on and the holiday honky-tonks purport to be offering the tourists the real thing as they stagger from Tootsie's to Kid Rock's Big Ass Honky Tonk. The vacationers no longer care if they don't know who Chet Atkins was, if there's a chance of seeing Luke Bryan or Morgan Wallen over at the mall.

For me, I am happy to leave that part of town to the holiday makers. There are songs to be found, and they are all being written, quietly but constantly, in America's Music City.

28

A Wedding on the Bay

On my first-ever visit to America in May 1988, I arrived in New York City with our A&R man Gordon. Once we had 'deplaned', he headed straight for the helicopter ride into Manhattan. 'It's as cheap as a yellow cab,' were his words, which, as I was not immediately responsible for the bill, I took as gospel truth.

New York, that week, was covered in a raincloud that didn't disappear for the entire time I stayed there. I was there to oversee two mixes of songs for a subsequent final single release from our debut album, *Raintown*. Michael Brauer was working out of Quad Studios in Times Square, and I was staying near the park on 57th Street. On our first night, Gordon had arranged for us to have dinner with a music business colleague down in the Village. Louie, the colleague in question, fulfilled very stereotype of the music businessman I'd have expected if I'd had to describe one at that point. Checking in with Gordon, he'd enquired if I had a girl with me. Gordon told him I was on my own.

'Does he want one?'

I enjoyed the night, but was grateful for the cloud that had rolled in, as Louie, discovering it was my first night in New York, told me he had a friend who flew a helicopter around the city and was keen I should sample the experience.

'He flew 'copters in 'Nam. This guy's the best. Wait till I call him. His big thing is flying you through the Twin Towers of the World Trade Centre.'

Louie confirmed the bad/good news that the weather had grounded the 'copter excursion, so when he asked what I'd like to do instead, I expressed an interest in driving round the island of Manhattan. We all got in the back of a yellow-checkered cab: Louie, his young female friend, and me. I was still getting over the helicopter idea when we were streaming down the FDR Highway and pulling up to lights in a rather dimly lit area. Louie leaned across the rear seat and locked my door. 'You can't be too careful around here.'

It was Manhattan and I loved every minute of the ride, even managing to say 'Thanks, but no thanks' to the cocaine as it got passed between Louie and the girl in the back seat. Louie was rolling by now. Soon, we were back at an apartment close to Central Park, Louie's weekday bolthole, and I was filing through his brilliant record collection while he chopped out the Charlie on the coffee table. He had great stories of his promo days, working for legendary labels and artists, and I soaked it all in. I came to his blues section and the name of an artist I'd never heard of before: Homesick James. I loved the name and filed it away for an idea that would come good a few months later.

I left Louie's place and took a cab home, but before I left his friend passed me her business card, 'Give me a call if you're ever lonely.'

I was learning quickly about the ways of the city.

I was sitting with Ewen, the Deacon Blue bassist, at a breakfast table in Denver, Colorado. He'd asked over the waiter for help, as there seemed to be no cutlery on our table. By now, Ewen had explained the problem twice, and it was obvious the waiter had no understanding of what was required. Ewen tried again, this time elongating the word 'CUT-LERY'.

This met with a blank look.

Ewen sighed. 'You know,' he said, adopting a slight mid-Atlantic twang, 'knives and forks and shit.'

'Oh . . . you mean silverware!'

Jovan Mrvos (our Columbia A&R man who would later introduce me to the Stones) is still a great friend. I remember going to see him at his office and proudly showing off a new biker jacket I'd just bought at Urban Outfitters. It was in pristine condition.

'That jacket needs to be tied behind a car and pulled along the road for a few miles,' he correctly observed.

Jovan lived on the Upper East Side, and I was invited over to his place one night. The warm spring rain was still coming down, but the plane trees on the sidewalks were in full foliage, and somehow it all felt like a scene from a Billy Wilder movie. The windows from his apartment were open, and I could hear the soundtrack from once *Upon a Time in America* drifting down to street level as I walked up the stoop to his front door. That night, sitting in Jovan's place, looking out on the newly christened trees and the brownstone street, I realised I'd come good on that dream of America I'd held for so long.

It was only a few months later that we all got to come back to the US as a band. We'd started work on our second album, and I'd had the rough idea of working with different producers for appropriate songs. We'd already completed two songs with Warne Livesey, and we'd heard there was an A&R staff producer for Columbia based on the West Coast who was interested in working with us.

His name was David Kahne, and, in true eighties style, he was flown to Glasgow to meet us, bringing his bicycle in his hold luggage and staying at Glasgow's only five-star hotel at the time, No. 1 Devonshire Gardens.

It was agreed we'd work on some songs, and by June of 1988 we were in North Hollywood, staying in two rented condos along the road from Sunset Sound, where we were to record the tracks. As a recording session, it was pretty forgettable. I didn't enjoy working with David, and he felt – probably accurately – that we'd not given him the best songs either.

However, it did allow us to be in California for a while, and towards the end of the session, on a long weekend, our friends Dave and Wendy, who we'd known in the UK, were getting married up the coast in the grounds of Berkeley University in the Bay Area. Looking back now, with no mobiles or smartphones, I can't work out how we found them, but Lorraine and I took our rental car up Highway 5 through the desert and met the pre-wedding party, who were all enjoying a beach barbecue at Santa Cruz near a friend's apartment.

At the barbecue, I found myself walking along the shoreline with a friend of theirs named Brett, who sadly is no longer with us. An intense and dedicated survivor of peak Haight-Ashbury hippiedom, he started to explain the pains of his recent divorce to me. His wife had chosen to elope with a Jesuit priest, who had clearly abandoned holy orders.

'The worst thing, Ricky, was she took my Macintosh.'

This was 1988 and I could only imagine why he was getting so needlessly worked up over a raincoat in one of the sunniest places on the planet.

It took me a few more hundred yards of beach to twig he was referring to a computer.

The wedding was to be in a small outside auditorium in the grounds of Berkeley University. On the night before, Wendy, who is Australian, asked if I could play something for her coming up the aisle, having already agreed that Lorraine and I would sing at the ceremony. I hastily cobbled together some ideas that would sound a little like 'Tom Traubert's Blues' by Tom Waits, which includes the refrain from 'Waltzing Matilda'. I was sitting on the front row with Lorraine, and was about to go up on to the stage to play the piano, which had known better times, when Lorraine whispered in my ear, 'I don't want to put you off, but Bono's here.'

I turned to see Bono, the Edge and a whole group of other folk, who included Maria McKee (for some reason), all arriving as one to enjoy the ceremony. As I played, rather tentatively, Wendy walked up the aisle with her dad, Barry, to be met by Dave, who'd ridden up to the altar on a Yamaha motorcycle. It was California, so there was no need for a helmet, and for similar reasons no one batted an eye at any of these disparate events.

I can't remember much about the wedding, but we stayed for the next day too, when there was a lunch. Again, the U2 guys joined in the festivities. I enjoyed Bono and Edge's company and got to know them a little, not least because Dave and Wendy decided to spend part of their honeymoon down in LA with us after the session had ended. A couple of years earlier Dave, who then ran a charity that addressed civil rights in Central America, had taken Bono and Edge round some of the places in San Francisco where exiles from Nicaragua and El Salvador had come and told their own stories in murals that adorned the walls of the Mission District. Wendy's friend, Pete Williams, U2's lighting director, had suggested to them they might want to see what was going on in 'America's backyard'. Bono and his wife Ali had been so taken with this visit that they arranged to go down to Nicaragua and El Salvador and see some of the work Dave and his colleagues were doing there. Hence, a friendship had commenced. For us, however, it was all just another mind-blowing American moment.

Back in LA, Dave was in his element, and, before we knew it, we were all down in A & M studios in Hollywood, hanging at the mix as Jimmy Iovine assembled the *Rattle and Hum* album. For

Dave, this was all just part of a life he cruised through meeting famous folk. For us, we were starting to feel like groupies. On one memorable day, Dave arranged for us to join Ali at Malibu for a swim at the beach. I felt I was holding my life together fairly well, until I entered the water and was pummelled by a ten-foot wave, which hurled me back on to the sand. Dusting myself off and trying to act cool, I walked as casually as I could up the steep bank towards our party as they sat staring at my bedraggled figure. It was only at this point, resembling a man with grossly engorged testicles, that I realised a good two or three pounds of sand and shingle were lodged in my Speedos.

Along with many of our liberal friends, we loved San Francisco, but back then we loved LA much more. I suppose it was because we got a chance to work and belong there. Just being in Sunset Sound for a couple of weeks was enough in itself, but driving along Hollywood Boulevard, listening to the radio and going twice round the block until a song had finished also seeped into our souls. We loved the drives to Santa Monica and Melrose Avenue, lunchtimes at Johnny Rockets and the second-hand clothes at Aardvark, as well as the record and guitar stores. The only thing missing was the chance to play our own music there. The next time we came back to LA, it would be to headline at the Roxy.

We were in Ralph's on Sunset, filling up a large supermarket trolley on our first night in California. I was scouring the dairy shelves, but I couldn't seem to find what I was looking for. I asked one of the staff.

'Where would I find butter?'

Blank look.

'BUTTER. BUTTER.'

Still blank.

'You know . . . to spread on your bread.' I mimed the action.

'Oh. You mean budder.'

I came back to New York that summer for another remix. This time it was Bob Clearmountain who was to re-vocal and remix 'Real Gone Kid' for release a couple of months later. That summer in New York there had been a heatwave, and although it was starting to ease as I arrived, the streets still smelled of uncollected garbage, and the heat seemed to ooze out of every crack in the walls and pavements. We were working at the Hit Factory, which wasn't far from where I was staying, and I noticed the likeness to Glasgow that so many music people had remarked upon when they first visited us in Scotland. The sandstone and the grid system are both common features, especially in Glasgow's main business centre. In years to come, Glasgow would be used as a stand-in for New York in Hollywood movies, as it was often cheaper to film there than in the Big Apple itself.

As a band, we finally returned to the US after our Australian tour in 1989. As we got over our jetlag, we made a video for the fourth single to come from our second album, *When the World Knows Your Name*. We'd asked our friend Wendy to scout some good locations, and we eventually filmed most of the shots in and around the Pacific Coast Highway, just south of San Francisco.

With the filming complete, we began our first US tour. The opening gig was one of those truly great nights. A sold-out show in Boz Scaggs' club, Slims, in San Francisco meant that people were crammed into a tiny space, and I have a strong memory of audience members hanging out on window sills as we played through our set. The second show in LA, however, didn't go so well. It felt stuffed full of industry people, and we never really established ourselves in the way we should have. By the time we reached the East Coast though, we had got our show in shape for two brilliant sets at the Bottom Line.

We'd return later that year for more shows in America, which went well, although without achieving any breakthrough success with our record. It was to be one of the most frustrating stories of our career that despite our willingness to come over and tour, we were not given the support necessary to do it in the same way as we had done at home. Perhaps, in retrospect, we should have just done what many acts before us did: got in a cheap van and done whatever was necessary to reach the audience. Perhaps, by that time, we had become too cosseted with our travel requirements, and I doubt we would have endured such a journey successfully. So, these two tours in 1989 became Deacon Blue's only successful live appearances in America.

Despite this, in the following years, we came back many times. We mixed a record and returned on various promotional outings, always enjoying the adventure even though we were subjected to the usual round of rock humiliations:

Tour manager: 'Today we're over at the folk from the Gavin Report (or some other music mag) for coffee and doughnuts.'

Cut to us stopping at Dunkin' Donuts on the way over. Yes, we were bringing the coffee and doughnuts.

Then there was the summer of 1995, which I spent in LA with my family recording my solo album. By the end of that year, I'd been over three times to finish the record, before heading to Massachusetts after Christmas to mix the album at Fort Apache.

Although I did come back again in 1996 for a long weekend to shoot a video in LA and Las Vegas, it wasn't until 1999 that we returned as a family for a proper holiday in California. We came back a few years later too, not working but simply enjoying travelling, treating ourselves to a beach holiday and visits to old friends in the Bay Area. We fooled the kids into believing they had to salute every time they heard a train whistle and they dutifully fell in line, even confessing years later that they'd do it in bed to make sure they obeyed the law.

In 2012, my eldest daughter moved to San Francisco to work for a charity. Although that job didn't last too long, it opened up new opportunities for her, and she continued working in the Bay Area, where, in due course, she met her future husband. In 2019, we all returned for another wedding by the Bay, although this time the venue was inland, and up the coast a little towards the Napa Valley. On a perfect July day, they were married in a beautiful ceremony under a clear blue sky, with a lake and the green hills of the valley as a backdrop. We sang and danced the night away as it grew dark, and we sat with our old best friend, Wendy, and reminisced about how our friendship had remained intact, with more adventures to come, some thirty-five years after we'd met.

In the meantime, I'd travelled north, south and east of where we were, and still not experienced much of the US. I get annoyed when people try to conflate an entire country with one set of politics. It happened in the eighties with Reagan, then again with the Bush family, but we don't expect people to assume that the UK is full of people like Margaret Thatcher, or, for that matter Tony Blair or Boris Johnson. So, despite the liberal voices huffing and puffing, I love America. I love its spirit and its ambition, and I love too its self-reflection. I love the music and I love the literature and the movies, and most of all, I love my American friends. Now, I have every reason to go often, with a daughter and a fine son-in-law who live, near their boat, right beside the Bay.

29

To Africa

When I was a kid, my mother took me to an exhibition held to celebrate the life and work of the Dundee missionary Mary Slessor. It was held in the halls of her home parish, the Wishart Memorial Church, above where my father's old warehouse used to be situated on the Cowgate in Dundee. I remember the replica bush huts and native villages representing the life Mary had encountered in Nigeria, and I recall too my mother's own admiration for this young Dundee millworker who had gone off alone to Africa.

Both sides of my family had missionary connections. My father, generous to a fault, had invited his old uncle, a missionary to China who had been forced to leave after the revolution, to come and stay with them in their new home in the early days of their marriage. Uncle Alec stayed with the family for a few years, and he died shortly before my birth, explaining my middle name, Alexander. In the loft of our second family home, his old trunk sat beneath the rafters until we finally moved house for the last time. It contained books and belongings, and a family keepsake still treasured: his Chinese Bible.

China didn't figure highly on our radar as youngsters, and it would skip a generation as a place of interest until my youngest daughter studied the language and culture and spent significant time there many years later. It was Africa we got to hear about most.

On my mother's side, my Uncle Jimmy had served in Zambia and my Aunt Margaret had been a missionary in Tanzania, while my father's cousin had married a Belgian man, and they were both on the mission field in what was then the Belgian Congo. Stories of the adventures of all these family members abounded. The one I enjoyed most was my dad's cousin and family getting out of the Congo as the independence movement grew in strength. Stopped at a checkpoint with someone poking a gun at their car, the family story ran that one of their offspring asked, 'Is that a real gun?' We sat in awe at the kitchen table as my father or mother read from the blue airmail letter in a fever of excitement. 'And the soldiers let them on their way,' my mother declared triumphantly.

Each of these little miracles would be recounted at length on furloughs by the families, and I remember the Belgian second cousins all coming to visit in their seven-seater Peugeot, driven all the way from Africa. It was too far for us to visit (we never went abroad as a family at all) and so distant that our relatives would only return every few years. My mother would ready a house, extra winter clothes and school places for the children.

'I've got them some anoraks,' I remember her telling her puzzled elder sister, who had no idea what she was talking about. She'd left Dundee as a nursing sister, heading out to meet a husband with whom she had only ever corresponded by letter. By the time I remember their first proper long visits, they were a family of eight, although there was only one male cousin, Charlie, who was a little older than myself. Despite the random nature of their courtship, Margaret and her husband Alan enjoyed a long and happy marriage. Eventually, they went to live and work in Bath, Somerset, where I'd spend glorious summer weeks with my cousins, and help my uncle harvest the fruit from his allotment down by the river that ran along the back of their house. By then, he worked for the missionary society, but despite the regular job, their life had always been one of 'living by faith'. They owned very little and rejoiced in the giving of people who supported their work. They adhered to a fundamentalist Christianity but seemed, to me at least, to have inherited none of the restrictive and coercive aspects of what can often be seen as a very narrow form of religion. Instead, their large family oozed life and joy in all they did, and each of them seemed grateful for everything they had, and never resentful of what they might be missing.

My Uncle Jimmy was similarly blessed with a sunny nature. His own role was that of the preacher or evangelist, and he spent almost all his life in Zambia, even suffering from recurring malaria for long periods in his early days there, when they'd been at the mercy of the native mosquitos. He had come to the country then known as Northern Rhodesia via Kenya, where he had been stationed as a conscripted soldier during the war. Far from home and away from the faith he'd known as a child and youth, he encountered an open-air preacher and rededicated his life back to God. He had been a worry for my grandmother, who'd watched her eldest and only son become estranged from his faith. His conversion that night in Nairobi gave him the impetus to return to Africa and dedicate his life to God through serving as a missionary. Like his younger sister, Margaret, he would sail far away and return only occasionally to Dundee, where he'd spend much of his time preaching around various Brethren Assemblies, showing slides of his work in Africa. How we loved the nights when Uncle Jimmy or other missionaries would speak instead of the usual – and rather dull – itinerant preacher. The missionaries seemed to dress more informally, and told stories of funny African misunderstandings, spectacular car journeys and accidents, and occasionally described dangers we could never imagine. From Uncle Jimmy's perspective, the furlough wasn't always the relaxing break from service it might and should have been. 'Here comes the missionary, let's kill him,' he once quipped.

It was the stories we loved. In Dar es Salaam one warm night, as the house was sleeping, my uncle had seen his best trousers disappearing through a bedroom window as he looked up from his bed. It seemed an elaborate fishing pole and hook had been assembled by a few locals in order to remove some valuables from their house.

Uncle Jimmy's stories, though always told with a sparkle of humour, had a darker side which involved visits to the prisoners on death-row in the Kabwe Jail. In the dark of Hermon Hall (the mother church of the Brethren in the centre of town), he would show slide upon slide of African men and women in white garments, all ready to be baptised in local rivers, his own trousers and sleeves rolled and ready to take to the water to carry out the full immersion. Stories would be told around each successive slide, and Jimmy would implore the congregation to pray for the brother in question. It all passed in a blur, and it would take some of the cousins to fill in the details about what life was really like in Africa on a day-to-day basis. In all honesty, though, it was their stories of life in boarding school in England that we really craved.

My grandparents were proud of their son and daughter serving abroad, and I always loved to see my grandfather's face as he read Jimmy's airmail aloud, laid out in print, courtesy of his portable typewriter, and carefully sliced open by the letter knife in the dresser. My grandmother would sit attentively at the table to catch up on all the news, dressed in the 'pinnie' she wore around the house on all ordinary days.

Africa remained only as a dream to me. My sister went to live there for a year in early married life as her husband worked in a hospital in Malawi, but again neither my parents nor I were able to visit. I met African friends, and in the years when new citizens arrived in Scotland, we got to know exiles from the DRC and Burundi.

A few years ago, I was asked to help with some publicity for a great Scottish Charity, the Scottish Catholic International Aid Fund, or SCIAF. It was established not long after the war to be the main means of the Catholic Church here supporting aid and development in poor countries around the world. They work in Asia and Africa, and each year they focus on one particular project for their Lenten appeal, which brings in a large chunk of income from parishes and schools in Scotland. In 2017, as they were preparing to make their work on organic farming in Zambia their main priority, Val Morgan, their then head of PR, who I'd got to know a little, asked if I would join them to see the work they were doing and try to report back as much as I could on my return.

At the time, I hosted a Sunday morning radio show for BBC Scotland that was based around religion and ethics and, because I could guarantee some direct feedback from the visit, I decided to accept the invitation to go on the trip. It wasn't my first visit to a developing country (I'd already been twice to Brazil with Christian Aid), but it would be my first visit to the continent of Africa. To go to the place from where my uncle had sent these typed airmails was an incredible opportunity for me. Neither of my parents had ever managed to see the land where Jimmy had worked, and I felt strongly that if there was to be a trip to Africa, then Zambia or Tanzania were the places I wanted to see most.

Despite the briefings, modern communications and preparations before we left, Zambia and the primitive existence of so many of the people we met outside the cities still came as a surprise to me. Half an hour to the west of Livingstone in the south

of the country, we arrived, via a potholed main road followed
by a few hundred yards of dirt track, at a small settlement of
houses. It was less than thirty miles from the airport we'd flown
into the day before. There, a new terminal had been built that
looked fit to grace any modern European city. Despite those
small signs of investment and modern technology, the village
into which the CARITAS (SCIAF's worldwide partner) vehicles
rolled could well have been very similar to the kind of place my
uncle had first visited seventy years before. Mud huts, occasional
tin roofs (a sign of success), small plots of land and a scattering
of goats, chickens and cattle were all they could show in terms
of assets. The villagers assembled to meet us and explained the
changes in farming they were being taught by the SCIAF partners, and we dutifully recorded the stories on video or tape, with
the various journalists and our group photographer collecting
stories and images to send home.

At one point, I looked around and became quite bewitched
by the simple beauty in my surroundings. We had assembled
in a house belonging to a woman called Vainess, and I was
enchanted. As the fire for cooking burned gently, I gazed around
at her maize fields and her three small properties, and took
photos of a brood of chicks scurrying after a mother hen.

I recorded a translated conversation with her for future
broadcast, and then we both waited as one of the team took
some video of her land. Her English, not quite good enough to
be able to conduct an interview, was, however, strong enough
to convey her biggest need. Moving closer, in her quiet voice she
said, 'I have a vision.'

I was curious.

'I would like to have water. Here, at my house . . . my own
water.'

Lost in the beauty of the landscape and the warmth of the
clutter of children and animals, I'd failed to notice the lack of

any basic amenities. Water for Vainess came from a pump a couple of kilometres back down the road. To get it, she and her children would walk there and carry back gallons of the stuff, two or three times daily. All this – just to have water. Add to that the only power is from batteries charged by solar panels; enough to light up homework time for the children, but little else. No bathroom, no shower, no toilet, no electricity, no phone, nor any other modern 'luxuries'. What had seemed an enviable, ascetic retreat from the big, bad world was simply a very tangible example of the poverty we'd come to see.

That story was told over and over again in Zambia, and it was a responsibility but also a real joy to be able to write, talk and share video about the work SCIAF were doing to make people's lives better on our return. As I got to know and trust Val, I grew closer to the SCIAF community, and three years later they invited me on another trip back to Africa. By that time, Lorraine and I had made the decision to make any future charity visits together. In preparation for this one, we'd already spent a few days visiting Sarajevo with a Scottish group focused on keeping the remembrance of the massacre at Srebrenica at the forefront of people's thoughts. Beginning to hear the harrowing stories of genocide proved to be an appropriate primer for the visit to one of the poorest and most dangerous places in Africa: South Kivu in the Democratic Republic of the Congo (DRC).

It was, again, a country with some family connection for me, but it is so large there is no way of knowing if we were retracing any familial steps. The nature of SCIAF's work there was helping women who had been victims of rape. Sexual violence as a weapon of war was – and still is – a huge factor of everyday life for women in the DRC. Across the border is Rwanda, where we flew into and left from, which, twenty-five years before our visit, had undergone the worst genocide since the Second World War.

The fallout from that conflict helped fuel much of the violence still affecting the South Kivu province we were to visit.

With that knowledge, and some particularly grim stories Val had shared with me that I still find troubling to think on, we set off with some television and print journalists. It was January 2020, barely six weeks before the coronavirus pandemic was set to close down the UK, and we moved through our visit seeing precautions such as temperature checks and constant handwashing in Africa that had been completely absent back in Europe. That the DRC had recently been fighting Ebola was very clear, but the lessons they had learned seemed to be largely ignored back at home.

Lorraine's presence was central to our trip. The visits we made were all to women who had suffered sexual violence at the hands of groups of militia in the lawless chaos surrounding the city of Bukavu. It was Lorraine who would interview the women, while I listened and recorded at a distance. The company on the trip was good, but the sheer demonic nature of the violence and horror carried out on those we met made it a particularly arduous week of travel. January and February are rainy seasons, and getting from one place to another was tricky, even in the four-wheel-drive vehicles provided. Cars slewed across the road, and instructions were given on what to do should the vehicle topple. Add into that random roadblocks set up by villagers suspicious and often slightly hostile to anyone from an NGO. That our hotel had a twenty-four-hour armed guard told us much of what we needed to know.

However, as much as Bukavu is a vision of hopelessness, it is also a triumph of the human spirit. On top of a hill where, days earlier, shanty houses had all collapsed on top of each other in the January rainstorms, we visited a church celebrating its first Mass of half a dozen or so to be held that Sunday morning. This one was at 6 am, and even as we made our way there, locals were up and exercising along the mud-strewn roads of the makeshift city. Bukavu, like many cities in Africa, has grown without any real infrastructure as a gathering and sheltering point for many rural people who have fled from the violence being carried out in their isolated countryside villages. Thousands arrive each month to swell the numbers, despite the local priest, Father Justin, who heads the parish ministry team, encouraging many to return to their home villages. He fears there is little in the city for them, and, inevitably, poverty, crime and disease become bigger dangers.

On this morning, however, for at least a couple of hours, the minds of the locals were elsewhere, as singing like nothing we had ever heard before filled the church, about a thousand voices soaring around the sanctuary. All around us locals, dressed in a mixture of native costume and football shirts, danced and blew vuvuzelas, while a choir of hundreds of male voices took up another anthem. That morning, Father Justin preached in a local language, and after the service I spent time walking with him through the ghetto, where he is trusted and loved by the community. They joined in our small promenade, and if they caught my eye, they'd mime the money sign. We had been warned against ever giving out cash here, though, as even if it seems safe, others might take revenge on recipients if they feel themselves excluded.

There were great moments of acceptance and understanding that we were among them to hear their stories and to tell people at home of life in the DRC. We didn't pretend to be special, but as we came from an organisation that was doing its best to channel appropriate aid and support to those in need, local people seemed to accept us in good faith.

At home, a few years earlier, we had befriended a family of refugees from Burundi. Caught up in the genocide carried out by

Hutus on the Tutsis, our friends had found themselves in Glasgow starting a new life. It took a long time for their full story to be told, as recalling it always brought back the horror of those times, and with it, inevitable trauma. We thought of them as we heard stories from Rwanda of how the two tribes were learning to live together again.

We had assembled in a small house about two hours outside Kigali (Rwanda's capital city), which belonged to a woman called Claudette. The house had been a gift that victims of genocide who had somehow survived the slaughter were given by the government to start a new life. It was small, but compared to some of the housing we had seen on earlier visits, better appointed and fairly well furnished. Beside Claudette sat a man who said nothing during the long story Claudette told, via our translator, of how she had survived the many attempts to kill her twenty-five years earlier. That she had survived when so many of her family had not was something of a miracle and yet, as we paused for the translator to dry her tears and for all of us to catch our breath in the small living room, I don't think I was the only one who wondered if, at any point during her journey, death would not have been an easier option. Degradation upon degradation had been inflicted upon Claudette, and there's almost nothing you can imagine that was not suffered in her weeks of torment. As she completed her story, it felt as if there was no air in the room. It was then that the greatest shock came. The silent man sitting next to her had listened attentively, and yet we had seen almost no emotion from him. His name was Claude, and it had been Claude, she told us, who had carried out much of the brutality upon her that she had just described.

Claude had, in his own words, been a killer for the Hutus. Caught up in the fever of poisoned propaganda, he had killed more than he could remember, and had even attempted to kill

Claudette, who still bore the scar from the machete wound he had inflicted. So, we wondered, how had they come to both be in this room together?

Claude told us of the hatred of the Tutsis he had been taught growing up. He explained how little he knew, and how killing men, women and children during the hundred days of genocide became second nature. When the new government finally took control, he fled over the border to Congo. It was a few years before he heard there was what Rwandans called Gacaca – the truth and reconciliation programme designed to allow the country to move on, accepting the facts about what had happened. Signing up to return, he committed himself to re-education and rehabilitation. On realising that a survivor lived nearby, he presented himself at Claudette's house on several occasions. Each time, Claudette would scream and cry out to neighbours for help. Still, he returned. Finally, one day, he brought his wife and stood in her garden, determined to apologise and repent of the evil he had committed. Claudette accepted him in.

In the most remarkable story of mediation any of us could recall, the two became friends. Claudette, having no surviving family of her own, now regards Claude as family. It is similar for Claude. 'She even attended my mother's funeral with me,' he told us.

There was silence in the room as we all took in the true cost of beautiful forgiveness. Percy, SCIAF's representative in Rwanda, summed it up perfectly later in the garden outside the house. 'It's Saul becoming Paul.'

Claude's own précis is perhaps even more eloquent: 'She gave me a human heart,' he told us.

I am reflecting on that last African journey now, some eighteen months after we came home. It was the last long journey we made before the pandemic took over the world. In some ways,

I am glad it was the last. Travel has been impossible during the pandemic years, and I am grateful that other journeys and experiences have not clouded our memories of Srebrenica, Rwanda and the DRC. They were journeys that allowed us to see, at first hand, in the abandoned bloodstained church with its charnel house of skeletons in the basement, or in the autopsy centre in central Bosnia where human remains are identified and catalogued, what becomes of hatred. We are children of parents and grandparents who endured world wars, and we have some deep duty to speak up against the organised evil they fought against. It's not enough to let it simmer and assume it will go away. It's often closer than we imagine.

It was a relief to leave behind some of what we witnessed in Bosnia and Africa. There are only so many stories of evil you can hear without beginning to feel the oppression of the darkness that brought them into being. And yet Africa, especially, wormed its way into my soul. No Sunday morning passes that I don't think of that crowd of believers singing in the parish church of Mater de Dei at the top of the mud and mayhem of Bukavu's main roads. So often I see the logos for 'Visit Rwanda' on the Arsenal football tops and think, 'Yes, that's really what I want to do and where I want to go.' It is a place full of tragedy and brutal colonialism, but also one capable of unalloyed joy – and joy is always worth the search.

I have experienced a deeper happiness in Zambia, Rwanda, the DRC and Brazil than I have ever known to exist in the so-called 'developed world'. It's hard to explain, but possibly easier to imagine once you get your head around what is and isn't possible. It's not, I trust, a glib take on the simplicity of life in such places either. It's a recognition that for so many people who inhabit our planet, life revolves around an interdependency we don't understand any longer. Community is about mutual need, and that reliance on the help of a neighbour and their equal dependence on you is absent for most of us living in these northern lands.

The lockdown started soon after our visit, and I often wonder whether I will return to Africa. If I do go back again, I want to see Burundi, where our friends are from, and there's another stop I need to make in Malawi to see some other friends. Tanzania would be good too and I have always wanted to visit Kenya. But it's Bukavu in South Kivu that calls me most. That Mass, that singing and the kindness and openness of people who have been so wronged, but still had so much love to give; that still has the strongest pull.

Part Six

LET'S LIVE
OUR FIRST FEW LIVES
ALL OVER AGAIN

30

The Second Coming

When a popular band splits up, the first thing people want to know is when you'll be getting back together. With Deacon Blue, we never ruled it out, but neither did we expect it.

In 1999, I was trying to help a small charity raise some money, and realised that the figure they needed was perfectly achievable if someone performed a sell-out gig at the Royal Concert Hall in Glasgow. So I called everyone up, and we were surprised by how quickly the show sold out. This was still mainly pre-internet times, and within a couple of hours of the phone lines opening, all the tickets had gone. Having rehearsed and successfully negotiated a gig, it was suggested we might want to do a few more shows. So, in the autumn of that year, we toured the UK, playing the repertoire we'd left behind in 1994.

After that, it became slightly disjointed. For one thing, Graeme became quite ill. He'd been feeling unwell towards the end of the tour, and shortly after we came home, he was diagnosed with pancreatic cancer.

We didn't have any further plans to do much more touring. However, I'd been offered a new solo record deal. Papillon, an imprint of Chrysalis, offered a good deal for me to record a solo album if I undertook to deliver a Deacon Blue album first. I suggested that I had all the songs ready for my solo album, so could record that one almost immediately but release it after the Deacon Blue record, which would be recorded second.

This was a huge mistake. I now know that it's almost impossible to write and record separate projects like this. The only way to approach any album is to give everything you have – in songs, production ideas and energy – to the task at hand.

I gave everything I had to my solo record, but in all honesty, had an incomplete set of songs for the Deacon Blue album. Not only that, but there was no sense in which I brought people together to make the album and for these reasons, along with Graeme's absence and a certain indifference from the new label, the whole enterprise felt doomed. The label itself had ceased to exist by the time my own album came out, and there was no publicity and very little marketing budget for what was – and still feels like – one of the best records I've ever made.

Deacon Blue toured on the *Homesick* album, and there were times when I enjoyed what we achieved, but there was a sense from all of us that our attention was on the work we were each undertaking away from the band. Ewen had joined Capercaillie by this time and decided not to tour with us. Graeme was very ill, and, for the last part of the tour, Dougie had accepted television work that he needed to fulfil, making it impossible for him to join us. It no longer really felt like the band we'd all once worked so hard to create.

Not long after this, Lorraine accepted a role in a BBC Scotland TV drama that made it difficult for her to get time away with the band. Meanwhile, I had put most of my creative energy into songwriting projects, which I was enjoying with some success in the early 2000s.

A Sony release of a new compilation album in 2006 brought a new focus and we found time to tour again that year and in 2007. By the time these tours had been completed, though, I found myself as unhappy as I'd been in 1994. I knew that you can't be in a successful performing band without enjoying some fresh creativity. In short, we couldn't be a band without making some new music. This time, however, I wasn't prepared to throw everything away as easily as I had first time around. If we were going to come back, we were going to do it with some style.

In 2008, Deacon Blue were invited to be the special guests of Simple Minds for a short arena tour of the UK. It involved being paid well to play for forty-five minutes to a fairly positive audience. It also gave us the chance to witness a great band who were continually updating themselves while keeping the essence of what they'd always done. There was so much I was to learn from that short tour, which would probably shape my musical career for the next twelve years and (hopefully) beyond.

That Simple Minds had never split up was an interesting story too. Jim Kerr and Charlie Burchill were clearly the core of the band, and they'd kept moving it forward in their own image despite numerous personnel changes. As far as the audience were concerned, it was and always had been Simple Minds. Ten thousand people bore witness to this every night of that tour.

I loved getting to know Jim a little. We'd met and spoken before, but now, on the road together, I got more of an insight into who he was, how he'd led this great ship through many changes, and also how he brought the audience into the whole event. It's never too late to learn, and I watched, listened and relearned some things I'd needed to know better. I understood how, fundamentally, the band – or the appearance of being a band – still mattered. It gave him the showcase for his songs and ideas, and it gave the audience a familiar handle with which to grasp the concept of what they were trying to do. In those few days of touring, I found that I wanted our band to matter as much. But first, I had to show the same energy and commitment to our project as Jim had to his.

I found myself reflecting on my deep desire to get out of Deacon Blue in 1994. Why had it been so important to do that then? And if the whole point had been to make something special, unique, adventurous and widescreen back in the early days, why were we simply treading water now? In 2008, it seemed we were going nowhere, and we had no ambition to be anywhere other than nowhere. If splitting up had been such a priority, why were we just drifting around now? I often reflected that there might have been a better way.

I've been as honest as I could when I've told people why Deacon Blue split up in 1994. The simple truth was there was no easy way to make another record together. I'd lost whatever I needed to have to make that happen, and having thought it through in every different way, I don't think we could have done much else at the time but stop.

However, with the benefit of hindsight, we might have simply taken some time to think it all out. Doing so may have allowed us to do the different projects we all wanted. That five-year break allowed Dougie to become a TV star, Jim to play to huge audiences in France as the legendary Johnny Hallyday's pianist, Ewen to discover and star in the world of folk music, and Graeme to marry the woman who would bring happiness into the short remainder of his life. Lorraine, about to become a mother for the second time, would eventually meet Ken Loach, appear in a movie and become a dedicated actor. I'm glad all of this happened, as all these people were and are brilliantly talented individuals. I'm also glad we managed to reconnect, and that in that reconnection, I rediscovered in Graeme the soulmate and dear friend I'd had back in the early days of the band. It also meant that when we reconvened in 1999 with a vague agenda, the idea that the band was the dominant vehicle in all of our lives disappeared. No one was relying on Deacon Blue to be their main source of employment. This meant we had to work around each other's schedules, but also to work at a pace with which we could all feel comfortable.

The downside of this was that, for the subsequent ten years or so, we failed to do anything significant other than release an album that was half-hearted (at best) and put on a few tours for which we mined our back catalogue. Tours had their moments, but there was more relief than gratitude when they came to an end. Phase two of Deacon Blue was a slightly rickety machine. All of us had now discovered other things in our lives, which was good. I, however, had found no creative mojo for taking the band forward. In the early days, it had consumed me. I was still an ambitious songwriter, I still wanted to play these songs live; why was it so difficult to do that with the band I knew and loved? By the time we got to 2007 and the final proper tour, we were feeling a decision was looming.

Finding the spirit of what Deacon Blue was and could be took a little longer, and it involved someone coming in who could make us value each other in fresh and exciting ways, and who also made me believe that being in a band, and making music together was what everyone outside expects it to be: one of the best experiences ever known.

We were putting together a compilation album a couple of years before this. I'd expressed to Scott Fraser, our then bass player who worked with me a lot in my home studio, that I didn't know how to write a Deacon Blue song any more. I really didn't know where to start. It's so strange how small conversations come back to you, but Scott gave me the best advice I'd ever had on this subject: 'Just go back to the start; do what you did then.'

At first, I recoiled from the idea. What did that even mean? Then it clicked. At the start, I didn't think these songs were in categories. There were no other avenues or outcomes. Each song was a Deacon Blue song because that was the band I was putting together around the songs. It was simple. Just write the song that's in your heart.

Meanwhile, we still had other plans. Lorraine and I had signed a new deal to make a record under the name McIntosh Ross, and we were heading to Los Angeles in the new year to work on that. As a way of trying out ideas for that record, we'd assembled a few musicians in Glasgow to record some tracks. Our old friend, Ged Grimes, (originally part of the band Danny Wilson) came in to play bass on the session and we loved having him about. When the late offer came in to do the support tour for Simple Minds, we decided it was time to change the session musicians, so we asked Ged and his good friend Gregor Philp to come in. Dougie had played with Gregor in the band Swiss Family Orbison and had been suggesting for ages that we ask Gregor to play guitar. It was Ged and Gregor's enthusiasm and dedication that gave me the spur I'd been needing to think creatively about Deacon Blue again. At the end of the dates, I began to think about how we could move forward. One thing was certain; either we moved forward creatively, or we gave up. I knew there could be no more greatest hits packages and tours. It was create or die.

As often happens with creative processes, it was a circuitous path. Lorraine and I made our record and enjoyed a tour. The whole project had been a refreshingly new experience for us both. By the time we got to the end of that period, I'd started to think about the two of us making another album, and had kept Deacon Blue at some distance. I'd gone down to London to meet potential new managers for our project and was in conversation with various individuals, including Nick Stewart. Nick had been a boss at Island Records, and still worked out of that beautiful space in Chiswick where the label was first based back in the seventies. At my meeting with Nick, he ignored the McIntosh Ross project and concentrated on Deacon Blue.

'My dear boy, you have to make an album.'

Like Scott's advice a few years before, it was hardly ground-breaking information, but, for whatever reason, it inspired me. I went back to Glasgow the following day and put two ideas together that had been on my computer desktop. One was a little string riff that I'd recorded on my Dictaphone, and the other was a file which said two words: 'The Hipsters'.

I'd no idea what this really meant, but recognised there was something eating at me. The title amused me, as we had always been the uncoolest band on the block. What if we were to come back, with a new album – and on it, a song about us, celebrating ourselves, my friends, my band members? And what if the song – maybe even the album – was called 'The Hipsters'?

All of this was tumbling through my head as I started to write it. I kept working on it until I didn't know how to get any further. I needed help. Gregor had a great background in playing guitar (and every other instrument), as well as programming and recording. He started coming over to my house from his home in Dundee. Lorraine was touring with a play at the time, and in between me getting the kids out to school and organising the house, we spent days and nights making extended demos for what would become a new album.

Suddenly, thanks to the advice and the enthusiasm Gregor had for the concept of the band, it seemed that all I wanted to do was write for Deacon Blue. I was writing the songs of my heart, telling stories of who I was now, but embracing the scale and the scope of what the band would bring to the track. It could sound so majestic – grand, even – and we knew the people to make that happen. If this sounds obvious, it had taken me years to find it. However, I was grateful. In the years that followed, it has been Gregor who has made all the difference: not simply his musicality, but also his persona, his outlook on life, his sense of humour and his enthusiasm. I took too long to take Dougie's advice and get him on board, but as ever, I'm so glad I did.

Before we got into the studio, we still hadn't found our manager. Nick did the job for a year or so, and I will always treasure his advice, but he still wasn't the right person. The search continued as we went back on the road. We hadn't played at Glastonbury as Deacon Blue for twenty-one years, but having tried it out the previous summer with McIntosh Ross, Lorraine and I thought it would be great to come back with the band properly.

It was solid, squalid rain in June 2011 when we made our way through the roads of Somerset towards Worthy Farm. We were to play in the Acoustic Tent, a huge marquee that had a few hundred souls spread out over the arena as Nick Lowe played his set before ours. I love Nick's music and was enjoying his set, but was equally concerned that if Nick only drew in a few hundred, we might get even less. It wasn't looking good, and we also knew that when we went onstage, Coldplay would be headlining the Mainstage. As the rain continued outside the tent, Mick, one of our guitarists, shouted out that a strange phenomenon was taking place: 'All these people are heading towards the marquee . . . it's weird.'

It was. They were coming in their hundreds and eventually their thousands – and they were all coming to see us. That night was the true second coming of Deacon Blue. It was the night when we realised what we'd missed and what we needed to do next. The tent felt like the Barrowlands, and everything we did seemed to work. I still look back on that night and our big tent revival as being the awakening I'd needed.

That Glastonbury weekend, we were also joined by a new bass player. Lewis Gordon was this brilliant kid who would occasionally ask my advice about the various bands he was in at the time. As our great friend Ged had now joined Simple Minds, we needed a bass player. Lewis was so good, so cool and such an easy fit that we felt sure he'd be off to join a young, new band or be heading out with his own project without us any time soon. That he's now been with us for over ten years has been one of the best things about what our biographer, Paul English, calls Deacon Blue 2.0.

In the months that followed Glastonbury, we finally found the management we'd been looking for. Paul Loasby came on board, with the help of the man who now runs all our affairs, Tom O'Rourke. We had a re-release schedule lined up in which all our albums would be remastered and repackaged properly, while the surprise bonus, a brand-new Deacon Blue album, would be recorded and released in 2012, followed by a tour. It was the start of a creative period involving extensive touring, the release of four new albums, a live album, a DVD, a mini album and an EP, all in the space of eight years. By 2019, we were back in Australia for the first time in thirty years, with a return visit planned in 2022.

It was the second coming and I am, even now, enjoying it more than the first.

31

The Guisers

All the way up the road, they were caught in the headlights. Little packs of guisers, picking their way from house to house. These days, they'd call themselves trick-or-treaters, but when we grew up, and in Scotland, they were always guisers. With one hand on a patient parent and the other clutching a carrier bag or a little plastic bucket, half filled with the swag, I saw them as I drove my mother home. On that Hallowe'en, even she noticed the pavements were a little busier than the usual odd sprinkling of joggers and late, tired commuters returning to suburbia.

It was almost silent as we drove back to her small flat, ten minutes away from my own house. Occasionally, I would remind her of days gone by, and she smiled as we reminisced. In my childhood, it had been she who'd organised everything about Hallowe'en. It was she who policed the front door as the children from the council estate came calling two days too early. 'You can come back on Hallowe'en proper, and we'll give you something then.' We'd be embarrassed, peeking out at the assembled urchins with their Guy in a pram as they trundled back down the garden path in oversized bonnets, scarves and painted moustaches. Inside, we waited for the day to come, with excited discussions about where we'd call and what we would be on the night. Tales of our classmates' rich pickings would determine new routes on the date in question.

Sometimes, my mother would hold an informal Hallowe'en night of our own. Apples would be placed in a basin and a rudi-

mentary string hung across the kitchen so treacle scones could
be eaten without the aid of our fingers. Little was made of the
supernatural elements of All Hallows' Eve; it was enough just to
dress up, learn a poem or a song and walk around the houses of
our small estate.

All this passed like a film in my head as the car took us back
to my mother's on that last evening. It must have been more
than fifty years since we'd celebrated Hallowe'en together, and
even memories of my own children's guising were beginning to
fade. As we walked along the corridor to her small flat, she told
me how the words of 'Sweet Molly Malone' were going round
her head as she'd thought about one of her granddaughter's
Hallowe'en turns.

She sat down in her chair and I turned on a few lights, then
made sure she was settled before we kissed and I said goodnight.
We'd spent a good part of this week together, between one thing
and another. A check-up on her eyes at the hospital on Wednesday, and a lunchtime visit to see a podiatrist at the health clinic
today. I'd acted as the driver and sometime translator, as she
would hear very little of what the health specialists were saying,
and even if she did, she found keeping the information organised
fairly taxing.

'Did you write that appointment on your calendar, Mum?'

'No, I forgot.'

And so, I'd go into the kitchen and take the flimsy date book
off the wall. It was a homemade affair with months beginning
to fall out, given to her by one of the girls (that could be anyone
under sixty) in the church. There was a sunset or landscape on
each month, with an accompanying text across the top of the
page. That month's reminded the reader that the 'wages of sin
is death'. A message I'm sure didn't need over-emphasising with
my own mother.

That day at the health centre, the podiatrist (a girl who might well have been about the age of one of my daughters) had seemed a little uncertain of the correct protocol for dealing with a nonagenarian. It took her a while to find me a seat as I hovered clumsily over the chair in her practice room. She plonked my mother down on an extended dentist's-style chair, which caused even my mother (the most forgiving and gentle of patients) to mutter a complaint that it was almost impossible to draw herself up. The girl meant well, but spoke so fast that nothing really went in, and it took me all my concentration to remember what had been said and why. Mum's circulation was poor, and by the time we sat down in the café in the foyer afterwards, she passed her hands into mine to warm them up. Cold and thin, it struck me how far we'd come in swapping the roles of parent and child. For years, it had been she who'd taken me to dentists, doctors, piano lessons and Cubs. Now it was me walking her to the car, quietly turning her in the right direction.

'It's strange that everyone has gone now,' Mum had remarked to me the other day as we sat over lunch. 'Why am I still here?'

She knew the answer, of course. She was the youngest of four, and her sisters and elder brother had all passed on. The phone calls to Mary in Cardiff and Margaret in Cheltenham could no longer be made, and there were few friends of her own age with whom memories could be shared. An older friend of over 100 had died a couple of months back, and enquiring whether she wanted to attend the funeral, she dismissed it out of hand. 'It's too far. I'll not bother.'

I wanted to say that it might have been good to go, for fear that others might adopt a similar line on her own final farewell, but sensed she'd already anticipated that and was willing to take her chances.

As I made my way back down the quiet corridors of her building, there was very little noise from anywhere. Driving back down the road, I passed more tiny, be-costumed travellers and the odd adult in full pantomime outfit, slightly worse for wear. I imagined no such night would pass like this even over the coming Christmas and New Year seasons. It would be next October before the guisers and their adult minders would be out again. For some, it would be their last such night, as the self-consciousness of adolescence kicks in. As for others, next year may afford them their first chance to go out unchaperoned.

A year is a long time for an elderly lady of ninety-one. Driving home alone, it was hard to imagine such a night passing as peacefully again. Now, I'm grateful for that evening being our final, gentle Hallowe'en together.

32

I first read C.S. Lewis's autobiography more than forty years ago during a cold Easter holiday, sitting leaning against an unpainted radiator of the downstairs study in the house where I grew up. I remember that holiday well, as it was one of the first times my parents elected to go away without me and entrust the house and the dog to my care.

The study had been a key room for me growing up. In the early days, it had been a spare bedroom and occasional play-room for me and my sister. After a floor was put down in the attic, my train set was moved out of its dominant position in the study and put out of sight at the very top of the building. Towards the end of primary and beginning of secondary school, my cousin from Tanzania came to stay for a year, and the study became Cilla's room. On one notorious night, it became the secret door to the house to avoid frightening my parents. My sister, Anne had knocked on the window in a bloodstained ballgown, having been rescued from a car crash in a Perthshire field involving some school friends on their way home after a Christmas formal dance. Anne's gentle but determined knock at the window to Cilla's room was the best way to break the news to the sleeping family.

After Anne left home to go to university in Glasgow, and my cousin went down to England, the small study was allowed to become a convenient hangout for me. In my late teenage years, it housed the family piano, assorted musical instruments, my first proper HiFi and an expanding record collection. On the Easter in question, all of these factors would have come in to play, as the room became my cave for one week of splendid isolation.

I can't remember why I picked up the Lewis biography, save perhaps that his version of Christianity was as close to mysticism as I had ventured, and I was keen to get closer to and understand what made him believe. I loved the bits about 'northernness' and falling in love with the poetry of Matthew Arnold in the form room of Octie (his teacher), but I also wanted to know why, in amongst all the magic and myth, there was this deep longing for faith.

I also loved the title. It was a quote from Wordsworth, but it spoke to me about something that I had never associated with the faith I had inherited: joy.

The first 'good' song I ever wrote was a response to that book and a reflection on faith, sometimes blind faith. I'd been captured by Robert Frost's 'The Road Not Taken' when I first came across the poem at school, and I would often go back to it, probably reading it to unsuspecting English classes as a student teacher. My song dealt well with the idea of choice and making decisions (evangelicals were good on all of that); what it was less certain about was the idea of happiness and how to enjoy it.

In the years to follow, I'd have to console my father that the depression he was suffering from did not negate his core belief in his simple conversion experience and life of devoted service in the church. 'How,' he would ask me, 'can I be someone who has been saved and yet have all this doubt and unhappiness?' I felt his pain. He had once told me he wanted someone to adapt the words of Max Bygraves' song, 'Happiness' to make it into a gospel chorus. It begged the question that was always lurking below the surface with such matters: 'How can anyone be joyful without Jesus in their life?' Coming from their faith standpoint, it's a legitimate point; from anywhere else, it seems paranoid, clannish and patronising

The answer to all these points was brilliantly answered one day by the man who became a wise and deep influence on my life at a critical time, Father Roland Walls. In a talk to a stuffy Church of Scotland committee I'd been invited to attend while working for the church, he reflected on the scene where the mother of James and John wants to ensure their place at either side of the Saviour in the kingdom to come. Roland laughed heartily as he unpacked the full impact of Matthew's Gospel. 'You realise, of course what he's saying?' He beamed into the rather nervous group of ministers, elders and Women's Guild stalwarts, who were beginning to doubt the wisdom of inviting a Catholic priest into their retreat. 'Don't get any big ideas. You might not even make it there!' How Roland laughed.

Everyone in the room was rather taken aback. Despite our varying interpretations of theology, the one thing we'd all imagined was a humble, but reasonably strong, probability of heaven. Of course, Roland wasn't trying to deny any of that to them, but rather saying: 'It is not for us to judge anyone. Judgement is for someone else at another time.' That information brought true joy, and a sense of release, at least for me, that the business of proselytising was not for me. Roland, on the other hand, was someone I wanted to get to know more.

He'd been an Anglican Brother who had formed a tiny order called the Community of the Transfiguration, who set up camp in three huts around a disused miners' welfare hut in Roslin, near Edinburgh. In his later life, he made the logical step to convert to Catholicism, as he was, in most respects, at home in the form and spirituality of that tradition. He was a tiny man who smoked a pipe and looked as if he might well have brothers called Bilbo and Frodo. That he was also a great theologian who wrote almost none of it down would come as a surprise if you happened upon him on some form of public transport (his only means of travel). It was public transport that begat his great story, which is brilliantly told in Ron Ferguson's biography of him, of a train journey he took to England while still uncertain about how the next part of his life might unfold. Looking for spiritual guidance, he looked out the window to see a passing coal truck emblazoned with the instruction: 'Return to Scotland empty.' Roland did, and lived out his life in one of those small huts in Roslin, along with any passing homeless folk or those who simply didn't seem to fit into to our accepted forms of regular life and work.

In around 1985, he came to visit the small community of Christian folk I was attached to in East Pollokshields at that time. I'd talked to him about trying to make a go of things in music, fully expecting his disapproval. The opposite happened. He'd heard something I'd recorded and responded with delighted enthusiasm, even though, by his own admission, he knew nothing of pop music or its associations. Roland was great at disarming almost everyone. To the powerful, he spoke truth, and to zealots who wanted to bring down the temple on everyone's heads, he offered pithy ripostes. 'Oh, it's good that God made them bishops,' he'd chuckle 'because they love getting dressed up in robes and large hats.'

Years later I'd come across a priest who had a similar impact on my life. Father Joe Boland had been my wife's school chaplain in her final years of secondary education at Kilmarnock's St Joseph's Academy. They reunited and Joe invited her to take part in a year-long retreat called the Spiritual Exercises of St Ignatius. At the end of her journey, I too undertook the exercises, and the impact of these two years were huge in both of our lives. For one thing, the things we expected to be revealed were often still as opaque as when we'd started, but other parts of life were celebrated anew. Religion can feel like someone has placed a wet blanket over all the great bits of life, but in Ignatian teaching, all of life is celebrated and thoroughly enjoyed. Before that, I'd imagined that any kind of spiritual awakening would involve narrowing my horizons and taking on abject suffering. Joe would have none of that. Instead, he invited us into the jail.

Joe was chaplain at Kilmarnock Prison. It is Scotland's only privatised penal centre, but is still run along fairly orthodox lines. He suggested we come in and play some songs in the chapel to a selected group who were all 'lifers', These were men of all ages who had committed crimes so serious they'd been handed life sentences. They'd all had the chance for some long reflection and knew the truth that separation from their own families and communities was the hardest part of their punishment. I played a few songs from my solo album of the time, *Pale Rider*, which concentrated a lot on the bonds I had with my own children and, in many ways, was a celebration of the life I enjoyed within the love of my family. Each song seemed to land in the right place, and I can't remember a better audience for the songs of that time. I loved playing the show, and can still see the faces of the men as they leaned in to the narrative behind each lyric. Lorraine came to sing too and joined her brother, John, who is a beautiful singer and guitarist, to play some cover versions of songs they loved. There were two interesting outcomes after the concert.

It was still the days before Facebook, and I'd written a small reaction to the show on an online message board. To our surprise, there was a post from the prison's Church of Scotland chaplain, who had taken issue with a song John covered on the day. Ron Sexsmith's brilliant 'God Loves Everyone' didn't sit well with the minister, with its echoes of universalism and also, perhaps, its clear condemnation of religious homophobia (the main reason, Ron told me, years later, why the song had been written). This pernickety, almost cruel reaction killed off for me any sense that this narrow fundamentalism could ever reflect what I'd come to believe anymore. That he wanted to take part in a nuanced debate about the rights and wrongs of an idea of a generously loving God when we had all experienced deep joy at music bringing us together, said everything about why Fundamentalism has been a roadblock for so many for so long. It was great to clarify what I had left behind, and to realise God was so much bigger and better.

The other interesting outcome was the positive reaction to music in the jail. The governor was an imaginative woman called Wendy Sinclair Gieben, who later became Scotland's chief inspector of prisons. With her blessing, I'd suggested to Joe we do a proper gig inside and bring in the band, including all the production and the lights, for all the prisoners to enjoy.

At the start of our 2007 tour, Kilmarnock Prison became the opening show. It wasn't quite the Barrowlands, but it was a proper gig where the inmates were allowed to let off some steam. At the end, there were votes of thanks to everyone who'd made it possible, and I made a point of thanking the prison staff, to which there were loud boos and jeers. However, when I also thanked the prison chaplain, Father Joe, there was a standing ovation. The prisoners knew Joe was someone they could trust and who took time to listen to what they were saying. Joe was (he is now retired) a man who took almost no time off, so he had never found the time to come up to a proper gig before. This had been his first experience of a Deacon Blue concert, and I wanted to know what his reaction had been.

'I loved it.' He smiled as he reflected on the whole experience.

'Do you think we did any good out there?' I asked him, not really sure whether it had all been worth it.

'Oh yes,' Joe affirmed. 'In that room today there was joy, and where there is joy, there is God.'

It was a defining moment for me. In the typical way in which these things happen, that prison show and Joe's reaction to it changed everything about how I saw performing. Examining myself closely, I realised I had been sniffy about joy. When we played shows, I didn't mind people having a good time, but sometimes I felt I had to be dragged reluctantly towards allowing an audience to enjoy the hits like 'Real Gone Kid' and 'Dignity'. Somehow, I'd been condescending about this simple endorsement of our most popular songs, and wanted, for whatever reason, always to stretch for the difficult moments, the darker, more 'serious' passages. I rejoiced in the unexpected and the downright obscure, forgetting that people often wanted to come out and leave a lot of that behind. Joy, for them, was a song they'd heard a million times in their house or car or on the radio, but that they really, really needed to see us perform one more time. How difficult was that for me to understand? If I'd only listened to the rest of the band, they could have told me this too, but my brow would furrow when it came to giving people something they wanted.

So, what changed?

I think the fundamental change was understanding and empathising with an audience. Rather than looking down on them – which it is very possible to do – I wanted to celebrate their love and be more in step. Did the concerts get any better? I'm not sure anyone could measure the difference, but there was a difference in me. We gathered before shows, and I'd pray. I'd pray for us and for the audience and I'd pray that, for the next two hours, people would experience the same thing Joe had glimpsed in the jail: real joy.

33

The City of Love

The strongest musical memory I have is being upstairs in my bedroom while my mother prepared food in the kitchen below, singing hymns. Her singing was a soundtrack to my childhood, and it was always hymns or simple children's choruses. It's the choruses I remember best, and in my later years, a new one will pop into my head every other morning.

The one I loved the most was one I mentioned that we sang with my mother in her final days. 'Away Far Beyond Jordan,' imagined heaven as the promised land; a peaceful sanctuary only accessible by a wide river whose shore would be a haven, welcoming to the weary traveller. It's that vision of paradise I still cling to when I am confused and tired of trying to make sense of everything.

> If you get there before I do,
> look out for me, for I'm coming too.
> Away far beyond Jordan,
> we'll meet in that beautiful land.

The song has stayed with me all of my life, but has gained an added poignancy in the last few years as I watched my elderly mother, the youngest of four, say goodbye to each of her sisters. So often, she'd tell us how she wanted to phone one of them up and share a story or news of a happening in their hometown, only to realise they were no longer there to listen. Similarly, with the passing of friends, it almost seems that there are fewer and fewer to mourn when an old acquaintance finally departs.

When we sang 'Away Far Beyond Jordan' in Sunday school, it was dressed up with actions. Our hands would move with the music and lyrics to illustrate the story; we'd shade our eyes to peer from the shore to see who was coming next. None of it, to children like ourselves, had any meaning, and it's only in later years that the lyrics and the idea of the song has meant anything to me. Families get broken up, loved ones lose loved ones, and the hope of a reunion keeps a fire lit for all those lonely, last days.

A couple of years ago, I remembered a story I'd heard about the Gorbals in Glasgow. In the church of Blessed John Duns Scotus, there is said to be some of the remains of St Valentine. As the Gorbals was always a slightly mythical place for me, I became fascinated with the idea that in the heart of Glasgow, such a strong symbol of love endured.

The Gorbals had been a place I'd only read about until I moved west from Dundee. Even when I lived here first, the old tenements of that part of town had been pulled down and sixties high-rise flats had replaced them. No one seemed to love the flats, and everyone I spoke to agreed that the demolition of the old area had been unnecessary, as the housing stock could have been refurbished and the community kept in place. Instead, the people were scattered across Glasgow and beyond, and one of the strongest, most tight-knit neighbourhoods of the city was destroyed. In case it sounds like I'm romanticising poverty, I witnessed all of this at first hand when my wife's aunts returned from Ireland and America, and always headed straight back to the old community they'd first joined in Scotland. They talked about Crown Street and Cumberland Street as the centre of their world in the early sixties. A place of refuge, family and welcome, to which they always returned on any visit.

As the idea nagged away at me, I wanted to bring these two threads together. I wanted to celebrate the symbolic heart of a city that has been my true home for thirty-five-plus years with the hope of those overheard childhood hymns. I wanted to celebrate the possibility of mercy, love and kindness being not just dreams of paradise, but ideals we need to believe in if we want our world to be a better place for everyone. In short, we envisage the future to be the best of what our imaginations can contain. In turn, our hope is not in the consolation of life after death, but in the true expectation of life before it.

So, *City of Love* became an idea about finding a place of hope; a city we somehow knew but hadn't yet been realised; a dream that had been cruelly disturbed, and one that we couldn't quite remember but still remained in our heart as a place of true happiness. The *City of Love* was on that far shore. Rooted in this dark, soot-drenched jumble of houses, where light had to fight to break into the back courts, was a heart of love that, despite all the efforts to diminish or remove it, continued to beat.

In Richard Holloway's memoir, *Leaving Alexandria*, he tells a great story about a time he asked his friend, the Church of Scotland minister John Harvey, to help him find something appropriate to say for the coming celebration of Easter. Both men were based in the Gorbals, and the crushing reality of the poverty of their fellow citizens meant the future bishop couldn't believe there was any possibility of resurrection on that Easter Sunday to come. He paced the streets of the Gorbals, fuelled by whisky, as they both raged at the darkness around them. When there is no belief in even the rumour of resurrection, it seems as if all hope is lost.

That truth never occurred to us as we sang lustily and looked out to see who was coming to the warm, sandy shores of our

promised land. The thought that we would one day be waiting or
being waited on would not enter our minds. And yet we all must
have imagined a reunion, a time when we'd been lost somewhere away from our parents, and panic would set in. Any of us,
even then, could imagine the relief of seeing a familiar face in a
crowd of strangers. It's that consolation, as simple and as final as
that, that I wanted to strive to talk about in *City of Love*.

> If you've got the will to keep on going
> No matter what the world is saying
> No one can stop you, not until
> You reach the end and lay down your burden

34

Coda

If you've got this far, you'll have noticed there's very little mention of my wife, Lorraine, or our children. I have always taken the line that they would be much better at telling their own stories. I'm also very grateful for their patience with me and have no right to expect them to extend that kindness any further.

Your parents cast long shadows. In 1990, I got to know a man whom I liked very much. Originally from the business side of the Sony empire, Richard Rowe had been brought in to run the brand-new Sony Music Publishing. At the time of buying over the CBS labels, Sony didn't buy out their publishing arm, so it was Richard's job in the UK, and eventually in the US, to establish the catalogue for the new company.

When we met, he was charming, funny and very generous. He explained a little of his back story. His father was Dick Rowe. Dick Rowe was a by-word for an in-joke within the music industry; he had been the man who had turned down the Beatles for Decca back in the early sixties with the notorious sign-off, 'Guitar groups are on their way out, Mr. Epstein.'

This story, however, did not do justice to the ground-breaking musical path Richard's father had forged, and in conversation he would explain how his father would receive a pile of forty-fives from the States and brilliantly match the songs with his roster of British acts: 'This one's for Cilla Black.' I loved Richard's affection for his dad, and his warm recollections explained perfectly why a headline story isn't always the deeper truth.

A few years after we first met, I happened to be in Los Angeles with my manager, Peter Felstead, and Richard and I hooked up for a breakfast at the Beverley Wilshire. It was lovely to see him again and enjoy his own slight puzzlement at running Sony's flagship operation in their largest territory. I reminded him that my family were grateful for the advances I'd been given, and that, as things stood, it seemed they might not all be recouped. He shrugged blithely and laughed. 'Listen, Ricky, at the end of the day, it's not my money. Anyway,' he went on, 'I've given some money to some nice people, and that makes me very happy.'

Richard had heard about the record I was making in LA, and I, in turn, was interested to know what he was doing there. It turned out that Sony were buying the ATV catalogue, which actually included my early Deacon Blue songs, but more interestingly for them – and for him – also contained the Beatles Northern Songs catalogue. At the time, it was all still owned by Michael Jackson, who, seemingly a little short of funds, was selling it on. I didn't want to pry on a private moment, but I knew that for Richard, this was a way of rationalising the story about his father that had hurt him so much. Here was young Richard, finally signing the Beatles.

I'd meet Richard off and on over the next twenty years or so, and I was always glad to see him. Though he's now moved on from his Sony position, he is still in the heart and soul of the music business. One time, we caught up in New York, and he let slip that part of his role had been to spend extended time with some of his biggest writers, including one Bob Dylan. Inevitably, I wanted to know what his take on Bob was, having had the chance to spend significant time with him. Richard paused and thought carefully. His answer wasn't any of the ten or twenty I might have guessed.

'I think what I can tell you is he is a man who loves his children very much.'

I have never met Dylan, and I have no desire to do so, but I love his music completely. I also have no desire to write anything profound about him here, as there's no need to add anything to the screeds that are already out there. In fact, I wish people would write less and enjoy more – that's the only thing I could safely be quoted on about Bob. So I carry Richard's wise encomium with me, knowing it's as good a fact as I'm ever likely to need.

I like it so much, I'd wish for it to be said of me too. I love my children very much, but on days like today, when they are far away and I'm allowing myself to miss them, I know a deeper truth that brings me greater comfort. I am truly loved by them, and for that I will always be grateful.

It's now three weeks since I returned from the last tour. It was to have been the biggest number of dates, playing in front of the biggest number of people, since our heyday in the nineties. We almost made it too. The first week in Germany and the Netherlands had been cut early as the Delta variant of Covid made its way across Europe. The final week was to be in Ireland, followed by two final shows in Scotland, with the very last – the biggest of the tour by some distance – at the Hydro arena in Glasgow. It was not to be. By the time we were approaching the final week, the Omicron variant was causing Covid infections to rise at an unprecedented scale, and going to or enjoying gigs was becoming a needless distraction for many folk who were simply keen to have an infection-free Christmas with their families. So we postponed the final week and came home.

I walked the dog out to the park this morning on a bright January day, as, like most people, I was still on the final leg of the New Year holiday. I was hailed by a passing fellow dog walker. He was keen to tell me how he'd come to the tour for the first night down in England, as he'd been unable to get the tickets he'd wanted in Glasgow. As we chatted, I had the strange yet familiar feeling that he may well have been talking about someone else. In fact, I almost felt as if I (as the dog walker) had no memory of what I (as the performer) had been doing, or how he did it – and it was only three weeks ago. What will it feel like in a couple of months? Did I enjoy it? Yes . . .

categorically. Could I survive without it? Much more easily than people might suspect.

The truth about my own way of seeing live performance is that it is something so all-consuming and demanding that I can easily imagine it never happening again – until the moment when it does. It's also the most ephemeral experience I know of; so transient are its charms that one can feel an audience in ecstasy, and then, within a heartbeat, they are readying themselves to leave the theatre and run for a train or hail a cab home. There is, from them, no lingering farewell, no extended coda. Even as we walk offstage after the last finale, we are aware that the audience have more important things to do than clap you to the wings; there are buses to catch and parking to be paid for, and concerns that have been abandoned for the two hours of the gig come calling quickly.

On the tour and shortly after, we spent time watching Peter Jackson's *Get Back* documentary. Watching it on a tour bus with your bandmates is, perhaps, the most meta way one can ever experience such a thing. Up until its release, most people assumed that it would be all about the Beatles falling apart. What came over instead was the essence of four musicians who needed each other badly. Their need for each other's approval, harmony and opinion was palpable. That so much of their post-Beatles life was defined by the fact they were once one of the four tells its own story. There is, dare I suggest, also something beautifully universal about the band experience to be gleaned from watching the Beatles put together the project. Everything about being in a band for ten minutes or thirty years is in there: the painful silences, the awkward nods of distrust or praise, the sheer exhilaration of a song taking off when it is least expected, the hours of tedious noodling and distraction, and the pain of delivering a song to the only audience that can make or break it before anyone even knows it exists – your own band mates. There is too that great sense that there are two kinds of people in the room. Those in the band and everyone else. No one wants to be in the second group; no one picks up a guitar and dreams of being George Martin.

All of these thoughts went through me as I watched with my musical siblings, and then again at home, as I watched alone or with my family. Sometimes, and my colleagues will bear this out, I've done everything I can to put a cool, firm remove between myself and my bandmates. I desire the space to create, think or dream on my own, but despite this, I am acutely aware that the magic only happens with everyone. The trick is to know how to play your own part well . . . and that is a lifetime's struggle. Like the other five people in Deacon Blue, I've walked away at the end of a tour grateful that the last show has passed. The intensity of the time can be too much, and all of us have gone round all the familiar discussions a few too many times. We are happy to decompress alone. This time, it was different. We woke every morning to the possibility that one positive Covid test would bring a halt to the whole circus. That sharpens things up a little. As well as this, however, there was something deeper and stronger within the group, notwithstanding the fact some of us have been doing this for some thirty-five years, in good times and bad. There was a love and mutual admiration that went beyond anything I'd experienced before: a need – because that's what it is – and a deep reliance on each other.

Perhaps too I had to ask myself the question: can I still do this? I turned sixty-four at the end of the tour and, yes, the words of *that* song went round my head a few times over the course of those weeks. Is it possible to bring the same sense of discovery, spontaneity and danger that is the high wire of live performance when you should be 'dangling grandchildren on your knee'? I guess that is for others to judge, but for me, the deep satisfaction of singing songs that had embedded themselves into people's lives wiped away any self-doubt I'd had leading up to the tour. What brings me the greatest satisfaction was the range of moods and emotions we covered over the two and a quarter hours we were onstage. There were recurring highs, but also beautiful, quiet moments when we strummed our way through the campfire songs or sang to pin-drop silence on deep album cuts. More than anything, the worldwide pandemic returned each performance to the precarious nature of our early days on the road. The only certainty on any given day was that we hoped to get through one more night, until it became obvious we could do more. Believe me, that adds an edge to any gig, and a deep gratitude as the curtain falls on successive nights.

I was flicking channels over Christmas and happened upon Jimmy Stewart in *The Glenn Miller Story*. There is a telling scene where Glenn witnesses a nightclub band and singer destroy one of his compositions. Over drinks at home, his wife gives him the advice he needs to hear: 'You need a band, your own band.'

How right she was.

To be in a band, the right band, all going in the same direction, is one of the best feelings ever. It's not hard to imagine how getting either of these things wrong can bring misery to everyone, but it's also satisfying to see something through. I never had the patience to work through what was wrong before, but recently I've tried to hold on to the essence of what brought us together. I guess I have learned to accentuate the positives and eliminate the negatives . . . how ironic that, in the course of the tour, as we completed our lateral flow tests each morning, we were only interested in a negative outcome!

I loved *Get Back*. I loved all of it, even the frustrating points when they never finished a song or teased us with glimpses of the final version. I loved the arrow that shoots through the whole picture: the promise of a performance. That they know how capable they are of delivering a gig is so commendable; that they are desperately aware of why they stopped playing live three years earlier is beyond reproach, but the sheer exhilaration and energy of the Savile Row rooftop gig makes up for everything. It's so true of so much of the life of a band. Rehearsals are tedious, noisy. It's frustratingly difficult for everyone to hear themselves or hear each other properly; they're annoying to whoever hears them through the wall, and are usually scarred by endless navel gazing. Then comes the gig, and suddenly it's all OK. Mistakes are brushed aside, and you carry on right through to the end, because that's what you have to do – and somehow, somehow, it's all brilliant. People love it, and you, for that brief twenty minutes, hour or four hours, fall back in love with each other, knowing it's only possible because they are all there, facing the same way, playing as much or as little as is needed, literally *in concert*.

I felt this in November and December 2021. So, to those bandmates who made it happen: Jim, Dougie, Gregor, Lewis and my lifetime companion, Lorraine. Thank you. To those who put us onstage and amplified or lit us up, thank you. And to Graham, our endlessly patient tour manager, and Tom, our manager, fellow traveller and dear friend, thank you. And to you, who came and listened and rejoiced with us: thank you all.

You made it all so good, I think I might just do it again.

ACKNOWLEDGEMENTS

To Lorraine, who knows all the stories and so much more.

To Caitlin, Emer, Georgia and Seamus: Thank you for being my best friends.

I'm indebted to Richard Roper at Headline for believing in the idea and being an ideal editor.

I want to thank Kevin Pocklington for opening the door to this book. To John Walsh for his early encouragement and to Chris Deerin for spending some time with these stories.

Tom O'Rourke as my manager and friend has been a valued sounding board at every stage.

The only reason anyone might want to read these stories is because I managed to be part of a great group of musicians called Deacon Blue. I'd like to thank Lorraine Mcintosh, Dougie Vipond, Jim Prime, Ewen Vernal and the late Graeme Kelling for allowing some of these tales to take place. You have been great travelling companions.

Gregor Philp and Lewis Gordon have joined the circus and it would be impossible to imagine making music without them.

Huge thanks to Bob Morton and Elaine C Smith for giving me a place to write.

INDEX